VC-126

Markus Jachtenfuchs/Michael Strübel (eds.)

Environmental Policy in Europe

Assessment, Challenges and Perspectives

Nomos Verlagsgesellschaft
Baden-Baden

Die Deutsche Bibliothek – CIP-Einheitsaufnahme

Environmental Policy in Europe: Assessment, Challenges and Perspectives / Markus Jachtenfuchs; Michael Strübel (ed.). – 1. Aufl. – Baden-Baden: Nomos Verl.-Ges., 1992
  ISBN 3-7890-2635-2
NE: Jachtenfuchs, Markus [Hrsg.]

1. Auflage 1992
© Nomos Verlagsgesellschaft, Baden-Baden 1992. Printed in Germany. Alle Rechte, auch die des Nachdrucks von Auszügen, der photomechanischen Wiedergabe und der Übersetzung, vorbehalten.

This work is subject to copyright. All rights are reserved, whether the whole or part of the material is concerned, specifically those of translation, reprinting, re-use of illustrations, broadcasting, reproduction by photocopying machine or similar means, and storage in data banks. Under § 54 of the German Copyright Law where copies are made for other than private use a fee is payable to »Verwertungsgesellschaft Wort«, Munich.

Table of Contents

Introduction   7

Authors   13

Part I
Efforts and Perspectives of European Organizations   15

EC Foreign Environmental Policy and Eastern Europe
Markus JACHTENFUCHS   17

Current Situation and Perspectives in Resolving
Transboundary Environmental Problems at Regional Level
Mikhail KOKINE   43

Problems of Environmental Cooperation in Europe:
A Non-Governmental View
Hans-Peter DÜRR   57

Part II
Regional Cooperation and Ecological Modernization   69

Conditions for Environmental Policy Success:
An International Comparison
Martin JÄNICKE   71

*Environmental Cooperation between
the Nordic Countries and Eastern Europe*
John STORM PEDERSEN/Troels NORUP PANILD   99

*Economic Development and Ecological Crisis
in the Former GDR: Opportunities Offered by Change*
Peter PICHL/Uwe SCHMIDT   133

*East European Countries Facing Ecological
Cooperation in Europe*
Marek PIETRAS   155

**Part III
Perspectives of an All-European Environmental Policy** 175

*Geographical Aspects of East-West
Environmental Policy*
Frank W. CARTER   177

*The Principle of Spatial Responsibility: Understanding the
Background of Cooperative Environmental Policies in Europe*
Barbara RHODE   197

*Regulation Problems of a General European Environmental
Policy*
Kurt TUDYKA   231

*The End of the East-West Conflict and the Ecological
Challenge for Europe*
Michael STRÜBEL   241

Introduction

All European countries suffer from a variety of environmental problems. Meantime, it has become a commonplace to say that pollution does not respect the political borders of nations and of ideological blocs. However, despite the end of the Cold War and the disappearance of the East Bloc as a coherent unit in world politics, borders and divisions in Europe still exist and will continue to do so in the foreseeable future. The guiding question of this book is therefore how to create or establish ecological cooperation under the present widely differing ecological, economic, political and geographical conditions in Europe.

With the collapse of the authoritarian regimes of Eastern Europe, symbolized by the destruction of the Berlin Wall in November 1989, we have a unique opportunity to build a cooperative Europe of democratic states. Domestic changes in the former communist states, the transformation of existing international institutions, such as the Conference for Security and Cooperation in Europe (CSCE), and intensified intergovernmental as well as transnational cooperation provide the basis for creating durable peaceful relationships between the formerly antagonistic blocs which go beyond the pure, simple absence of armed conflict. Firstly and foremostly, these changes have to be introduced in the field of security and economic policy, and, fortunately, there appears to be a growing awareness that a linkage exists between economic recovery in Eastern Europe and international stability.

However, this is no more than an opportunity which can also be missed, for Europe is still divided economically and ecologically along the old lines. One scenario for the future would certainly be a cooperative Europe that tries to bridge the gap between the West and the East as well as to harmonize democratization with the goals of economic development and the preservation of environmental health. But another alternative is also possible: a Western Europe with the European Community as its focal point, highly integrated economically, increasingly able to act internationally, beginning to tackle its environmental problems and to reform its production systems, and gradually reducing its democratic deficit; and an Eastern

Europe torn between nationalist eruptions, economic crises and ecological disasters.

Cooperation with and assistance to Eastern European countries in the field of the environment is thus important not only for purely conservationist purposes but also for broader political reasons. It is not claimed here that environmental policy is the most important area of cooperation or a *conditio sine qua non* for successful trans-European cooperation. On the other hand, environmental policy is not one policy field among many equally important other areas. When the notion of "sustainable development", which is now entering the international agenda, is taken seriously, economic development and environmental protection are only two sides of the same coin. Economic growth, if not seen simply in terms of production, creates the conditions for environmental protection. On the other hand, economic growth which "externalizes" (i.e. disregards) its negative effects on the environment undermines its own basis. In the most technologically advanced countries, environmentally sound technologies and products are today less seen as a cost but increasingly as an opportunity.

Thus, there is a possibility that these countries will slowly shift their production towards products and processes that require a smaller input of energy and materials. By tightening up their production cycles, it may be possible to significantly reduce the environmental costs of the production process. Thus, by introducing the environmental component into their economy, countries which are already winners now will even further increase their technological advantage, minimize their costs and thus become more competitive on the world market. On the other hand, countries facing severe economic crises today might not be able to resist short-term calculations which lead to the conclusion that environmental protection only costs money. As a result, they might install technology which is already outdated and will be even more so in the future. Such a response would only contribute to the maintenance of the welfare gap between Eastern and Western Europe.

This means that protection of the environment is crucial for the long-term economic recovery of Eastern Europe. In this new situation, the success of environmental policy can no longer be measured against the standards developed during the Cold War when any cooperative agreement between East and West had a value in itself. Environmental policy success must be assessed also in the light of its contribution to a sustainable economic growth in Eastern Europe. When decent standards of living are a condition for stable democratization in Eastern Europe, environmental protection contributes to the creation and maintenance of democracy in those countries. It is important, however, that not only Eastern Europe but also Western Europe, which has repeatedly declared its solidarity with the East, be aware of that link and conceive and adjust its policies correspondingly.

The following contributions should be seen in this context. They do not pretend to have technical solutions at hand. Instead they try to give a picture, admittedly incomplete, of the prospects for and the problems associated with ecological cooperation in Europe.

The first part focuses on the role of organizations. Whereas Markus Jachtenfuchs analyzes the prospects of an active foreign environmental policy of the European Community for Eastern Europe, Mikhail Kokine presents the work of the United Nations' Economic Commission for Europe which has done path-breaking work in the past but is likely to remain important even in the aftermath of the Cold War. Both organizations are rather state-oriented. This is less the case for the Council of Europe which, although a classic intergovernmental organization, is quite active in creating transnational links between municipalities and other regional entities. Hans-Peter Dürr gives an account of the opportunities and difficulties, underlying conflicts and cleavages of non-governmental organizations working in the field of transnational environmental cooperation.

The second section is devoted to ways and means of achieving ecological modernization. A comparative study of the environmental policies in several European countries (contribution of Martin Jänicke) shows the different political conditions for a successful environmental policy. Troels Norup Panild and John Storm Pedersen consider the patterns of cooperation between the Nordic Countries as a model for new patterns of cooperation between them and Eastern European countries. Both Eastern and Northern Europeans could profit from such cooperation. Marek Pietras sees a considerable potential for ecological cooperation in Eastern European states, presently hampered by a large gap between the objective environmental situation and subjective awareness of the problems as well as by financial constraints. Peter Pichl and Uwe Schmidt analyze the structural deficits of former East Germany and point to the crucial importance of the energy sector for environmental recovery.

The third section assesses from different angles the perspectives of an all-European environmental policy. Frank Carter shows that while pollution does not respect political borders, it is subject to geographical constraints. Barbara Rhode stresses the interaction of man and nature and concludes that for this reason, different pollution media require different cooperative policies in Europe. Differentiation is a subject taken up also by Kurt Tudyka who analyzes the inherent tensions between the international character of environmental pollution and the national character of regulations set up to deal with this pollution. Finally, in a comparison of different environmental protection regimes in Europe, Michael Strübel concludes that the long-term periods which ecosystems need to recover make it difficult for institutions depending on short-term political cycles to act effectively. There are good prospects for cooperation due to the unideological character of environmental policy, but the financial perspectives appear rather gloomy. Critical points are discussed concerning the introduction of a new concept of security including the ecological dimension.

This book was prepared at the European University Institute in Florence. It brings together thirteen authors from seven different European countries. Having as a principal approach the build-up of an interdisciplinary scientific network, colleagues came together not only from all over Europe but also from different fields: economics, geography, physics and political science. The effort here has been to find a common language for the common problems, and to discuss the environmental problems in a broader context than that afforded by individual disciplines.

The editors would like to express their thanks to President Noël and Secretary General Buzzonetti of the European University Institute as well as to the Commission of the European Communities for their generous financial and personal support, and to the Academic Service, especially Shelley Buckwater and Brigitte Schwab for providing invaluable organizational and editorial help. The interdisciplinary Working Group on Environmental Studies was a permanent forum for stimulating discussions and for efficient conference organization. It constituted a unique forum for bringing together students and research fellows who work throughout Europe on different facets of environmental policy. Without this collective effort, this publication would not have had the broad approach and – we hope – the quality that must be judged by the reader himself.

Heidelberg/Florence
Summer 1991

Authors

CARTER, FRANK W., Ph.D., Dr., Head of the Department of Social Sciences, School of Slavonic and East European Studies, University of London

DÜRR, HANS-PETER, Prof., Dr., Director of the Max-Planck-Institute for Theoretical Physics, Munich

JACHTENFUCHS, MARKUS, M.A., Ph.D. Fellow at the European University Institute, Florence

JÄNICKE, MARTIN, Prof., Dr., Professor at the Department of Political Science, Free University of Berlin

KOKINE, MIKHAIL, Dr., Secretariat of the Economic Commission for Europe, Geneva

NORUP PANILD, TROELS, M.A., Ph.D. Fellow at the European University Institute, Florence

PICHL, PETER, Dr., Institute for Economic Sciences, Academy of Sciences of the GDR, Berlin

PIETRAS, MAREK, Dr., Assistant Professor at the International Relations Department, Marie Curie-Sklodowska University, Lublin

RHODE, BARBARA, Dr., National Expert at the Directorate General for Science, Research and Technology, EC Commission, Brussels

SCHMIDT, UWE, Institute for Economic Sciences, Academy of Sciences of the GDR, Berlin

STORM PEDERSEN, JOHN, Dr., Assistant Professor at the Institute for Social Economy and Planning, Roskilde University

STRÜBEL, MICHAEL, Dr., Assistant Professor at the Institute for Political Science, University of Heidelberg

TUDYKA, KURT, Prof., Dr., Professor at the Center for European and International Studies, Catholic University of Nijmegen

Part I

Efforts and Perspectives
of European Organizations

EC Foreign Environmental Policy and Eastern Europe

Markus JACHTENFUCHS[1]

1. Introduction

In the relations between Eastern and Western Europe, the European Community is playing an increasingly important role. After the decade-long refusal of socialist Eastern Europe to accept the EC as a political reality was eventually overcome by the signing of a "Common Declaration" between the EC and the Council for Mutual Economic Assistance[2] in June 1988, the European Community is now establishing relationships in a wide range of policy fields with all Eastern European countries. Partly due to the severity of environmental destruction in those countries, but partly also for reasons internal to the EC, environmental policy cooperation is occupying an important place in these relationships.

This article attempts to analyze the bilateral relationships between the Community and the different Eastern European countries in the field of the environment by employing the concept of *foreign environmental policy*. It thus covers a field which is rarely treated in the rich literature on the EC's external relations. The use of this concept raises, however, two problems, the first of which is to conceive an operational definition of the concept. Foreign environmental policy has a normative-political as well as an analytical

---

[1] The author would like to express his thanks to his interview partners in the EC Commission who provided some helpful information used in this paper.

[2] OJ L157, 24.6.1988, p. 34.

dimension which must not be confused. The second problem is the application of the concept not to a nation-state but to the European Community. This raises several questions stemming from the specific political and legal framework under which the EC operates. The fact that the EC does not neatly fit into long-standing traditions of thought in international relations theory and foreign policy analysis should however not lead to neglecting an actor of growing influence in an increasingly important policy field. The proposal made here is that EC foreign environmental policy can only adequately be understood by moving away from the analysis of "classic" types of that policy, i.e. the negotiation of international environmental protection agreements, and by adopting a comprehensive approach which also takes into account the growing integration of environmental elements into other policy areas, especially with regard to trade. As a consequence, this view makes the distinction between internal and external aspects of environmental policy almost disappear. Although this undermines to a certain degree the foundations of the original concept, the term is maintained because it implies an actor-oriented view not shared by other approaches.

2. Conceptional Framework and Institutional Setting

Before applying a rather diffuse concept to the analysis of the relations between the European Community and Eastern European countries, some clarifications are in order. In a first section, I will try to contribute to a better operational understanding of foreign environmental policy; a second section deals with the specific conditions of foreign environmental policy-making in the European Community.

2.1. *The Concept of Foreign Environmental Policy*

The term "foreign environmental policy" first appeared in the context of analyses dealing with the classic type of transfrontier pollution, namely air pollution. The 1979 Geneva Convention on Long-

Range Transboundary Air Pollution[3], concluded in a period of strong tensions between East and West after a campaign led by Scandinavian states (which were suffering most from acid rain coming from Great Britain), and with the explicit support of the Soviet Union, served as a model for propositions which held that states should put environmental concerns on their diplomatic agenda (Prittwitz 1984, ch. 1). The main task of a national foreign environmental policy would be to protect the citizens of a state from pollution imported from abroad. Environmental matters, it was argued, should not be left within the domain of specialists and technicians in the competent ministry but become an integral part of the overall formulation and operation of a state's foreign policy. An institutional consequence of this approach is to involve the ministry of foreign affairs increasingly in international environmental questions and thus contribute to a greater politicization of transboundary pollution.

The concept as it was developed in the mid-eighties is essentially a normative one. It argues that transboundary pollution has reached such a level that foreign policy, whose aim is in the last resort the continuity of the state and the well-being of its citizens, could no longer ignore the problems posed by it. Policy-makers should react to that challenge by using traditional strategies and instruments of foreign policy, either by adopting conflictual strategies (intervening via diplomatic channels, trade restrictions, refusal of financial or technological assistance, public accusations) or by pursuing co-operative policies (financing environmental protection measures, entering into negotiations, transferring technology). One might be tempted to say that the concept is a plea for the inclusion of environmental considerations into the calculation of the "national interest" of the respective state (Wirth 1989; Myers 1989).

The idea of a foreign environmental policy described above, partly criticized by scholars as establishing too close a link between old, conflictual or even violent modes of policy-making and areas which would need new forms of cooperation (Tudyka 1988: 16/17), and partly advocated as an urgently needed solution for pressing

---

[3] Text reprinted in OJ L171, 27.6.1981, p. 13.

problems (Mayer-Tasch 1985), has in recent years found its way into the political arena.

Policy-makers do not only accept environmental questions as a now established part of international relations (Clinton Davis 1987) but also advocate a strong foreign environmental policy in order to tackle urgent problems of a mostly global scale (Schevardnadse 1990; Voigt 1987; von Weizsäcker 1987). This corresponds to an increasing number of international conferences partly or exclusively devoted to environmental questions and increasingly attended by foreign ministers or even by heads of government. Since 1984, the world economic summit regularly deals with environmental affairs. The Conference on Security and Cooperation in Europe, in its beginnings primarily concerned with security affairs, human rights and economic relations, has progressively devoted its attention to environmental questions (CSCE 1989: 147-149) and even organized a special meeting on "ecological security". Major conferences on specific issues, such as the 1989 London meeting on the protection of the ozone layer and the 1990 World Climate Conference in Geneva, have definitely put environmental issues, at least those related to global deteriorations, on the diplomatic agenda of the main countries of the world. This trend will most likely continue in the coming years, especially with a view to the 1992 UN Conference on the Environment and Development. In the process leading to the phasing-out of ozone-depleting substances, the European Community has even played a leading role (Jachtenfuchs 1990). It is likely to be a crucial player in the negotiations on a future climate convention.

Although it is still too early to judge whether the recent proliferation of high-level conferences in the field of the environment is merely an example of symbolic politics or, on the contrary, the beginning of a general shift of emphasis in international relations towards the cooperative management of global threats, the recent developments show that foreign environmental policy is now recognized as an important area of a country's foreign policy, and is becoming an important issue not only for the respective ministers but also for heads of government.

The acceptance of the fact that environmental policy has also an external dimension which has to be explicitly taken into account by policy-makers and analyzed by scientists is however only a first step towards a more comprehensive view of environmental considerations in the area of foreign policy. In most cases, international environmental policy is still mainly concerned with a rather narrowly defined issue area. Foreign environmental policy then deals with reducing sulphur dioxide emissions, curbing CFC concentrations or combatting the discharge of harmful substances into the sea. This classic environmental diplomacy is however not sufficient for solving the problems at stake. More appropriate is an approach which regards environmental policy as a "cross-section issue" (Weizsäcker 1987: 196) relevant for all other policy fields. From a problem-oriented point of view it is thus not sufficient to simply conclude an agreement on the reduction of a specific pollutant without taking questions of technology, trade and finance into account. A modern foreign environmental policy would thus not separate foreign trade policy, development aid, financial transfers and transfer of technology but assess and alter the impact of those policies on the level of environmental protection and, vice versa, the consequences of environmental protection measures on those policies.

Analytically, this normative statement implies a strong emphasis on the interaction between the internal and the external dimension of a policy; in other words, between the external consequences of domestic policy measures and the domestic consequences of foreign policy action in the respective fields. Most of domestic environmental policy has also an external component; for instance, stronger environmental requirements for products in one economic area will inevitably affect trade relations with third countries and a tighter process regulation within a country might well lead to a relocation of polluting industries to other countries. Domestic environmental protection measures may thus have the characteristics of unilateral foreign policy measures. As a consequence, this strong interaction between the internal and the external sphere increases the impact of non-governmental actors (interest groups) and of public opinion on the conduct of foreign policy, which is, according to the traditional view, sheltered from such factors.

The concept of foreign environmental policy has thus a normative and an analytical face. It has first been formulated as a demand: environmental policy *should* become a matter of high political concern not only in the domestic arena but also in the field of foreign policy. This view has at least partly been adopted by political actors. Its focus can be widened from environmental policy in its pure sense to the integration of environmental policy considerations in other policy areas.

On the analytical level, the concept focuses on the consequences of actors' behaviour and their explanation. In the last resort, it is therefore only of secondary importance whether actors perceive themselves as pursuing a foreign environmental policy or not. What counts are the reasons and the results of such a policy by taking into account the interaction between environmental policy and other policy fields on the one hand, and the link between internal and external dimensions of such a policy on the other hand.

In the last resort, the term foreign environmental policy could therefore be self-destructive if its scope is too broadly defined. It would probably be more advisable to term it "environmental relations" or to speak of an "environmental protection regime" between the EC and Eastern European countries. Although there are some good reasons for this argument, I believe that the main difference is one of emphasis. Whereas the regime-approach would concentrate on the *interaction* between the constituent parts of the regime, the concept of foreign environmental policy stresses more the role of single *actors* within a regime. Both approaches are thus not mutually exclusive but complementary. The actor-oriented approach seems, however, more suitable for an analysis of the so-far neglected role of the European Community in international environmental policy.

2.2. Political and Legal Framework within the European Community

In an analysis of the foreign environmental policy of the EC, due account has to be taken of the fact that with regard to its internal structure and its external performance the European Community is neither comparable to a fully-fledged state nor to an intergovernmental organization. Its external conduct cannot be adequately understood by looking at it as a monolithic entity in the tradition of rational-actor theory but only when the political and legal conditions which shape and limit the conduct of its foreign relations are taken into account.

Environmental policy in the European Community developed only slowly after 1973 (Bungarten 1978: 119-236; Johnson/Corcelle 1989). While the Community forged its internal environmental policy in a step-by-step proceeding, and still does not cover all fields of it in equal depth, external environmental policy as a consequence hardly existed and remains up to now less developed than external relations in other policy areas. As long as there was only a weak internal policy in this field, there seemed to be no need or opportunity to formulate an external policy. Environmental agreements were concluded and negotiated by the member states. The first major convention where the Community was allowed to become a contracting party alongside its member states was the 1979 Geneva Convention on Long-Range Transboundary Air Pollution. Other agreements followed (Johnson/Corcelle 1989: 294 seq).

An expansion of the Community's external environmental relations can be expected from the internal market programme launched in 1985, which is accompanied by a strengthening of policies aimed at alleviating its negative effects. The dynamics of the internal market programme and the corresponding pressure towards a stronger environmental policy within the Community is thus likely to result in a more active external policy in this field. The Single European Act, in force since 1987, which strengthened the EC's decision-making procedures in order to ease the adoption of the measures necessary for the implementation of the internal market programme, for the first time explicitly provides that the Community possesses the capacity to act internationally in environmental affairs (art. 130r, 5)[4].

Besides these internal reasons for a strengthening of the Community's foreign environmental relations, external reasons also exist. Whereas the EC is developing its internal structures, it tries to establish cooperative relationships with the rest of Europe, namely the EFTA countries and Eastern Europe. These cooperative relationships, partly aimed at not excluding Eastern Europe from the emerging internal market and partly at strengthening the Commu-

---

[4] If not otherwise indicated, references are made to the EEC Treaty.

nity's internal cohesion by acting and speaking uniformly, do already have a strong environmental component. This component consists of the financing or co-financing of environmental protection projects, research cooperation, transfer of technology, and data gathering.

If a strengthening of a policy within the Community is generally accompanied by a parallel development of external relations in the respective policy field, one might expect the foreign environmental policy of the EC to expand in the future.

The European Council, whose task is to assure the overall consistency of Community policy and to give general political guidelines has in recent years made itself an advocate of a stronger involvement of the EC in international environmental affairs. After the declaration of the Summit at Rhodes in December 1988, the Dublin European Council in June 1990 adopted a long "environmental imperative declaration" which put special emphasis on the international dimension of Community environmental policy (EC 1990). Despite a long list of plans and resolutions without concrete results, the value of these declarations should not be underestimated. The conclusions of the European Council, especially when it endorses concrete measures or proposes specific actions, have a guiding function for the Commission and the Council of Ministers. For the national ministers united in the Council, it is hardly possible to ignore the orientations (which are often very detailed) endorsed by their own heads of government. As the European Council is not limited to the framework provided by the EC treaties but also embraces the intergovernmental part of the Community, authorizations to act can also address areas of policy coordination by the member states in which the Commission does not assume a leading role. The dividing line between the two areas is sometimes difficult to draw.

Finally, it is important to analyze any EC policy, internal or external, in the context of the general development of the Community's institutional balance. The European Community is not a static organization in equilibrium but a dynamic system in an unfinished state of development. Quarrels between different players within the EC about power sharing and division of competences are therefore frequently linked to highly specific policy issues without a direct relationship to the institutional debate. Sometimes, the end-product of the Community's policy process can hardly be understood if the ongoing inter-institutional debate is not properly taken into account. In general, the Commission and the European Parliament can be considered as driving forces working in favour of a progressive transfer of competences to the European level whereas the Council of Ministers (i.e. the organ representing the member states) is only reluctantly prepared to give in to such demands. In a longer time perspective, the European level, despite individual drawbacks, acquires successively more competences in an increasing number of areas either at the expense of the national level or in collaboration with it. As a consequence, the Community is acquiring a steadily increasing capacity for external action.

The reasons for this are not exclusively political but also rooted in the legal structure of the EC. In the European Community, progress in integration is codified, sometimes with long delays, in (mostly written) legal form. On the other hand, progress in integration has frequently been furthered by changes in the legal sphere, very often through judgments of the European Court of Justice. After the so-called ERTA-judgment which the Court delivered in 1971 (ECJ 1971), it has been reluctantly accepted that after the Community has enacted internal legislation, it is also competent to act externally in this specific sphere when uncoordinated member state action would endanger the unity of Community law. The Single European Act, adopted 16 years later, formally gives the Community the right to conclude treaties with third countries in the field of the environment.

As a result, when it comes to negotiations on a specific agreement, the Community may be competent in some parts of the subject matter whereas the member states retain competences in other parts. As the scope of an agreement being negotiated rarely fits neatly with the Community's internal division of competences, the so-called "mixed agreements" have been used (O'Keeffe/Schermers 1983). In this case, the Community together with the member states concerned both sign and ratify the agreement in question and thus avoid difficult and long-standing debates about the exact dividing line between Community and member states competences. On the other hand, this also implies that in some cases individual member states are no longer free to act internationally in a given area because they have given the legal competences for doing this to the Community. Due to this complicated legal-political background in which neither the European nor the national level can act independently, the Community's decision-making process in international negotiations is often very cumbersome and its negotiating position relatively inflexible.

As stated earlier, foreign environmental policy should not only mean the conclusion of environmental agreements but also the integration of environmental elements into other policy fields. The Single European Act provides a legal basis for such a development when it states that "(e)nvironmental protection requirements shall be a component of the Community's other policies" (art. 130r, 2).

In external relations, the most important field of application of this "integration principle" is commercial policy. Commercial policy is one of the rare areas in which the Community possesses exclusive competence for external affairs (art. 113). At the same time, it is certainly one of the most significant fields of the EC's external relations. To the extent that trade will be increasingly based on environmental considerations or that environmental protection measures will be implemented by trade measures, the Community is the only competent actor in that field.

The same is true for association agreements which the Community can conclude with third countries (art. 238). These agreements establish a special relationship between third countries and the Community.

The European Community thus in principle possesses the competences and tools to conduct a foreign policy in the field of the environment. Political and legal considerations indicate that this policy is likely to be expanded in the future. However, this tendency finds its limitations in the internal structure of the EC.

3. Recent Developments and Possible Future Actions With Regard to Eastern Europe

The following section has as its aim to present an inventory of EC foreign environmental policy towards Eastern Europe, assuming that the scope which these activities have reached in the last two years is not generally known. This necessarily somewhat descriptive part will be followed by an assessment of this policy not only in terms of its internal coherence but also in a broader perspective with a view to the internal foundations of such a policy and its future development. For the purposes of the present analysis, it is useful to distinguish between what could be labelled "classic-type policy", i.e. actions targeted at specific environmental problems such as the conclusion of environmental protection agreements, and a more integrated policy-making which does not assume a contrast between environmental and, say, economic policy, but instead tries to realize environmental benefits by modifying other policies and even to achieve advantages in other policy areas by taking environmental considerations into account.

3.1. Classic-Type Policy

Major impulses and support of a stronger foreign environmental policy of the European Community come from the European Council. Although it is not fully incorporated into the institutional web of the Community, the declarations of the European Council should not be considered as mere wording without concrete and immediate relevance. On the contrary, the endorsement of a specific policy action by the European Council implies at least that this specific action or policy is now a part of the *acquis communautaire* and will not be put into question by the Council or by other bodies representing the member states. The European Council can also go further and give a new impetus to hesitating national ministers. This seems to be true for the "environmental imperative declaration" of the European Council, adopted in Dublin in June 1990, which calls upon the Community "to play a leading role in promoting concerted and effective action at global level" while recognizing that internal and external aspects of environmental policy are "inextricably linked" (EC 1990).

A real environmental policy for Eastern Europe which is worth its name has only started to emerge after the signing of the "common declaration" between the Community and the Council for Mutual Economic Assistance in June 1988 which ended the decade-long mutual ignorance of the two organizations and, most notably, after the breakdown of the political structures of the former Eastern bloc. A major event in that respect was the first special environmental conference convened by the Conference on Security and Cooperation in Europe (CSCE) in Sofia in October and November 1989. At this meeting, which marks also the definite entrance of environmental policy on the agenda of an institution which previously had diplomatic and economic questions as its main area of concern[5], the Community was represented by the President-in-office of the Council and the Commission. Only a few member states were represented by high-level delegations. On that occasion, the EC offered administrative and technical support for existing or planned industrial plants with a view to a future application of equal environmental standards throughout Europe[6]. Comparable environmental protection requirements were considered necessary in order to avoid the relocation of industries into Eastern European "polluter heavens". As a main prerequisite of such an assistance, the publication of reliable data on the state of the environment in Eastern Europe was stressed (EP 1989: 11). Objections of Romania, at that time still under the Ceaucescu regime, prevented the publication of a final communiqué.

Environmental relations between the EC and Eastern Europe have been shifted to a high political level by the meeting of the EC Environment Council with seven ministers of the environment from Eastern Europe, including Yugoslavia but without Romania, in June 1990. On the basis of a presentation of the disastrous environmental situation in Eastern Europe and its severe economic consequences[7], the concluding document of the meeting identifies "priority" areas of cooperation. This document resembles, however, more a com-

---

[5] At its Dublin meeting, the European Council stressed the need for the CSCE to have environmental questions included among its themes.

[6] In the beginning of September 1990, a "regional environmental center" was inaugurated in Budapest. This center, which receives considerable financial support by the EC and the US, shall act as a coordination and information center on environmental protection measures for Eastern European countries.

[7] For instance, the Czechoslovakian minister estimated that approximately two million people will have to change their job in his country alone because of intolerable pollution levels.

prehensive listing than selected priority items[8]. In order to meet the urgent need for more reliable data, the Community offered the Eastern European countries participation in the newly created European Environmental Agency[9] and in the CORINE information network[10].

Although the modalities of this participation will only become clear after the Environmental Agency has become operational, the admission of third countries to a Community institution is unprecedented. This seems to indicate the will to lay the basis for what the conference called "a coordinated environmental policy at continental level"[11], i.e. the beginnings of an all-European environmental policy.

The necessity of such a policy lies not only in the need to avoid leaving Eastern Europe as a heavily polluted region with low life expectations. It is also in the interest of the European Community, for instance in the field of transboundary air pollution where the air quality within the Community could more cheaply be raised by a reduction in the still considerable emissions of Eastern European countries than by a drop of air pollution originating within the Community.

The EC has been trying to participate in regional environmental protection agreements. After laborious negotiations, it was allowed to become a contracting party to the 1979 Geneva Convention on Long-Range Transboundary Air Pollution. The particular political circumstances of the convention - it was negotiated within the CSCE framework - gave rise to strong resistance against EC participation which was only accepted in a special formula. The Community is also involved in the financing of the trans-European air pollution

---

[8] Summarized in *Agence Europe*, No. 5278, 20.6.1990, p. 12.

[9] See Council regulation 1210/90, OJ No. L120, 11.5.1990, p. 1.

[10] Established by Council Decision 85/338, OJ L176, 6.7.1985, p. 14; for a recent modification see OJ L81, 28.3.1990, p. 38.

[11] *Agence Europe*, No. 5277, 18/19.6.1990, p. 7.

monitoring network (EMEP)[12]. The Geneva Convention being a framework agreement, the more substantive parts are contained in two annexed protocols on the reduction of sulphur dioxide and nitrous oxides. As there was no internal agreement about compulsory reduction, the Community is not a party to those protocols. On the other hand, the international negotiations stimulated the internal decision-making process which had been blocked up to that time and promoted the adoption of internal legislation[13]. The fundamentally divergent approaches to combatting air pollution existing in the Community, mainly the debate on emission versus air quality standards in which the United Kingdom opted for the latter and the other member states for the former method (Haigh 1987: 20 seq), prevented the adoption of a uniform Community position, however necessary for the signature of an international treaty on the environment.

The maintenance of the ecological balance in the Baltic Sea has been another matter for East-West cooperation since 1974. Due to the rejection of any form of EC participation by the former East bloc countries, only the member states concerned became a party to this convention. The convention is a classic example of the approach which tried to overcome East-West tensions in the Cold War era by concentrating on "functional" subjects such as transport or environmental protection. Its ecological effectiveness has however been limited. At a conference in Rønneby (southern Sweden) in September 1990, the process was re-launched. The countries bordering the Baltic Sea, together with Norway, Czechoslovakia, and the EC Commission have decided to tackle the measures necessary to restore the ecological balance in the Baltic Sea. There seem to be no

---

[12] The Council decision to ratify the protocol is reprinted in OJ L181, 4.7.1986, p. 1. Whereas the member states contribute with more than fifty per cent, the Community as such provides only three per cent.

[13] See for instance the directive on air pollution from industrial plants, (84/360), OJ L188, 16.7.1984, p. 20, the directive on air pollution from large combustion plants (88/609), OJ L366, 7.12.1988, p. 1, the directive on air quality limit values for sulphur dioxide (80/779), OJ L229, 30.8.1980, p. 30 (modified by OJ L201, 14.7.1989, p. 53), and the directive on air quality standards for nitrogen dioxide (85/203), OJ L87, 27.3.1985, p. 1.

more objections to the participation of the EC in the Helsinki Convention.

A typical tool of international environmental cooperation at a rather low level is monitoring and data gathering. The above mentioned EMEP network falls into that category, but also the Community's CORINE network, and, on a higher institutional level, the European Environmental Agency. As insufficient data are widely considered to be a major problem, cooperation in this field is foreseen in the framework of the association agreements to be negotiated with the Eastern European countries[14].

Pollution control agreements normally regulate cases in which substantial damage to the environment has already materialized or where it is expected to materialize within a relatively short time period. An environmental policy which is not exclusively oriented towards short-term results but also towards medium-term improvements and an approach which prefers prevention to ex-post cure will try to decrease the possibilities for damage to materialize. One area, where this approach could yield high results especially with respect to Eastern Europe is research. Research in the field of energy savings or material savings (e.g. in the steel industry) coupled with the possibility of technology transfer could lead to the use of more environmentally sound technologies, in particular in the heavy industries in Eastern Europe[15]. Research cooperation in the above-mentioned fields is possible according to the provisions of the 3rd framework programme on research and technological development. In the field of research cooperation with third countries, several models of cooperation exist. The member states retain, however, considerable competences in this area, and financing of projects by Community funds is possible only to a rather limited extent.

A specific area of cooperation, and one in which the Community possesses a sound legal capacity for action laid down in the EURATOM Treaty, is the field of nuclear safety. The recently concluded cooperation agreement with the Soviet Union[16] contains a clause on

---

[14] See COM (90) 398, p. 14.

[15] See the Commission outline of possible areas of cooperation in COM (90) 257.

[16] OJ L68, 15.3.1990.

cooperation in the field of nuclear energy. On this basis, the Commission has asked from the Council the authorization to go ahead with negotiations on three agreements, namely on nuclear safety, on the exchange of fissile matter and on nuclear fusion[17]. Although nuclear energy is highly contested in many Western European countries and increasingly also in Eastern Europe, it may continue to play a significant role for the generation of electricity when greenhouse gases, i.e. mainly carbon-dioxide, are to be reduced significantly in the next decade. Improving the poor safety record of Eastern European nuclear power plants will then become an imperative irrespective of one's personal position towards the exploitation of nuclear energy.

3.2. Integrating the Environment in Other Policy Areas

Economic development and environmental protection are inextricably linked. With the ever increasing level of industrial activity, the challenge for policy makers today is no longer to decide how much environmental protection is tolerable without hampering economic growth and the international competitiveness of a country but how sustainable economic activities can be introduced that do not hamper the natural resource basis and thus undermine the very basis of any economic activity. To give just one example: in Poland, one third of the rivers are now too polluted even for *industrial* uses. Due to excessive pollution, the installation of new industries is barely possible in the old industrial areas.

When the "Group of 24" decided in July 1989 to entrust the EC-Commission with the coordination of the emergency aid to Poland and Hungary (PHARE programme) (Ehlermann 1989), which was later extended to the other Eastern European countries with the exception of the Soviet Union, it consequently made environmental protection one of the five priority areas of the aid scheme[18]. One sixth of the total amount of aid for 1990 (49 out of 300 million ECU) are intended to finance projects on the monitoring of pollution,

---

[17] See *Agence Europe*, No. 5308, 2.8.1990, p. 3.

[18] Art. 3 of the regulation implementing the PHARE programme explicitly mentions environmental protection; see Reg. 3906/89 of 18 December 1989, OJ L375, p. 11.

improving water quality, the treatment of waste, etc. The main aim of this aid is to enable the local authorities to deal with the most pressing environmental problems. Consequently, all projects are conceived and managed in close collaboration with local authorities in order to avoid inefficiencies which would occur if too many decisions were taken in Brussels.

The environmental section of the PHARE programme still constitutes an example of classic environmental policy but it has a special political significance in so far as it has been decided at a very high political level to include environmental assistance in an important *political* package to support the transition from a centrally-planned to a market economy. It can thus be regarded as a first step towards integration.

Similar plans, although still in a less concrete form, exist for the conclusion of "second generation agreements" between the European Community and Eastern European countries[19]. In its programmatic outline of the future association agreements[20], the Commission includes environmental protection among the areas where closer cooperation is desirable. Amongst those, the association of Eastern European countries to the future European Environmental Agency occupies a special place. Again, environmental protection is part of a political package in an important area. It remains to be seen, however, whether the other areas of cooperation will be shaped in a way which is coherent with the notion of sustainable development[21].

The most important field of action perhaps for the development of environmentally sustainable policies is probably the Community's trade policy. The EEC-Treaty, in its article 113, attributes wide-ranging *exclusive* competences to the Community. Although their

---

[19] "First generation agreements" mainly deal with trade and economic cooperation, whereas the new type of agreements envisaged by the Commission covers a whole range of political, economic and institutional questions.

[20] See COM (90) 398.

[21] As one of its first actions in the framework of the aid for Poland and Hungary, for instance, the Commission has sent large quantities of pesticides to Poland; see *Agence Europe*, No. 5142, 30.11.1989.

reach is not clear in any specific case, member states have lost their capacity to act in most fields. In addition, decisions are taken by qualified majority. Given its legal competences and its political and economic importance as the world's biggest trading power, the external trade policy of the EC has a strong impact on environmental protection measures either in a positive or in a negative sense. Trade regulations could be used to achieve environmental goals, and environmental restrictions on trade, which are likely to be utilized increasingly in the future, will have an impact on the trade balance of third countries. The following remarks do not attempt to present a comprehensive analysis of existing trade patterns and policies and their impact on the environment but merely to outline the main areas in which conflicts between environmental protection requirements and trade could arise, as well as the fields in which commercial policy could serve as a powerful tool to achieve a better protection of the environment. It is, however, submitted that these areas are of special importance for Eastern European countries to the extent that those countries become integrated into the world economic system and thus vulnerable to changes in trade patterns. The three main areas where conflicts as well as synergies between commercial and environmental policy exist are industrial relocation, the impact of product standards on trade flows and direct restrictions on trade[22].

Industrial relocation could become an important issue for Eastern European countries in the future, although it is very difficult to assess its concrete significance. Even if in general a relocation of industries to regions with a higher absorptive capacity of the environment is accepted, the case is different for Eastern Europe. Polluting industries might be attracted not by the absorptive capacity of the environment in those countries (which seems to be extremely damaged) but by the need to create new jobs. Polluting industries would thus in the short term help to cope with the economic crisis but at the same time exacerbate the ecological crisis. In the medium and long term, such a development is likely to have a negative im-

---

[22] A very solid study of these interactions, although concentrated on the environmental effects of the completion of the internal market via trade relations with third countries is contained in a report prepared for the Commission (Task Force 1989, ch. 11).

pact on the economic situation as well because it leads to the conservation of an outdated industrial infrastructure. It seems, however, that at least in general terms, the principle of not having two levels of environmental protection standards in Europe is accepted. The conclusions of the meeting of Eastern and Western European ministers of the environment provides that effective procedures to assess the environmental impact of new industrial installations shall be developed. The installation of EC companies shall be encouraged, but those companies should follow a code of conduct based on Community protection standards[23]. An important step in this direction would be the extension of the procedures for environmental impact assessment existing in the Community[24] to new installations in third countries. This means the extension of internal Community standards to third countries and the pursuance of foreign policy goals by internal legislation.

A perhaps even more important area is the impact of high environmental standards for products on trade flows. In general, EC product standards are higher than those existing in Eastern European countries. Those standards could thus act as a barrier to export from Eastern European countries, exports which might be vital for economic recovery. As derogations from those standards are unlikely to be applied, the only solution for Eastern European countries to avoid permanent trade disadvantages is to adopt levels of protection which are roughly comparable to those of the European Community. Although this could in general lead to the adoption of high environmental standards by the trade partners of the EC, a huge conflict potential is hidden here. Environmental protection standards could be used mainly for protectionist reasons, thus not serving the environment but hampering the economic development in third countries. In any case, trade conflicts because of environmental standards are likely to increase in the future. It might therefore be appropriate to create fora in which such questions can be discussed at an early stage in order to avoid or to minimize conflicts. Although such institutional arrangements are most urgently

---

[23] See *Agence Europe*, No. 5278, 20.6.1990, p. 11.

[24] On the basis of the Directive on Environmental Impact Assessment (85/337), OJ L175, 5.7.1985, p. 40.

needed in the trade relations with the United States and Japan, they might be increasingly important for Eastern Europe.

Besides these indirect restrictions on trade (which do not have trade impacts as their *aim*), increasing use is being made of direct restrictions on trade. A number of international agreements use trade limitations for the achievement of their regulatory goals[25]. In a number of specific areas, the EC has pioneering internal legislation which it should also apply in its relations to Eastern Europe. This is the case for the transfrontier movement and the export of hazardous waste[26] and for the export of dangerous chemicals[27]. These measures, again of an internal nature, offer strong tools for environmental protection in specific areas.

When regarded from a more political perspective, there seems to be no alternative to the seemingly utopian conception of a Europe with equal environmental standards. A European Community with high standards opposed to Eastern European countries with a low level of protection would be a conflictual construction. The more the integration of the two halves of Europe progresses, the more vulnerable this process becomes for disruptions. With increasing trade flows, the likelihood of trade conflict will also increase. A closing of the Community frontiers for Eastern European products because of environmental standards is, however, a highly undesirable outcome. Given the legal, political, and economic capabilities of the EC, the Community should press for the realization of all-European environmental protection standards without imposing them by virtue of its overwhelming economic weight. Indeed, Eastern European countries have a long-term interest in such standards: If they now, under the pressure of the economic crisis, were to opt for lower environmental standards, they would risk installing an in-

---

[25] Examples are the CITES-Convention (Convention on International Trade in Endangered Species), implemented by regulation 3626/82 (OJ L384, 13.12.1982) and the Montreal Protocol on Substances that Deplete the Ozone Layer, OJ L297, 31.10.1988, p. 9.

[26] See directive 84/631 (OJ L326, 13.12.1984, p. 31), as amended by directive 86/279 (OJ L181, 4.7.1986, p. 13), and the Council Resolution of 21 December 1988 (OJ C9, 12.1.1989).

[27] Reg. 88/1734, OJ L155, 22.6.1988, p. 2.

dustrial structure which is already outdated today and even more so in the future. The necessary adjustment costs would then be even higher.

4. Conclusion

The above analysis has shown that the European Community is active in many fields with regard to environmental protection in Eastern Europe. Its policy covers pollution control, information gathering, research and economic assistance. This result is even more surprising when the mutual ignorance of EC and Eastern Europe prior to 1988 is taken into account. The EC not only acts in the field of its own proper competences but also as a co-ordinator of the PHARE programme which provides Western aid to Eastern Europe. This is not only a major political success for the Community but is also likely to make a contribution to the amelioration of the environmental situation in Eastern Europe because the environment is a major issue in the PHARE programme. The European Community is thus directly or indirectly controlling a large part of the environmental assistance to Eastern Europe.

However, the argument put forward here is that a gradual shift from classic environmental policy (i.e. mainly pollution control agreements) to the restructuring of economic activity will happen in the future. Pollution control is necessary but not sufficient. In this phase of the reconstruction of their economies the Eastern European countries have a unique chance to lay the foundations for industries which are less resource-consuming and less polluting. There is, however, the risk that short-term policies and severe financial constraints will lead to the installation of an industrial infrastructure which observes lower environmental standards than in Western Europe. These industries could then become the problem sectors of tomorrow. Neglecting the environmental factor could lead to economic backwardness by conserving outdated production structures while the world's main trade blocs, the EC, the US, and Japan are increasingly tightening their environmental protection standards. The establishment of a model of environmentally sustainable development is thus an important factor for the political relations between the EC and Eastern Europe. It is inconceivable to build up new all-European structures and to bridge the gap between the two parts of the continent without fighting the environmental disasters in the East and their economic reasons. Helping Eastern European countries in coping with ecological disasters and in preparing the grounds for sustainable growth is a central issue of European politics. A new concentration on ecological security could replace the traditional but outdated fixation on military security (Senghaas 1990: 31/32).

Given this context, the question arises whether the Community has the competence to tackle these matters. The chapter in the EEC treaty dealing with environmental protection is the only one to mention the subsidiarity principle according to which the Community is only entitled to act when a specific goal can be better attained at Community than at member state level. The subsidiarity principle will certainly play a major role in the intergovernmental conference on political union which will revise the EEC treaty. The subsidiarity principle which plays only a minor role as long as decisions are taken unanimously, thus leaving a veto right to each dissenting state, will become much more important when majority voting is introduced for environmental protection. A clarification of the external competences of the Community would indeed be of use in the field of environmental protection where until now the heavy machinery of mixed agreements has been put into place. In the trade sector, however, which is going to play a larger role in environmental protection, the competences of the Community are very wide.

In the latter field, it seems that contrary to the situation in the sector of "pure" environmental policy, the Community has strong instruments at its disposal. The problem is not so much one of creating new ones but of properly using the existing ones. What is still lacking is a "prise de conscience" that environmental and economic policy, internally as well as externally, are inseparable. In addition to that, competences for foreign environmental policy in the sense used here are scattered within the Commission. Different directorate generals have largely diverging perceptions of the relative importance of environmental protection for their respective area of competence. A first occasion to do away with the artificial separation of economic and environmental policy are the series of association agreements with Eastern European countries which are now being negotiated. At present, there seems to be a risk that environmental policy gains importance but remains restricted to a specific area while economic and commercial cooperation continues in a business-as-usual manner. The main challenge for the foreign environmental policy of the European Community is therefore to leave its conceptual insulation and become an integral part of all other policy fields of the Community as it is stimulated by the Treaty. The new relationship with Eastern European countries provides a unique opportunity for this.

Bibliography

BUNGARTEN, HARALD W., 1978: Umweltpolitik in Westeuropa. EG, internationale Organisationen und nationale Umweltpolitiken (Bonn: Europa Union Verlag).

CLINTON DAVIS, STANLEY, 1987: International Affairs and the Environment, in *Studia Diplomatica*, pp. 99-107.

CSCE 1989: Abschließendes Dokument des Wiener Treffens 1986 der Vertreter der Teilnehmerstaaten der Konferenz über Sicherheit und Zusammenarbeit in Europa, 15 January 1989, in *Europa-Archiv 44*, pp. D133-D164.

EC 1990: Environmental Imperative Declaration of the European Council; Text reprinted in *Agence Europe*, Documents, No. 1632/1633, 29 June 1990.

ECJ 1971: Case 22/70 (ERTA), ECJ Reports 1971, p. 263.

EHLERMANN, CLAUS-DIETER, 1989: Aid for Poland and Hungary, First Assessment, in *European Affairs*, 4/1989, pp. 23-27.

EP 1989: Report on the Proposal from the Commission for a regulation on economic aid to the Republic of Hungary and Poland.

Opinion of the Environment Committee, Rapporteur R. Chanterie, EP-Doc. A3-90/89.

HAIGH, NIGEL, 1987: EEC Environmental Policy and Britain, (Harlow: Longman, 2nd ed.).

JACHTENFUCHS, MARKUS, 1990: The European Community and the Protection of the Ozone Layer, in *Journal of Common Market Studies 28*, pp. 261-277.

JOHNSON, STANLEY P./CORCELLE, GUY, 1989: The Environmental Policy of the European Communities (London/Dodrecht/Boston: Graham Trotman).

MAYER-TASCH, PETER-CORNELIUS, 1985: Die internationale Umweltpolitik als Herausforderung für die Nationalstaatlichkeit, in *Aus Politik und Zeitgeschichte*, B20.

MYERS, NORMAN, 1989: Environment and Security, in *Foreign Policy*, Spring 1989, pp. 23-41.

O'KEEFFE, DAVID/SCHERMERS, HENRY G. (EDS.), 1983: Mixed Agreements (Deventer: Kluver).

PRITTWITZ, VOLKER, 1983: Umwelt und Außenpolitik, in *Aus Politik und Zeitgeschichte*, B42, pp. 13-24.

PRITTWITZ, VOLKER, 1984: Umweltaußenpolitik. Grenzüberschreitende Luftverschmutzung in Europa (Frankfurt a.M./New York: Campus).

SCHEVARDNADSE, EDUARD, 1990: Ecology and Diplomacy, in *Environmental Policy and Law 20*, pp. 20-24.

SENGHAAS, DIETER, 1990: Europa 2000. Ein Friedensplan (Frankfurt: Suhrkamp).

TASK FORCE, 1989: 1992: The Environmental Dimension. Task Force Report on the Environment and the Internal Market (Brussels: EC Commission).

TUDYKA, KURT, 1988: Umweltpolitik in Ost- und Westeuropa (Opladen: Leske + Budrich).

VOIGT, KARSTEN D., 1987: Internationale Umweltpolitik, in *Die Neue Gesellschaft/Frankfurter Hefte 34*, pp. 951-955.

VON WEIZSÄCKER, ERNST ULRICH, 1987: Umweltschutz. Eine neue Dimension der internationalen Politik, in *Hans Dietrich Genscher (ed.)*, Nach vorn gedacht ...: Perspektiven deutscher Außenpolitik (Stuttgart: Bonn aktuell), pp. 195-209.

WIRTH, DAVID A., 1989: Climate Chaos, in *Foreign Policy*, Spring 1989, pp. 3-22.

Current Situation and Perspectives in Resolving Transboundary Environmental Problems at Regional Level

Mikhail KOKINE[*]

The Economic Commission for Europe (ECE) is a unique forum for East-West cooperation in the field of the environment. The Commission was established in 1947 as an integral part of the United Nations. It is one of the five regional commissions of the United Nations, and has 34 member countries (end of 1990). This membership includes practically all the countries of Europe as well as the United States and Canada. The Commission is engaged in 10 major programmes: trade, environment, science and technology, economic projections, transport, energy, agriculture and timber, industry, human settlements and statistics.

Regional cooperation in the field of the environment pursued under the auspices of the Commission has been shaped by a three-decade history of intergovernmental dialogue, negotiation and action. The response of ECE governments to the challenges of environmental degradation has in the past produced strategies, policy recommendations and multilateral regulatory instruments of a legally binding character. The list of selected ECE documents relating to the environment is enclosed (see annex).

East-West cooperation in the area of the environment has developed into one of the priority activities of the Commission. It is noteworthy that while at the beginning of this process only a limited number of ECE member countries actively advocated and promoted cooperative international efforts in this field, there is now a

---

[*] The views expressed in this article are those of the author and do not necessarily coincide with those of the United Nations Economic Commission for Europe.

broad consensus in the whole ECE region concerning the urgency and importance of environmental cooperation, as environmental problems therein are taking on a new dimension.

Transboundary pollution related to the use of the environment and natural resources is a growing concern in the ECE region. The effects beyond national frontiers of the long-range transmission of water and air pollutants, dangers connected with the transport and management of hazardous goods and wastes, the mismanagement of shared natural resources or biotopes and the extinction of migratory species are some of the issues which call for international cooperation, since individual countries acting alone cannot deal effectively with problems that are regional if not global in scale.

Concerted action at the regional level depends on the degree of compatibility of national environmental policies and standards. Such action can be very efficient for the optimal allocation of limited financial means and can help to avoid distortions in international trading patterns. Harmonization of policies is also being achieved through the coordination of the procedures for the environmental assessment of projects. This is especially important in the transboundary context. Standardization of environmental technology, control, monitoring and testing are other measures being applied. Cooperative research and management activities allow the financial burdens of technological development to be spread more equitably when costs of solving environmental problems exceed the capacity of a single country or even of groups of countries to bear this heavy responsibility. Enhanced international cooperation enables countries to deal effectively and amicably with shared natural-resource problems in a situation in which everyone benefits from the joint efforts.

The 1975 Final Act of the Conference on Security and Cooperation in Europe (CSCE) gave notable impetus to work by the Commission in the field of the environment. The ECE environment programme has been continuously adapted to implement the relevant provisions not only of the Final Act but also of the Concluding Documents of the Follow-up Meetings and to promote the outcome of the CSCE Meeting on the Protection of the Environment, held in Sofia (Bulgaria) in 1989. There have been a number of important initiatives within the framework of ECE, such as the High-level Meeting on the Protection of the Environment, which took place in Geneva in 1979. That meeting adopted the Convention on Long-range Transboundary Air Pollution and the Declaration on Low and Non-Waste Technology and Re-utilization and Recycling of Wastes. Thirty-one States and the European Economic Community have ratified the 1979 Convention on Long-range Transboundary Air Pollution and now actively participate in its implementation. Supplementary protocols have been adopted covering very specific subjects. In 1984 there was a Protocol on the long-term financing of the Co-operative Programme for Monitoring and Evaluation of the Long-range Transmission of Air Pollutants in Europe (EMEP). The following year, in Helsinki, a protocol on sulphur dioxide was adopted. By this protocol, which entered into force in 1987, Parties undertake to reduce their national annual sulphur emissions or their transboundary fluxes by at least 30 per cent by 1993. These reductions are based on the 1980 levels of emissions. The 1988 Sofia Protocol concerning the control of emissions of nitrogen oxides or their transboundary fluxes entered into force in February 1991. Preparations are well underway for another draft protocol on volatile organic compounds, the second major air pollutant responsible for the formation of photo-oxidants which are considered a key factor in forest decline. Furthermore, the Executive Body for the Convention decided, at its seventh session in November 1989, to initiate new proposals for the development of further international measures on sulphur emissions.

The EMEP monitoring programme, established in 1977, collects data on pollution levels in the air and in precipitation in Europe. It also collates the amounts of pollutants being transported from one country to another. This is done with coordinated measurements at 101 stations operated by 27 parties to the Convention. Model calculations are also used. These are based on information on emissions, meteorological conditions as well as chemical and physical processes in the atmosphere. The models simulate the transport and deposition of pollutants.

In addition to EMEP there are four other international cooperative programmes which monitor and assess air-pollution effects on forests, aquatic ecosystems, materials (including historical and cultural monuments) and agricultural crops.

Past efforts within ECE initially concentrated on pollution abatement. This focus has gradually evolved into a broader concept embodying environmental quality, natural-resource utilization, economic activity and social development. This view recognizes the close, complex and dynamic links that exist between individual sectors.

For this reason, ECE governments decided on a systematic reconsideration of their activities in the light of the environmental issues which are or could become of major concern particularly in a transboundary context. To this effect, in 1988 the ECE adopted the Regional Strategy for Environmental Protection and Rational Use of Natural Resources in ECE Member Countries covering the Period up to the Year 2000 and Beyond.

While this Regional Strategy deals with environmental problems of a transboundary nature and problems that are common to, or shared among, governments within the ECE region, it also reflects the interdependence of geographical regions and problems.

The Regional Strategy embodies a number of concepts and approaches. One of its key elements is "sustainable development". This concept reflects the view that the development process must be vigorously pursued, but that its continuation and expansion depend on mankind's ability to properly maintain the environment and the resource base which underlies such development. The concept of sustainable development is also a cornerstone of the report entitled "Our Common Future", by the World Commission on Environment and Development.

The critical concerns addressed by this ECE Strategy may be grouped under six headings: the Atmosphere; Inland Waters and Seas; Soil Protection and Land Use; Forests; Wildlife and Genetic Resources; and last but not least, Wastes, Toxic and Hazardous Chemicals. Not only does the Strategy identify problems and provide an analytical assessment of the various trends; it also sets goals to which ECE governments will devote attention in the medium and long terms. The Regional Strategy also establishes a series of policy and programme responses aimed at achieving these goals and sets out conditions necessary for its implementation.

The aspiration is to create in the ECE region, in the early part of the next century, a situation in which economic activity and social development can take place in an environment essentially free from: the degrading effects of pollution; the threat of hazards posed to human health by chemicals and wastes; loss of values and opportunities associated with a broad and stable natural-resource base; and disagreements over environmental issues of a transboundary nature.

The ECE's continuing cross-sectoral activities in the promotion of sustainable economic development include preparations for the Conference at Ministerial Level on the Follow-up to the Report of the World Commission on Environment and Development (WCED). This Conference was organized in Bergen in May 1990 by the Government of Norway in close cooperation with the ECE.

Uncontrolled amounts of hazardous wastes, dumped into nature or on ill-chosen landfill sites, have caused serious problems in a number of ECE countries. The ECE answer to this difficult problem lies in policies and strategies promoting low- and non-waste technology, in order to minimize the generation of hazardous waste. In this respect, ECE has been a pioneer. The Declaration on Low- and Non-waste Technology and Re-utilization and Recycling of Wastes adopted in 1979 calls attention to the use of energy- and resource-saving technologies as a means of reducing the amount of wastes generated per unit of product. This approach is based on the abatement of pollution at its source. Not only processes but also the design of manufactured products are factors examined with a view to decreasing those components which are potentially hazardous to the environment. Based on recommendations contained in the Declaration, broad cooperative activities are being pursued within ECE in the field of energy and resource-saving technologies and hazardous-waste management.

The elaboration of a regional strategy on integrated waste-management was initiated this year within ECE. It is expected to provide a concerted and systematic approach to harmonizing national waste-management policies, linking up the various objectives of waste management. These include: waste minimization at source, recycling, transportation, storage, treatment and disposal. Another ECE programme is aimed at promoting the production of environmentally sound products.

ECE also plays a special role in the field of the transport of dangerous goods, as it provides the technical support for the Economic and Social Council (ECOSOC) Committee of Experts in this field. This body, composed of high-level government experts, establishes the Recommendations for the Transport of Dangerous Goods, which cover all transport modes used throughout the world. Present work is oriented towards enlarging existing international agreements and provisions on the international carriage of dangerous goods, in order to include conditions and procedures for the safe transboundary shipment of hazardous wastes. The provisions and recommendations involved cover all transport modes and are designed for application not only in the ECE region but throughout the world. A convention on civil liability for damage caused during the carriage of dangerous goods by road, rail and inland navigation vessels has been elaborated and has been open to signature since 1 February 1990. It is based on the principles of strict and limited liability, the channelling of responsibility and compulsory insurance.

In the light of relevant provisions of the Final Act of the CSCE, ECE is paying increased attention to environmental impact assessment. A convention is being developed to regulate the application of such assessment in a transboundary context. The convention will stipulate commonly agreed provisions to carry out jointly or to coordinate national procedures for assessing environmental impacts and to arrange for those assessments to take place at an early stage of the planning of any activities likely to cause transboundary environmental impacts. At the end of 1991, the convention was open for signature but not yet in force.

There has been a growing sense of urgency in the region over the need to strengthen measures aimed at maintaining essential ecological processes and life-support systems. Preserving biological diversity in the interest of present and future generations is especially important in this regard. In 1988, ECE governments adopted a Declaration on Conservation of Flora, Fauna and their Habitats. The ultimate goal is to construct a framework for concerted efforts to conserve flora and fauna particularly threatened, and migratory species and their habitats. A number of cooperative programmes have been launched to promote the implementation of this Declaration. The elaboration of a European Red List of Threatened Animals and

Plants is under finalization, together with recommendations to ECE governments on its application at both national and international levels. The elaboration of comprehensive guidelines has also been initiated. Such guidelines, which will take the form of a code of practice, are intended to assist ECE governments in their efforts to strengthen the conservation of threatened animals and plants and to maintain, to the extent possible, biological diversity. Work continues on the elaboration of lists of species of particular conservation concern in Europe, thereby acknowledging species of flora and fauna for whose conservation a country, as a range state, has international responsibility whether or not those species are considered threatened in that particular country.

In the course of the past two decades, significant efforts have been made within ECE to strengthen cooperation in connection with transboundary waters. Intensive negotiation and cooperative action led to a number of ECE declarations of policy and decisions in the field of transboundary waters. Examples include the 1980 Declaration of Policy on Prevention and Control of Water Pollution, including Transboundary Pollution, and the 1987 Principles Regarding Cooperation in the Field of Transboundary Waters. In those Principles, ECE Governments recognized the significance of the harmonious development, use and conservation of transboundary waters. They declared that the prevention and control of transboundary pollution in rivers and lakes which crossed or formed the frontiers between two or more countries and in related ground-water aquifers, together with the prevention and control of floods, were urgent tasks which could only be accomplished by enhanced cooperation between riparian States.

A number of problems related to the abatement of transboundary water pollution cannot be fully resolved unless national policies and strategies are harmonized at the international level. Strengthened cooperation at the regional level, taking into consideration the various transboundary water agreements and aimed at preventing and controlling transboundary water pollution, would assure a better coordination of national water policies in all catchment areas.

Concerted efforts are also needed to bring about greater cooperation at a regional level in the protection of ground-water aquifers located beneath national boundaries against pollution and over-use.

Most existing bilateral and multilateral agreements do not contain provisions for the achievement of this objective. Governments need to consider the advisability of supplementing these arguments by provisions such as those contained in the ECE Charter on Groundwater Management, adopted by the Commission in 1989.

Complex and hitherto unresolved legal issues associated with transboundary water pollution exist, particularly in the areas of responsibility and liability; means of compensation; damage assessment, and attribution of damage to polluters abroad. The elaboration of a concept regarding responsibility and liability has been undertaken within ECE. Once endorsed, this concept will constitute a useful model for solving similar problems in other transboundary environmental fields.

The importance of further cooperation in the field of transboundary waters was emphasized in the pertinent recommendations of the CSCE Vienna Concluding Document. One recommendation called for the elaboration of a framework convention or specific conventions to improve the protection of transboundary water courses and international lakes. In the light of these considerations and the outcome of the CSCE Meeting on the Protection of the Environment (Sofia, 1989), the elaboration of a framework convention on the protection and use of transboundary water courses and international lakes was initiated within ECE in 1990.

In the Vienna Concluding Document, the participating states also agreed to cooperate bilaterally and multilaterally to improve and coordinate their arrangements for prevention, early warning, exchange of information and mutual assistance with regard to accidents likely to cause transboundary damage to the environment. The states also agreed to initiate the examination of key elements related to the transboundary character of industrial accidents, such as clean-up, restoration and liability.

The risk of accidents increases with technological advance, since such developments are generally less tolerant of human error in operations. Risks may also increase as the number, size and age of installations grow and the substances involved become more toxic. The possibility of industrial accidents with transboundary environmental impacts cannot be excluded. Emergency situations which have arisen clearly reveal a degree of unpreparedness both at national and international levels. Present means and methods for coping with emergencies have often proved to be inappropriate and inefficient.

Transboundary impacts necessitate the coordination of the flow of information between governments and to the public likely to be affected. They also call for contingency planning and the training of personnel in advance of the occurrence of any accident. It is essential to render compatible the procedures for notification and information exchange, as well as systems for early warning, alarm dispatch and post-accident monitoring, with a view to undertaking emergency response and rehabilitation measures either jointly or on a coordinated basis. It is equally important to achieve compatibility concerning techniques for damage evaluation.

Common procedures for providing mutual assistance are needed at the regional level, together with mechanisms enabling countries involved in emergency situations to obtain instant information on the availability of expertise, material and equipment in other countries.

Financial issues require negotiation and agreement before accidents occur. These deal with financing or sharing the costs of immediate measures to reduce damage to man, property and the environment; mutual response and assistance actions; compensation of victims; rehabilitation of damage; and other related issues.

In response to these pressing needs, ECE governments elaborated and adopted in April 1990 the Code of Conduct on Accidental Pollution of Transboundary Inland Waters. The Code provides guidance for the competent authorities in individual member countries in their task of reducing the risk of accidental pollution; it is aimed at improving the planning of preparedness to cope with emergencies and to handle accidents.

An *ad hoc* working group was set up in 1990 by ECE governments, with a mandate to elaborate a legal instrument on the transboundary impacts of industrial accidents. The *ad hoc* working group will study, *inter alia*, the issue of the possible establishment and operation of a centre and/or an appropriate network for emergency environmental assistance, the financial aspects involved and the possible participation of industry and the scientific community.

So while the record of achievement within the framework of the ECE in the fight against transboundary environmental problems is quite impressive, there is no room for complacency, since many urgent problems remain to be tackled. Indeed, East-West cooperation in the area of the environment is becoming a truly pan-European cooperation based on common concerns and objectives; this co-operation has developed into one of the most important priority activities of the Economic Commission for Europe. The time seems to be ripe for undertaking the updating and strengthening of the ECE Regional Strategy in order to assess and facilitate the solution of urgent environmental problems facing ECE member countries at both national and international levels. The encouraging recent developments in East-West relations create a unique momentum for concerted action of this kind.

Annex

Selected ECE Documents Relating to the Environment

- *Report of the High-level Meeting within the Framework of the ECE on the Protection of the Environment,* 13-15 November 1979, Geneva. 1980 (ECE/HLM. 1/2). This document includes, in the three ECE working languages:
  - Convention on Long-range Transboundary Air Pollution; and
  - Declaration on Low- and Non-waste Technology and Re-utilization and Recycling of Wastes.

- *National Programmes for Environmental Pollution Control. 1983 (ECE/ENV/41).*

- *Strategy for Environmental Protection and Rational Use of Natural Resources in ECE Member Countries covering the Period up to the Year 2000 and Beyond,* Part I: Environmental trends and policies in the ECE region. 1987 (ECE/ENV/49).

- *Statistical Standards and Studies No. 39: Environmental Statistics in Europe and North America – An Experimental Compendium* (UN Sales No. E.87.II.E.28). Part One: Time series data and indicators. Part Two: Statistical monograph of the Baltic Sea environment. 1987.

- *Environmental Series 1 – Application of Environmental Impact Assessment Highways and Dams* – (ECE/ENV/50 – UN Sales No. E.87.II.E.14). 1987.

- *Regional Strategy for Environmental Protection and Rational Use of Natural Resources in ECE Member Countries up to the Year 2000 and Beyond* (E/ECE/1171 – ECE/ENVWA/5 – UN Sales No. 88.II.E.26).

- *Environmental Series 3 – Post-project Analysis in Environmental Impact Assessment;* 1990 (ECE/ENVWA/11 – UN Sales No. 90.II.E.6).

- *Long-terms Perspectives for Water Use and Supply in the ECE Region.* 1981. (ECE/WATER/26) (Sales No. 81.II.E.22).

- *Policies and Strategies for Rational Use of Water in the ECE Region.* 1983. (ECE/WATER/31) (Sales No. 83.II.E.10).

- *Economic Bulletin for Europe, Vol. 36 No. 1 (March 1984). Drinking Water Supply and Sanitation in Rural Areas.* Published for the United Nations by Pergamon Press Ltd., Oxford, United Kingdom.

- *Strategies, Technologies and Economics of Waste-water Management in ECE Countries.* 1984. (ECE/WATER/36) (Sales No. 84.II.E.18).

- *Engineering Equipment and Automation Means for Waste-Water Management in ECE Countries* – (ECE/ENG.AUT/18 – UN Sales No. E.84.II.E.13). Vol I. A report on prevailing practices and recent experience in production and use of engineering equipment and automation means for preventing water pollution. Prepared under the auspices of the ECE Working Party on Engineering Industries and Automation. Part I.

– *Impact of Non-Conventional Sources of Energy on Water.* 1985. (ECE/WATER/41) (Sales No. 85.II.E.32).

– *Systems of Water Statistics in the ECE Region.* 1986. (ECE/WATER/43) (Sales No. 86.II.E.22).

– *Ground-Water Legislation in the ECE Region.* 1986. (ECE/WATER/44) (Sales No. 86.II.E.21).

– *Two Decades of Cooperation on Water. Declarations and Recommendations by the Economic Commission for Europe.* 1988 (ECE/ENVWA/2).

– *Water Pollution Control and Flood Management in Transboundary Waters.* 1988. (ECE/ENVWA/7).

– *Charter on Ground-water Management* (E/ECE/1197-ECE/ENVWA/12 – UN Sales No. E.89.II.E.21).

– *Code of Conduct on Accidental Pollution of Transboundary Inland Waters.* 1990 (ECE/ENVWA/16).

– *Water Use and Water-Pollution Control: Trends, Policies, Prospects.* 1989 (ECE/ENVWA/10).

– *Air Pollution Studies, No. 1: Air-borne Sulphur Pollution Effects and Control.* 1984 (ECE/EB.AIR/2) (Sales No. 84.II.E.8).

– *Air Pollution Studies, No. 2: Air Pollution across Boundaries.* 1985 (ECE/EB.AIR/5) (Sales No. 85.II.E.17).

– *Air Pollution Studies, No. 3: Transboundary Air Pollution, Effects and Control.* 1986 (ECE/EB.AIR/8) (Sales No. 86.II.E.23).

- *Technologies for Control of Air Pollution from Stationary Sources. Economic Bulletin for Europe.* March 1987, Vol. 39, No. 1.

- *Air Pollution Studies, No. 4: Effects and Control of Transboundary Air Pollution* (ECE/EB.AIR/13 – UN Sales No. E.87.II.E.36).

- *National Strategies and Policies for Air Pollution Abatement* – (ECE/EB.AIR/14 – UN Sales No. E.87.II.E.29). Results of the 1986 major review prepared within the framework of the Convention on Long-range Transboundary Air Pollution.

- *Air Pollution Studies No. 5: The State of Transboundary Air Pollution*, (ECE/EB.AIR/22 – UN Sales No. E.89.II.E.25).

- *Environmental Series 2: National Strategies for Protection of Flora, Fauna and their Habitats.* (ECE/ENVWA/4 – Sales No. E.88.II.E.2). 1988.

- *Declaration on Conservation of Flora, Fauna and their Habitats.* (E/ECE/1172; ECE/ENVWA/6).

- *Low- and Non-waste Technologies in the Production of Organics.* 1984 (ECE/CHEM/53).

- *Hazardous Waste Management.* 1985 (ECE/ENV/46).

- *Recycling of Used Tyres and Rubber Wastes.* 1987 (ECE/-CHEM/62).

- *Use and Disposal of Wastes from Phosphoric Acid and Titanium Dioxide Production.* 1988 (ECE/CHEM/65 – UN Sales No. 88.II.E./27).

- *Waste Energy Recovery in Industry in the ECE Region.* 1985 (ECE/ENERGY/9 (Sales No. 84.II.E.21).

- *European Agreement concerning the International Carriage of Dangerous Goods by Road (ADR) and Protocol of Signature*, done at Geneva on 30 September 1957; 1989 (ECE/TRANS/80 – UN Sales No. E.89.VIII.2). 2 volumes (Vol. II to appear shortly).

- *Convention on Civil Liability for Damage caused during Carriage of Dangerous Goods by Road, Rail and Inland Navigation Vessels* (CRTD) (ECE/TRANS/79) done at Geneva on 10 October 1989.

- *Recommendations on the Transport of Dangerous Goods*. 1989 (ST/SG/AC.10/1/Rev.6 – UN Sales No. E.89.VIII.1).

Problems of Environmental Cooperation in Europe: A Non-Governmental View

Hans-Peter DÜRR

1. Introduction

In my contribution I would like to present four different points.[*] Firstly, I will elaborate the argument that environmental problems are of a different nature compared to other societal problems we are usually dealing with, at least from a scientific point of view. To a large extent, the difficulties we are actually facing with international organizations handling these problems are caused by the very nature of the problems we are dealing with. In a second part, I would like to present some of the work of the non-governmental organizations I am familiar with. I will not talk very much about Greenpeace nor about the Pugwash Conferences on Science and World Affairs which has recently addressed environmental problems, but instead concentrate on the Global Challenges Network, an organization which was created three years ago. Although these organizations are not limited in scope to European problems but actually address global issues, they have European affairs as a focal point. In a third section, I will come to the practical problems and difficulties we have experienced in our daily work in dealing with the problems at stake. Lastly, I will elaborate briefly on prospects for the future.

---

[*] Professor Dürr's contribution was delivered as a speech at the European University Institute in Florence in June 1990. As its main intention is to give a practitioner's view of East-West environmental cooperation, the original style of a speech (and not of a scientific article) has not been changed.

2. The Atypical Character of Environmental Problems

Let me first address the difficulties we have in approaching environmental problems. You might be surprised to find a nuclear physicist dealing with environmental problems. To explain to you my political background, I must say that as a nuclear physicist I have been very engaged in the peace movement. By starting to work on the disarmament issue and trying to look for a solution to the problems of the arms race I found myself increasingly dealing with the dynamic aspects of this problem. At a certain point, I realized, when comparing problems of disarmament with those of the environment, that the latter are about one order of magnitude more complicated than disarmament issues. At this point, you have to realize that even with disarmament, we have not been very successful, although the situation has, of course, improved.

This finding can be explained very easily: in order to achieve disarmament, we know at least one solution, namely to disarm. It is only the method by which we can ultimately reach this that we do not know. But it is a possible solution. The situation is completely different in the case of environmental problems where the analogy to disarmament would force us to reduce our standard of living in order to consume less resources and hence to produce less pollution. In this case, we would have many difficulties to convince people in the political process to stop their commodity-intensive way of economic activity where large stakes are involved. This means that from the outset we are confronted with a very difficult constellation.

In addition, all environmental problems are closely interrelated. For instance, if you try to solve a problem in the commodity sector, you quickly have a whole range of problems from external trade, geology, domestic paths of development and development aid at hand. As a consequence, it is very difficult to disintegrate the problem, to cut it down into sub-problems which are of a size to make you confident that you can handle them. In our classic way of thinking, we are used to starting by breaking down a problem into smaller parts and dealing with each of the sub-problems separately, and only in a second step do we try to achieve a synthesis in order to solve the main problem.

For environmental problems, this is very difficult, especially with people coming from a science and technology background where they are used to breaking down problems, analyzing them, cutting them down into small pieces and trying to approach the problems at that level. In order to approach environmental problems adequately, we have to take a more holistic or global view from the beginning but at the same time continue to think in terms of local solutions. This is to be achieved in several steps. In the first place, we must have a *transboundary* cooperation. By this, I do not only understand a cooperation which crosses geographical borders but even more a cooperation between disciplines. In the past, there has been much discussion about interdisciplinary work. To my mind, all these efforts have failed because they are too abstract. It is essential to find practical ways to really implement interdisciplinary work.

In addition, it is necessary to cross the borders between *methods* for solving problems. We have to find new alliances between the people who think about the problems and the people who are working on the implementation of solutions. Coming from the academic world, I find that we have marvellous solutions to all kinds of problems, but unfortunately, these solutions are not workable. Thus, it is not surprising that if we propose our solutions to politicians or decision-makers, those people normally do not consider our solutions or find them unrealistic. It is therefore necessary to form new groups for problem-solving which from the beginning do not only think about how to solve a problem but also how to implement the solution we have found.

When dealing with environmental problems, we face the difficulty that we tend to concentrate too much on the symptoms and as a consequence we conceive our solutions in order to stop the symptoms or to repair the damage. What would be necessary, however, is to think about the underlying more fundamental processes. This is immediately connected to our entire system of values, in particular to the values of the Western industrial society. It seems to me that we have the wrong philosophy and that we will hence not be able to solve the current problems without changing the philosophy which is also closely related to the rules of our economy. Within the present economic system, our ecological problems cannot be solved. The system contains a certain *Eigendynamik,* an inherent dynamic, which to my mind nobody controls or is able to control. In fact, this system works as a destabilizing process, a process which nobody knows how to control or to confine it in order to avoid the difficulties it creates.

Although I am a scientist, I am personally convinced that the most important shortcomings do not take place in the field of fundamental research. This view does not neglect the fact that many problems remain to be solved, for instance in the sphere of economics. Obviously, there is an infinite number of problems for which we do not know the answers. Nevertheless, I believe that we know enough about the fundamental causes of the environmental crisis. The knowledge we have available is sufficient to start working on solutions. Therefore, I think it is not a good argument to say that one phenomenon or another should be researched more thoroughly. By doing this we will only waste our time.

The real shortcomings lie within the sphere of implementation of the solutions we find. I repeat it: we know enough about the basic problems and we have ideas and solutions at hand, but we do not know how to implement them. We still do not have very clear ideas of how to transfer these solutions into the political sphere. This is not only the fault of politicians, as one might be tempted to say, but it is also a consequence of the lack of an appropriate organization which would help us to achieve the desired results.

It thus seems to me that there is an urgent need to improve our political system. The main actors in this system today are the political parties. They tend however to act and think in short time periods, always having the next elections in mind. When it comes to long-term solutions, which are the only way to deal with some problems, political parties are unlikely to respond as they prefer to follow the perceived short-term interests of people. This leads to a vicious circle which is difficult to leave. Industry, for its part, declares itself unable to change as long as the political framework in which it operates is not modified because, it is argued, international competition prevents moves towards new models of production. For companies, it is impossible to disobey the rules set by international competition, as this would destroy their economic basis and threaten their very existence.

It follows from this that we need new tools in order to tackle the real problems. Especially, we need a new understanding of the *Eigendynamik* of the system. In my view, we tend to look at problems in a much too static way. In a first step we analyze and describe the problems and we think that we can solve them in a second step with some ready-made solutions. This approach will inevitably fail because most problems are part of a very strong dynamic system involving important power factors. Usually, any attempt to remove such powers will create strong countervailing powers. For those trying to change the system this means that they must dispose of much knowledge in order to achieve their aims. This cannot be accomplished by theoreticians alone but only with the help of people with practical experience.

A good illustration of this is the metaphor of a sailing boat. In former times, it was only possible to sail in the direction the wind blew. If you wanted to go in the opposite direction, you had to wait until the wind changed. In order to come to an end with this inconvenience, people used to think whether there was a way to make the wind turn when they wanted it to turn. In my view, a large part of our present discussions of environmental problems follows the same pattern. This approach will inevitably fail because of the inherent dynamics (*Eigendynamik*) of the system. Finally, people found out that by giving the boat a keel and setting the sails in an appropriate way they could sail against the wind. We now have to invent an equivalent of those keels in order to use the forces acting now to solve our problems. We will not be able to make those forces disappear and therefore we have to use them for our purposes. This is especially true with regard to the economic forces.

3. An Example: Global Challenges Network

Let me now talk about organizations. Greenpeace, for instance, is an excellent organization, but in my view they only show us what is going wrong without pointing out solutions. Nevertheless, this strategy is convincing because Greenpeace says that we cannot solve them anyhow. The mere size of the problems is such that they can only adequately be addressed by states, by the political or economic powers. The only thing organizations can do is to make the public more sensitive in order to exert pressure for change on governments. According to this view, any attempt to solve the problems by one's proper means will be too expensive and is thus most likely to fail. I basically agree with this view without being satisfied by it. As a scientist, I would like to help solve the problems and not only point out where they are. As governments are not capable of innovative solutions, much more external brain power is needed.

The Pugwash Conference on Science and World Affairs recently addressed environmental problems. As the conference had as its main topic the prevention of nuclear war, many nuclear scientists were present. These scientists are extremely capable and deep thinkers, but they are not very well known as they usually address governments directly. At present, their impact is not very important, with the exception of Eastern European countries where they have a considerable influence.

Three years ago, I initiated Global Challenges Network. This was the result of a certain agony stemming from my engagement against SDI, the Strategic Defence Initiative. I was upset about the speech of Ronald Reagan calling upon all scientists of the world to unite their forces in order to create a protective umbrella against nuclear missiles. I very much regretted that the President did not make a similar statement asking scientists to join their efforts in order to approach the global challenges of mankind, in particular the environmental problem, the Third World problem, the world economic problems and the energy issue. It is in this field that we need a combination of the capabilities of all kinds of scientists. When addressing this issue, I received only little resonance in the West but an important support in the East. President Gorbachev in particular took up the topic. This was the start of the Moscow Peace Forum in February 1987, which united a number of scientists, doctors, writers, etc. to concentrate on the above-mentioned problems. It was generally felt that the tension between East and West could much more easily be overcome if the meeting did not exclusively address disarmament issues. I have participated in many of those meetings and my experience is that the disarmament issue polarizes the debate even when all participants have a positive attitude towards each other. We thought that the East-West polarization could only be overcome if we concentrated on the global challenges humanity is facing. A concrete result of this thinking was the creation of Global Challenges Network. We called it a "network" because we were of the opinion that ecological problems cannot be solved by a global strategy but only by local activities. However, these local activities should not be isolated but form a network which is not so much conceived as a means of concrete cooperation but more as a way to stay in touch. A solution found in one place under specific circumstances can thus be communicated to other members of the network. Global Challenges Network is therefore to a large extent a communication network.

A few words about the history of Global Challenges Network might be appropriate. I was one of the initiators of the Moscow 1987 Peace Forum where we decided to found an International Foundation for the Survival and the Development of Humanity, which actually took place in January 1989. During the preparatory phase of the Peace Forum, we wrote to Mr. Gorbachev saying that it was very important for the Soviets at the Forum if Mr. Sakarov participated in their delegation. Sakarov was eventually allowed to attend the meeting, and this was the start of his later political role. Mr. Gorbachev himself played a very important role in setting up this international foundation. We had several meetings in the Kremlin with him on that subject. The International Foundation in a way also tried to create a general framework without limiting its tasks to environmental questions. It also deals with security, development, education, culture, social innovations and related questions. The Global Challenges Network on the other hand tries to set up a world-wide network on environmental issues.

Let me give you an example of the type of problems we approached. At the beginning, we tried to identify the major problems humanity is facing. In a second phase, these problems could be handed over to a commission which has the task to divide the problem into a large number of handy subjects which could be conferred to established organizations or institutions with experience in this specific issue. In all cases, the globality of the original question should not be lost from sight. At the same time, it seems important to indicate ways to tackle the problem and to identify its core. To come back to my metaphor, the task would be to invent the keel which is necessary to solve the problems and to create the political instruments to implement the solutions.

One of our initial preoccupations, for instance, was the cleaning of the Baltic Sea. We chose the Baltic Sea, and not the Mediterranean, because Eastern and Western countries border it. When we started our work in 1987, it was not yet easy to establish East-West working relationships. Concentrating on the Baltic Sea was a means to get East and West together in order to solve a problem which was important to them. Among the other subjects we identified were economic incentives for environmental protection, preservation of local crops in natural habitats as part of the preservation of genetic diversity, computer networks for environmental communication, arms conversion, and future transportation systems. Future transportation systems is a very important subject, especially at present, as we are transferring our transportation system to the Eastern countries. Although we know that our present transport system leads us to a dead end, we still try to export it instead of trying to install an appropriate system in the East which could serve as a model for countries, including our own countries, to show how a future transportation system could be organized with present technology. Other problem fields are the protection of rain forests and energy efficiency, which is becoming increasingly important.

4. Problems of Implementation

Let me come to the third point and tell you something about the difficulties we are facing. The main difficulty is not a new one: it concerns finance. As there is almost nobody specialized in financing a non-governmental organization we have to rely on a few sponsors. However, we are not linked to specific projects but are rather focusing on the initial steps. We would like to be a catalyst for projects and in this sense guide the work of organizations already in place. But precisely because we want to do only the first ordering of the process, the first management of the problem, without getting deeply involved in a specific project, we have difficulties raising funds. An argument frequently encountered is that our work is not really scientific and not connected to a particular project. Industry is not very interested because they think we are working against their interests. To a certain extent this is true because all the wealth we are accumulating now is in a way the product of the degradation of natural resources. We know that we will always have difficulties finding financial support with such an orientation but it is clear to us that we have to go in this direction.

Although it is highly important to finance a transboundary activity which crosses borders not only in the geographical but also in the methodological sense, it is very difficult to find support. I find myself in the situation that as a nuclear physicist, or more specifically as a particle physicist, it is relatively easy to obtain money for something the public does not even know about. I do not think that it is absolutely essential to find a new elementary particle, and I believe that this view is shared by many others. Nevertheless, I can find money to realize those projects because they are considered to be very important, for instance for our national reputation. I do not want to diminish the importance of particle physics, and I am convinced that its problems are important in a certain way but they are not urgent. We have been able to wait for four billion years on this earth to acquire our present knowledge, so we can wait two or three more decades to answer some of the questions it raises.

Whereas these questions can wait, this is not the case for the problems which humanity is facing. They must be solved in our present time. However, no money is available for accomplishing this basic task. It is clear that many of the proposals we make and many of the solutions we conceive will prove to be failures like numerous experiments in nuclear physics. We have to try again and again if we want to find appropriate solutions. But whereas the public is willing to let us go ahead with our experiments in nuclear physics, no money is available for experiments with regard to the very complicated social problems from which the survival of mankind might depend. This is the core of the problem, and it is not accidentally so as a success in the latter field would inevitably change the power structure of society.

In order to change this situation, we need horizontal coalitions, and we have to multiply our efforts to build up these coalitions. The aim is not only to get the different disciplines in the universities together, but also to make a joint effort of scientists, industrialists, politicians and the media. At present, we are rather successful in crossing geographical borders. Scientists talk to scientists across borders, and so do politicians. Industrialists have a much more internationalist approach from the outset, but there is no connection between the different types of knowledge. The basis of the problem, to give an example, is not how we could have clean water. We can of course easily agree on the need to have clean water, on the necessary technologies, etc. The real problem here is the calculation of costs. In our present economic system, the production of the damage contributes to the growth of the Gross Domestic Product (GDP) and the repair of the damage will again make the GDP grow. There is thus no economic incentive to avoid the damage as this will lead to a decrease of GDP when damage is avoided and repair not necessary. How can we convince people to tackle this basic problem?

5. Prospects for the Future

Finally, I will not give a broad outlook into the future but only indicate some perspectives. I think that we have to concentrate much more effort on the boundary conditions of the economy. Without changing the economic framework we will fail to solve our ecological problems. Even if we achieve good results in the present framework, these results can only be reparations. From a scientific point of view, however, I have to say that any repair will only accelerate the degradation of nature because of the fundamental law that any degradation is in a close relationship with the scope and the volume of an action. So if the reparative action increases, the degradation will increase even more.

The second point I would like to make is that at present, I see very good perspectives for cooperation with Eastern countries. This does not only include the transfer of our own inappropriate way of handling the problems we are facing but also the chances for a more intelligent way to do this. We can learn in this situation because we are presently at a starting point. Taking up this chance will however be very difficult because of our economic system which I call a "bank robber" economy. When we say that we create values, we are in reality not creating real values but only the values of a bank robber who invests his money in the welding torch which he uses for breaking into safes. Given this situation, we do not only regard this as the right way of living but even teach developing countries that bank robbery is the most efficient economic path. By doing this, we destroy all cultures which could actually teach us how to achieve a sustainable development which does not have bank robbery as its final aim. Sustainable development, however, is the only way out of our present bank robber economy, and by destroying other production cultures we might reduce or even destroy our chances to leave the impasse we have reached.

Part II

Regional Cooperation and Ecological Modernization

Conditions for Environmental Policy Success: An International Comparison

Martin JÄNICKE

1. Introduction

An international survey furnishes no instances of successful environmental policy. All industrialized countries are at pains to combat environmental degradation and still try to avoid it by installing end-of-pipe abatement technologies and the appropriate bureaucracies to administer them. Even in the most favourable of circumstances these efforts can only be partially successful. No systematic attempts are being made to introduce ecologically acceptable technologies and production processes and, as a result, environmental pollution continues.

Nonetheless, it is worthwhile comparing the differences in the relative success enjoyed by environmental policies in various countries. This is important as we need to know about relative success in order to progress towards more advanced environmental policies.

Unfortunately, the widespread interest in "bad news" has not exactly furthered the propagation of information about positive experiences. On the contrary, the learning process in environmental policy is awkwardly based on reactions to shocking experiences. It is hardly ever based on surprising positive experiences, on positive sudden insights. The speed with which news about bad experiences spreads is far greater than that of news about social innovations which reduce environmental pollution. In this sense we see the expression of a fatal imbalance; we should wish for better conditions for the diffusion of ecological innovations.

Positive experiences with environmental policy in specific sectors are not confined to certain pioneering countries. On the contrary, they are distributed widely in countries with varying overall ecological records. Between 1979 and 1989, East Germany, for instance, has reduced road traffic by more than a quarter. This was a remarkable achievement by international standards and reduced the pressure on a natural environment otherwise benefiting from very little protection. During the sixties, the USSR – also with a very poor overall record – introduced drastic clean-air measures in Moscow and relocated hundreds of enterprises from the city to other areas. Greece has introduced far-reaching traffic control measures to avoid smog, a move quite unthinkable in Germany.

My reason for mentioning this sort of partial success (under otherwise unfavourable conditions) is that it might be possible to devise a mosaic of such partial successes which would then constitute an overall concept for a viable environmental policy. Such an environmental policy success model consisting of the sum of all positive experiences in various countries would be better than the most successful existing national policy.

Beyond such an environmental policy on an empirical basis, however, lies the vast field of ecological problems requiring measures of which we have no practical experience today.

This chapter, therefore, deals with national environmental policies as a whole. There is no question of evaluating strategies, instruments or individual measures but, instead, of judging the conditions for environmental policy provided by the economic, political and socio-cultural framework. Thus, the initial hypothesis can be formulated: The conditions provided by the structural framework are more important than strategies, or individual instruments and measures; they are the more significant explanatory factors. They determine the probability and promptitude with which a country will develop an environmental strategy, or will confine itself to some isolated measures. The conditions provided by a given structural framework, according to this hypothesis, also determine more than individual instruments chosen. In other words, favourable conditions have a beneficial effect on all types of instruments and facilitate the revision of obviously flawed decisions.

Taking all this into consideration, our intention is a limited one, namely to explicate past processes in environmental policy. It is thus not simply a question of transferring the conditions for relative environmental protection success from one country to another. The topic is one of fundamental research rather than policy advice. The economic performance and political culture of a country (see below) are certainly factors that escape ecologically motivated control. Nevertheless, they too are conditioned and are not totally impervious to political influence. This applies with even greater validity in respect of the framework conditions for successful environmental policy to be discussed below.

2. Some "Obvious" Explanatory Factors in Environmental Policy

Why is it, then, that certain industrialized countries have been more successful than others in environmental policy, and what do these countries have in common that could be regarded as explanatory factors for this record of success?

1. The answer could lie in the role played by political parties. However, the party composition of the respective governments explains little. Sweden, predominantly governed by the Social Democrats, is, as regards the degree of improvement in environmental quality, more successful than Christian Democratic Italy. But conservative Japan has been even more successful. Conservative Ireland has a bad record, but conservative Holland ranks relatively high with respect to environmental quality improvement. In West Germany, the conservative southern states are in no way worse than the northern states predominantly run by the Social Democrats. It was the Social Democrat/Liberal Brandt government that initiated environmental protection in West Germany. But it was the Christian Democrat/Liberal government that – after a phase of stagnation in environmental policy – has since 1983 developed similar activities. There is little to be said for the assumption that, in international comparison, left wing governments as a whole do more for the environment than those on the right.

The existence of green parties has apparently been a favourable factor in focussing attention on environmental policy. But the trailblazers in environmental policy (see below) have been elsewhere. The Greens may best be interpreted as a "punishment" factor for inadequate environmental policy. Seemingly, the ecology movement as a whole plays a far more important role. Its strength, competence and institutional opportunities appear to be more important for success in the field of environmental policy than the special institution of a green party.

2. A successful environmental protection record could be determined less by party politics than by the point in time when environmental policy becomes anchored institutionally: whoever sets up environmental policy institutions at the right time and consolidates them within a legal framework could also be more successful in the realization of ecological objectives. Members of the Environmental Policy Research Unit of the Free University of Berlin have examined the question and established which industrialized countries have set up an environment ministry, a central environment authority, fundamental legislation on environmental protection, and when they did so; when and if environmental protection was laid down in the constitution and when the first national report on the environment was issued. This study (Fig. 1) (Lamm/Schneller 1989) shows that:

Japan, the United States and Sweden are clearly the pioneers in environmental protection. Between 1967 and 1974, Japan took four steps towards institutionalization. In the same period, Sweden set up a national environmental authority and passed a fundamental environmental protection act, and anchored environmental protection in the constitution. In the United States, three steps towards institutionalization were taken within a period of two years. These three countries today enjoy an overall relatively good reputation in the field of environmental policy. In certain vital sectors of environmental protection such as automobile emission regulations, they were international pioneers (OECD 1988: 87). On the other hand, Bulgaria, Czechoslovakia and Albania have not introduced institutions of the kind mentioned above. Among the industrialized countries, Czechoslovakia has had one of the very worst environmental records. Bulgaria is not much better.

However, the institutionalization hypothesis of success or failure in environmental policy is subject to exception. For among the pioneers in the field we find East Germany. As early as 1968, protection of the environment was laid down in the constitution. In 1970, a comprehensive fundamental act was adopted. In 1971, an environment ministry was set up. Up to 1973, the year of the oil crisis, some improvements (such as in air pollution control) were to be noted. Subsequently, there was a set-back that has continued up to the upheaval in late 1989 (which was also inspired by ecological motives). A report on the situation of the environment was presented in East Germany only after the revolution in 1989 – until then strict secrecy had been the rule (however, three members of the Politburo are said to have received regular reports on the environment). Today, the former East Germany ranks at the very bottom end of the international scale with one of the worst environmental records. We find a similar contradiction between relatively early institutionalization and environmental failure in Poland and Hungary, which between 1972 and 1976 had taken no less than four of the institutional steps mentioned.

We obtain more useful results if we weight the value of environmental institutions more clearly. Institutions are not all the same, nor are constitutions. Strictly speaking, the term "institution" applies only to stable, valued patterns of behaviour which can or must become reliable (Huntington 1965, Göhler 1987). Ministries without importance and competence, constitutional clauses that are not enforceable in the courts, laws that no-one knows about, or that have at least made no mark on social behaviour, are in this strict sense of no institutional significance. They are nothing more than political formalities. This was above all a problem in the Eastern European countries up to the revolution. The quality of institutionalization also depends on other criteria (finance and staffing, competence, degree of integration of the institution), which will be discussed below.

A second factor producing a contradiction between early institutionalization and an ecological record is apparently the *economic situation* of the country concerned: after 1973, East Germany, Poland, and Hungary suffered severe set-backs which displaced political priorities to the detriment of environmental protection.

This was particularly true of Britain, which in the sixties had indeed been a (relative) pioneer in air and water pollution control, but which in the course of the seventies abandoned these aspects entirely.

The considerable importance of the economic situation, however, is indicated in particular by the fact that, in the critical phase of economic structural change between 1974 and 1984, there was a marked slow-down in activity as measured by the speed of institutionalization (Fig. 1).

A third exception is suggested by countries that, although having produced often exemplary legislation, have been a great deal less successful in carrying it out (e.g. the United States and West Germany).

A certain exception is also suggested by countries such as Luxembourg and Norway that in respect of detailed regulations orient themselves towards larger neighbours (Sweden, Belgium/Holland), thus letting the latter take the lead. With regard to Switzerland and West Germany, it should in addition be noted that in the field of environmental policy, there had been activity below the federal level, to some extent, at an earlier date.

In spite of all reservations with regard to the schematic institutionalization pattern used here, certain suppositions appear plausible: environmental institutionalization is a necessary but not a sufficient condition fur successful environmental policy. In developed constitutional countries there is a connection between early environmental institutionalization and a trend towards relief of the environment only where a series of "interference factors" are eliminated. The reasons for early institutionalization will be dealt with below.

3. A third assumption also appears plausible: welfare states could be ecologically more successful than states that rather leave the solution of problems to society to deal with. This hypothesis, too, has a lot going for it. But it is also subject to restriction. If we take as a measure the relative rates of change established by major environmental indicators for Western industrialized countries for the period 1970 to 1985, the following picture emerges (Fig. 2): developed welfare state structures – measured as the proportion of the gross national product devoted to welfare expenditure (Schmidt 1988) –

and the relative success of environmental policy are clearly related only if one deals with three countries separately: Japan, Switzerland and the United States. These countries have a good record in environmental protection without evidencing developed welfare state structures. There are apparently two paths to relatively successful environmental policy: the welfare state and what can be vaguely adumbrated by the Japanese term "welfare society", a path with relatively well developed social self-regulatory mechanisms. In respect of labour market policy, this two-path thesis has already been established by Manfred Schmidt (Schmidt 1986).

3. Environmental Policy and Employment

It is possible to gain valuable insight into the conditions for success in environmental policy if a comparison is made with other national policy areas. This has already been done with regard to social policy. Two further sectors are of particular interest: structural policy (or also industrial policy) and labour market policy.

Insofar as it is a question of reducing old smoke-stack industries, structural change as such has rather had the effect of reducing pressure on the environment: steel or cement production, for example, directly involve a high degree of environmental pollution: indirectly, too, as they require large amounts of energy as well as causing considerable transport volumes. Thus, a positive link with environmental protection is hardly surprising. Nevertheless, there are countries such as Belgium, Great Britain and former West Germany, which although evidencing a high degree of structural change, nonetheless ranked centre-scale in environmental policy for the period 1970 to 1985. The price for structural change since 1973 has been high unemployment.

Japan and Sweden, on the other hand, have managed to achieve structural change with a high (Japan) and even rising (Sweden) rates of employment, not least because of an active structural policy. But also in environmental policy they have been relatively successful.

The connection can, with some degree of certainty, be diagnosed as follows: *countries that succeed in combining structural change with an effective employment policy are more successful also in environmental protection*. There are apparently conditions for success that favour a whole series of individual policies. The link between good environmental and labour market policies is quite striking (Fig. 3). In 1985, for instance, countries with relatively favourable rates of change in environmental quality had higher rates of employment than countries in which the quality of the environment had developed less favourably. It is usually the case that where the level of employment is unfavourable, the trend on the labour market is also negative, as in Spain, Turkey, Ireland and Italy. Only Holland forms an exception to the rule: its relatively successful environmental policy contrasts with a severe set-back on the labour market.

How is this link to be explained? In the first place it is reasonable to assume that countries with a relatively high level of employment will be less hesitant when it comes to shouldering the financial burden of environmental protection. Burdening industry with higher costs under such circumstances can less easily be rejected on the grounds that this would cost jobs than where mass unemployment sets the scene. Vice versa, environmental protection also creates jobs. Both links are uncontroversial, but they do not really suffice as an explanation.

A more powerful explanation can probably be sought in the framework conditions that favour *both* – environmental protection and higher employment rates. It is probably also the same framework conditions which make possible the successful structural move away from smoke-stack industries towards knowledge-intensive production methods. It seems more than likely that successful structural policy of this type is more easily achieved by countries in which the economic process is negotiated on a broad and long-term basis. In contrast, short-term perspectives and the dominance of special industrial interests are likely to be detrimental to policy success.

4. Problem-Induced Pressure Plus Capacity for Modernization

We follow this conspectus with a more systematic outline of the conditions for environmental policy.

The institutionalization of environmental policy in its initial phase, but also in phases of acceleration (for example in the confrontation with the dying of forests), requires a high degree of *ecological problem-induced pressure*. Unfortunately, environmental policy has nowhere emerged as a beautiful idea, but rather as a consequence of severe environmental damage. As elsewhere, we find a reactive political pattern in which a problem provokes a reaction once it can no longer be ignored.

In 1970, the countries that were the first to endow themselves with environmental institutions, such as Japan, the United States, East Germany, Sweden or Britain, evidenced a high degree of environmental pollution; this was also true of Sweden with its then highly developed heavy industry and the highest number of automobiles per capita in Europe.

Severe environmental pollution is however no guarantee for an increase in counter-measures. Czechoslovakia is a graphic instance. Severe environmental pollution is also no guarantee that the measures adopted and the institutions set up will be successful. East Germany is the prime example. A strong ecological problem-induced pressure has hitherto only been the necessary condition for the institutionalization of environmental policy.

5. Capacity for Modernization

Why is it, then, that some countries are relatively more successful than others in the field of environmental protection? To put it in a nutshell, they are countries characterized by what I would like to call the *capacity for modernization* (Jänicke/Mönch 1988). One could also speak of the capacity for reform. However, as it is also a question of technological progress – and, incidentally, more so than ever – I will adopt an existing and recognized term which also covers this aspect. By capacity for modernization I mean in general the achieved level of institutional, material and technical ability in a country to find solutions to problems. In this particular case we are concerned with a specific achievement of modernization: environmental protection and – moreover – the transition to ecologically better adapted production structures. The capacity of a country to modernize determines not least of all the level of problem perception. The connection, as Prittwitz in particular has stressed, arises thus: where the capacity for modernization is high, even a low degree of ecological problem-induced pressure can lead to the adoption of policy measures (Prittwitz 1990, cf. Jänicke 1990, Appendix).

As experience has shown, the capacity of a country to modernize can be determined by four factors which together form a mutually enhancing syndrome:
1) *Economic performance*;
2) *Innovative capacity*, as the sum of all opportunities for the advancement of innovators and representatives of new interests;
3) *Strategic capacity*, as a country's political ability to coordinate and, over an extended period, to implement long-term objectives, and;
4) *Consensual capacity*, as the ability of a country to achieve negotiated solutions within the framework of a cooperative policy style.

6. Economic Performance: the Ambivalence of Necessity and Possibility

In this connection, the effects of economic performance are initially contradictory. For a high standard of living usually results in more environmental problems, but also makes more counter-measures possible. One can speak of an ambivalence of ecological necessity and possibility. Rich countries evidence a relatively higher degree of motorization and electrification, more intensive production and employment of chemical products or utilization of concrete than poorer countries. But they also dispose of better technological, material and institutional possibilities for the application of measures designed to relieve the environment. (However, they are also in a better position to delegate undesirable production to other countries.) Where there is a lack of material resources because although the country is developed it is in crisis, this has a negative effect on the conduct of environmental policy. The critical post-1973 phase has already been cited in this connection.

Leaving aside such exceptions dependent on particular circumstances, a high level of economic development also favours environmental protection by the fact that the richer countries evidence a drop in the number of people employed in industrial production and a rise in the numbers employed in service industries. This relativizes the imperatives of industrialism. Consumption of goods also falls, in relative terms, in comparison to information, the quality of life and experience values. Education and increased leisure, too, promote this change in values and offer comparatively better preconditions for environmental mobilization. At least as far as the EC countries are concerned, there is an empirically demonstrable link between the standard of living and the level of environmental awareness (Pearce 1989: 39).

7. Consensual Capacity

Political science has relatively thoroughly examined the conditions for success in economic policy. It can be demonstrated that at least full employment and low inflation are more easily achieved in countries enjoying a smoothly functioning cooperative relationship between capital and labour (Schmidt 1986, Lehner/Nordhause-Janz 1988). Such structures are also referred to as "neo-corporatism". They are well developed in countries such as Sweden, Holland or Austria and less so in countries such as Italy, France and Britain. In Japan, cooperation between state and industry in industrial policy and the great importance of consensual mechanisms have much the same effect.

The common denominator, which also affects environmental policy, seems to be policy style: whether negotiated solutions on a broad basis or the predominance of the strongest special interests are the rule is of considerable significance for the outcome of policy.

Whether worker or environmental protection interests have a voice only on the streets or whether they can make themselves heard through well-established negotiation channels is quite certainly of importance for the matter itself. (Of course, if a negotiating stance is to be successful, the necessary capacity for conflict beyond the "round table" must also be in evidence.)

Where fundamental economic decisions are negotiated on a broad basis, it is not only the costs of the conflict which are lower. There is also a better balanced relationship between new and old interests in such a process of negotiation; new interests and ideas are taken into consideration earlier and are obstructed for a shorter period than where established special interests impose their own objectives. *It seems that, in cooperative industrial negotiation processes, environmental interests are also taken into consideration earlier.* If western industrialized countries are assigned to the categories consensual or conflictual (Schmidt 1986), it is quite clear that the consensual group is more successful in the field of environmental policy. Members of the group are Japan, Holland, Luxembourg, Sweden, Switzerland and Austria (Fig. 4). The argument becomes even more plausible when the conflict-ridden countries of Eastern Europe are taken into account.

An active, cooperative policy style is better for economy and ecology than a laissez-faire philosophy. According to a study by Katzenstein, this policy style is practised rather by small countries than by large ones (Katzenstein 1985). He attributes this to the necessity to constantly adapt to the pressure of the world market, a pressure to which small industrialized countries in particular are subject. But it could also be the case that the highly developed democratic institutions in these small countries produce a stronger *political* pressure to adapt and, to a certain extent, to better train the capacity for active reform politics (Jänicke 1989, 1990).

8. Innovative Capacity

This leads us away from policy style and towards the *conditions for innovation* in a country. In this respect there is considerable variation among the industrialized countries; this is clear even if we do not start by comparing Czechoslovakia (before 1990) to Sweden. And it seems that good conditions for innovation are equally favourable for economic and ecological success. It is, after all, a question of the institutional and material preconditions for political and economic innovators.

The institutional aspect involves a broad spectrum of state and lower-level institutions. It is a question of responsiveness to innovation and new interests:
- in institutions concerned with the political decision-making: where new objectives and interests – if necessary by referendum – gain rapid access to the political system, environmental protection has better chances;
- in the legal system (on which it depends whether new interests in conflict with old ones are granted equality of arms) (Weidner 1988: 84), but also:
- in information systems, from the media to science (the receptiveness of which towards new interests is an important factor in their competence), and:
- not least of all the economic system itself: where ecologically adapted new techniques are successfully obstructed by the established old technology, where for example energy-saving technology cannot assert itself against the electricity suppliers, environmental policy is usually blocked.

Good preconditions for innovators and the receptiveness of the political and economic situation towards them are, however, no sufficient condition for successful environmental policy. The United States, for example, has relatively favourable innovatory conditions of the above type. Environmental topics were tackled at an early stage by scientists (for instance at MIT). They were given wide publicity. And they resulted in legislation, which is to some extent exemplary (such as the Toxic Substances Control Act). But the implementation of this policy was a great deal less impressive. The United States policy on clean air, for example, produced rates of change between 1970 and 1985 that hardly correspond to the legislative fervour of the seventies.

9. Strategic Capacity

A good basis for innovators thus presupposes a further condition for success. I call it *strategic capacity* (see Scharpf 1987). It concerns above all the machinery of government. It refers to the capacity to implement comprehensive and long-term objectives in a well-coordinated manner and with sufficient staying-power. This is also a matter for institutions. Japan, for example, has a planning authority. Sweden has a system of medium-term orientation planning.

But it is also a question of the degree of institutionalization. To be able to achieve complex objectives, the competent authorities must be endowed with well-defined powers and calculable responsibilities. It is also a question of finance and staffing.

Countries that provide for only superficial institutionalization of environmental protection are from this point of view particularly remiss: the new minister has little to say, little finance and too small a staff. In this respect he also has little responsibility. This is a widespread problem in Southern and Eastern European countries.

Not the least important constituent of strategic capacity is the ability to coordinate administrative activities. Coordination problems can arise from forms of federalism in which (as in West Germany or – so far – in the EC) upper and lower echelons can easily obstruct one another (Scharpf 1988). However, coordination problems arise for the most part on the same hierarchical level between authorities with opposing interests. The degree to which the bureaucratic state tolerates substantial contradictions is generally underestimated: in the same ministry there can be sections for arms procurement and disarmament – the two often poorly coordinated. In another ministry, we find sections for the promotion of growth in energy supplies and for energy saving. Large sections of the government machinery promote growth detrimental to the environment, whether in agriculture or road transport. This co-exists with the environmental authority. The corollary of an additive environmental bureaucracy is an additive, end-of-pipe abatement technology (Jänicke 1989a).

In contrast, strategic capacity means that environmental protection really becomes a "cross-section function" of the administrative authorities. Generally speaking, strategic capacity must include the capacity to integrate partial sectors of the state with a view to new objectives, and to dismantle contradictions and defuse conflicts about objectives. In this regard, however, all industrialized countries have a lot of ground to cover. A cooperative policy style can help.

Just what an active and cooperative handling of industrial problem situations can achieve is demonstrated by the cases of Sweden and Japan, but also of Luxembourg (Jänicke/Mönch 1990).

After the 1973 oil crisis, Sweden suffered a massive slump in heavy industry. Steel production dropped sharply, cement production was nearly halved in the course of a decade. The industrial work force was drastically reduced. But total employment nevertheless grew, even though the initial level had been high. In this case, the active cooperation of state, industry and trade unions paid off. It is true that public debt grew, but, in present terms, Sweden can be regarded as an instance of relatively successful structural policy.

This is also true of Japan. As in Sweden, a long-term cooperative strategy was the answer to the structural problems of heavy industry. The industry's considerable energy problems were dealt with in partial sectors by a policy of well-ordered retreat, above all in cooperation between state and industry. Here, too, structural change was achieved while maintaining a high level of employment.

Luxembourg also experienced radical structural change. Steel production dropped by some 40% between 1970 and 1987, while nigh on half the work force became redundant. Other heavy industries − such as cement − suffered set-backs, but the level of employment could just about be maintained. Above all, a concerted broadly-based structural policy was responsible for this (Hirsch 1986). The heavy industry-centred Luxembourg is today one of the largest service industry centres in the EC.

These three countries have been relatively successful in the field of environmental protection. They render plausible the thesis that countries with an active, cooperative industrial policy also pay greater active attention to the environmental interest than countries in which structural change was left up to "market forces" (or was even − in vain − obstructed by the use of state subsidies). Such countries with environmental policy deficits are Britain, Belgium and the countries of Southern Europe.

10. Hypothesis of a Modernization Syndrome

Economic performance, institutional structures and socio-cultural factors are indeed generated independently. But they mutually reinforce each other in their respective effects in such a way that it is possible to speak of a modernization syndrome. This interdependence between the four components of an ecologically advantageous modernization capacity can be presented systematically as follows (Fig. 5):

1. Although developed national economies tend to have a more highly burdened environment, they nonetheless also offer better preconditions for environmental protection (represented as relation 1 in the diagram). This ambivalence between environmental needs and possibilities could be eliminated by a transition to ecologically less problematical methods of production (relation 9).

2. To a certain extent, the better off countries can more easily bring new insights and interests into play. There are at least more resources available (relation 2).

3. With a rise in the level of economic development there is also an improvement in the socio-cultural conditions for environmental policy: The quality of the environment and the quality of life are valued at least as highly as the consumption of goods (relation 3). Moreover, according to Inglehart, a high level of economic performance is accompanied by an increase in social satisfaction and, parallel to this, in the level of confidence – a good precondition for a cooperative policy style (relation 4) (Inglehart 1988).

4. It seems obvious that these socio-cultural preconditions favour a shaping of opinion and decision-making (input-level) sympathetic to the environmental interest. This is particularly true of the (already mentioned) inclusion of environmental interests in the processes of opinion-shaping and decision-making at an early stage (relation 6). A cooperative policy style is also advantageous to the strategic capacity of the state (as mentioned above): it is not only important interests that are more easily brought into balance. Environmental policy within the machinery of the state also tends to become a "cross-sectional function", thus not leading an isolated existence in the sense of a purely "additive environmental policy" (relation 5).

Of particular interest, however, are the remaining relations in Fig. 5. We will begin with the government administration (output-level).

5. Government can address the environmental problems in the sense of an end-of-pipe disposal strategy (relation 7), but it can also implement a structural policy with regard to environmental protection and work towards an ecologically better adapted method of production (relation 9). The previous link between a high living standard and "structural burdening of the environment" need no longer exist at all today. High value can, on the contrary, be produced precisely by means of knowledge-intensive production, by resource saving, cleaner and low-risk technologies. The latter is obviously an expression of a high degree of modernization capacity.

6. The state can not only implement these two strategies for environmental protection, it can also have two different *motives to act*: it can act under political pressure from below, transmitted by the system of opinion-shaping and decision-making. Reich refers to this as an "outside initiative model" (Reich 1984). In the past, however, there has time and again been environmental protection activity initiated by the state itself; for example, health authorities have become active when confronted with obvious environmental hygiene hazards. This "inside initiative model" shows the autonomous role of the government machinery should in no way be underestimated.

7. Similarly, the *independent role of social factors* in environmental protection should not be underestimated: ecological problems can be tackled directly, as it were by short-cut, without involving the state (relations 8 and 10).

This applies with regard to private litigation against those causing environmental pollution. The media can, however, also have a direct effect on the manufacturers of pollutants. A warning against a carcinogenic product today can lead tomorrow to the removal of the product from the shelves – an intervention which the state in terms of rapidity and scope cannot hope to match. This effect is enhanced by collaboration with, for instance, consumer associations. This can apply with regard to trade (which sifts out ecologically questionable products), but also with regard to competition by ecologically innovative enterprises. In West Germany alone there are two associations of environmentally aware entrepreneurs. Internal regulations of industrial associations that have been subject to effective public innovatory pressure can be of similar importance.

Finally, citizen action groups and ecological associations can exert direct pressure on polluters. Besides litigation as mentioned above, the possibility, above all in Japan, of negotiation between those affected and the polluters is of importance.

11. International Environmental Policy

A final remark on the conditions for success in international environmental policy. Today there is no question: environmental problems are global problems, from threatening climatic conditions and the hazards of chemical and nuclear plants to the international flood of automobiles. While, at least in the industrialized countries, the danger of military invasion has receded, the reality of ecological invasion looms ever larger. A shift from the problem of military security to ecological security in the system of international relations has become evident (and actuates a conversion of resources and capacities).

What form of international environmental policy does experience commend?

Two models should be distinguished: we shall call them the "vertical" model of international environmental policy and the "horizontal" model. In the first case, emphasis is placed on the international level: action is to be initiated at this level and implemented downwards. Only when the United Nations, the EC or other organizations have adopted binding resolutions for all, national and local measures will be adopted. This model is regarded as a guarantee against unfair competition and similar disadvantages.

In fact it hardly works. The higher the international level, the more environmental policy is reduced to verbal declarations. Distance from those affected and the proximity to multinational enterprises are also problems at the more elevated levels.

The horizontal model of international environmental policy on the other hand counts on environmental innovation taking place at lower levels, in individual municipalities, regions, countries. The national pioneer is also a particularly effective driving force for the ("horizontal") diffusion of its positive experience. Sweden, as the then pioneer in environmental protection, was instrumental in the calling of the 1972 Stockholm international conference on environmental problems. This had the important side effect that *national* environmental protection activity in Sweden (and in the United States) became known internationally. The rapid international spread of institutional innovation in these countries in the aftermath of the Stockholm meeting can well be regarded as a proof of the link between national innovation and international, "horizontal" diffusion. Most environmental ministries were set up between 1971 and 1972 (Fig. 1).

It appears to be a condition for success in international environmental policy that pioneers exist that do not wait until internationally coordinated measures come into force. The international organizations, but also the international network of the media, are important in the *second* phase as factors in the diffusion of national pioneering achievements (incidentally, the rapid "horizontal" diffusion of the United States constitutional model, via the French Revolution, required no international organization). While the pioneer may occasionally suffer short-term economic disadvantages in international competition (although this effect is much exaggerated), in the competition for innovative, forward-looking technologies he is at an advantage. And as experience shows, this advantage counts for more.

It calls to mind the story of everybody, somebody and nobody who are to tackle a problem: everybody says somebody should begin. Somebody says he will only begin if everybody does. So in the end nobody begins.

International and national environmental policy alike depend above all on an innovative somebody. It is easier to emulate a pioneer and his positive experience than to take a collective step into the unknown. It depends on international mechanisms how rapidly successful environmental protection measures are implemented world-wide.

Bibliography

GÖHLER, GERHARD, 1987: Grundfragen der Theorie politischer Institutionen (Opladen: Westdeutscher Verlag).

HIRSCH, MARIO, 1986: Tripartism in Luxembourg: The Limits of Social Concertation, in *West European Studies 9*, No. 1.

HUNTINGTON, SAMUEL P., 1965: Political Development and Political Decay, in *World Politics 7*, No. 3.

INGLEHART, RONALD, 1988: Politische Kultur und stabile Demokratie, in *Politische Vierteljahresschrift 29*, No. 3.

JÄNICKE, MARTIN, 1989: Ökologische und ökonomische Wandlungsmuster im Industrieländervergleich, in *H. H. Hartwich (ed.)*, Macht und Ohnmacht politischer Institutionen (Opladen: Westdeutscher Verlag).

JÄNICKE, MARTIN, 1989a: Über die Widersprüchlichkeit des Staates in der Umweltpolitik, in *H. Grebing; P. Brandt; U. Schulze-Marmeling (eds.)*, Sozialismus in Europa. Bilanz und Perspektiven. Festschrift für Willy Brandt (Essen: Klartext-Verlag).

JÄNICKE, MARTIN, 1990: State Failure. The Impotence of Politics in Industrial Society, (Cambridge: Polity Press).

JÄNICKE, MARTIN/MÖNCH, HARALD, 1988: Ökologischer und wirtschaftlicher Wandel im Industrieländervergleich. Eine explorative Studie über Modernisierungskapazitäten, in *Manfred G. Schmidt (ed.):* Staatstätigkeit (Opladen: Westdeutscher Verlag) (special issue No. 19 of Politische Vierteljahresschrift).

JÄNICKE, MARTIN/MÖNCH, HARALD, 1990: Ökologische Dimensionen wirtschaftlichen Strukturwandels. Eine Untersuchung über 32 Industrieländer, Free University of Berlin, Forschungsstelle für Umweltpolitik, FFU rep 90-10.

KATZENSTEIN, PETER J., 1985: Small States in World Markets. Industrial Policy in Europe (Ithaca/London: Cornell University Press).

KITSCHELT, HERBERT, 1983: Politik und Energie: Energietechnologiepolitiken in den USA, der Bundesrepublik Deutschland, Frankreich und Schweden (Frankfurt a.M./New York: Campus).

LAMM, JOCHEN/SCHNELLER, MARKUS, 1989: Umweltberichterstattung im internationalen Vergleich. Unpublished manuscript, Free University of Berlin.

LEHNER, FRANZ/NORDHAUSE-JANZ, JÜRGEN, 1988: Die politische Ökonomie gesellschaftlicher Verteilungskonflikte: Möglichkeiten, Grenzen und Defizite staatlicher Wirtschaftspolitik, in *Manfred G. Schmidt (ed.):* Staatstätigkeit, (Opladen: Westdeutscher Verlag) (special issue No. 19 of Politische Vierteljahresschrift).

OECD, 1988: Transport and the Environment, Paris.

PEARCE, DAVID, 1989: Blueprint for a Green Economy, London.

PRITTWITZ, VOLKER VON, 1990: Das Katastrophenparadox. Elemente einer Theorie der Umweltpolitik (Opladen: Leske + Budrich).

REICH, MICHAEL R., 1987: Mobilizing for Environmental Policy in Italy and Japan, in *Comparative Politics 16*, No. 4.

SCHARPF, FRITZ W., 1987: Sozialdemokratische Krisenpolitik in Europa. Das "Modell Deutschland" im Vergleich (Frankfurt a.M./New York: Campus).

SCHARPF, FRITZ W., 1988: The Joint-Decision Trap. Lessons from German Federalism and European Integration, in *Public Administration 66*, No. 3.

SCHMIDT, MANFRED G., 1986: Politische Bedingungen erfolgreicher Wirtschaftspolitik, in *Journal für Sozialforschung 26*, No. 3.

SCHMIDT, MANFRED G., 1988: Sozialpolitik. Historische Entwicklung und internationaler Vergleich (Opladen: Leske + Budrich).

WEIDNER, HELMUT, 1988: Vom Ausland lernen. Anregungen aus Japan, in *Udo Ernst Simonis (ed.):* Lernen von der Umwelt – Lernen für die Umwelt (Berlin: edition sigma).

Country	67	68	69	70	71	72	73	74	75	76	77	78	79	80	81	82	83	84	85	86	87	88	89	90
Japan	L				M			A																
USA		R	L								R													
GDR					M															M		(A)		R
Sweden	A			L					C		R													
Britain					M		A			C		R												
Denmark							L/A																	
Poland					M/R			A		C				L				R						
Hungary						C		A	R	L														
Netherlands					M	R		L										A				(A)		
Australia					M		L							R										
Yugoslavia							A/C					R							M					
Switzerland			A/C									C				L			L				(R)	
Spain						A					R			L				A						A
Norway			M			M					R				L								(A)	
Greece									C	A				M			L							
France						M		R			R								A					
Austria						M					R			M					A	(A)				
Portugal					A/M*					C		R					L	L/R						M^s
Canada					M							R						A	G					
Finland							R	M/A		R										M	(A)			
FRG								A		R														
Belgium								M				R				C	L	R						
Turkey															A	L	M			R				
Luxembourg																		M				M	R	
USSR											C								R	L/M				
Italy						M*		A												L				
Romania					M	L	A																	
Ireland					M																			
New Zealand																								
Bulgaria	C																							
CSFR					C					C														
Albania																								

A= National environment authority
C=Environmental protection in the constitution
L=Environmental framework legislation
M=Environment ministry
R=1st national environment report

Ranking of countries according to average year of the first three institutionalization steps.
Information in brackets = institutionalization confirmed by secondary source, year = publication of source
M* = Ministry later abolished; M^s = junior ministry
Source: Lamm/Schneller (1989), Additions (As of June 1990)

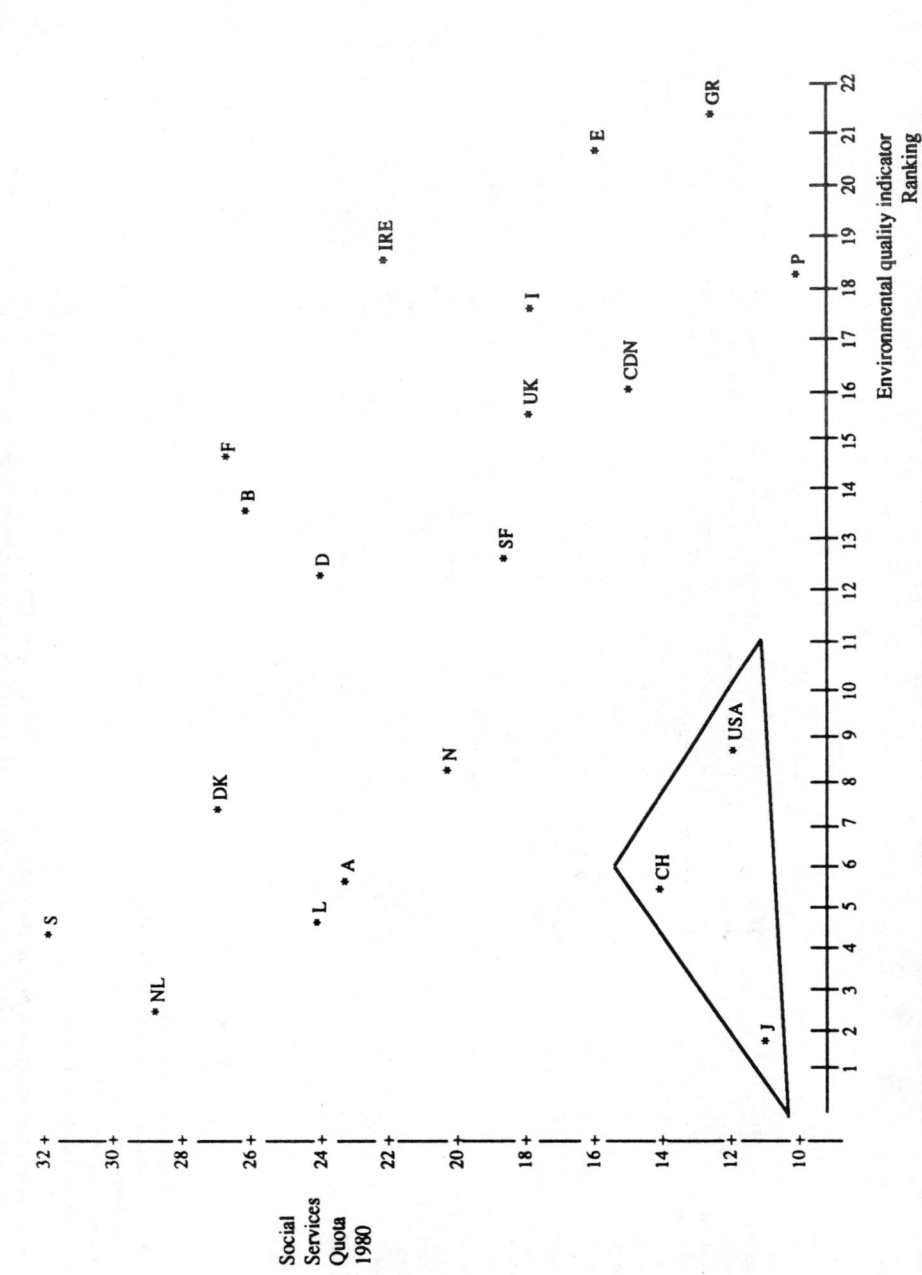

Fig. 2: Changes in Environmental Quality 1970 – 1985 and Social Services Quota 1980

© Forschungsstelle für Umweltpolitik (Environmental Policy Research Unit)

Environmental quality development: ranking for average rates of change in emissions of SO_2, NO_x, CO and CH_4 of the Biological Oxygen Demand (BOD) in selected running

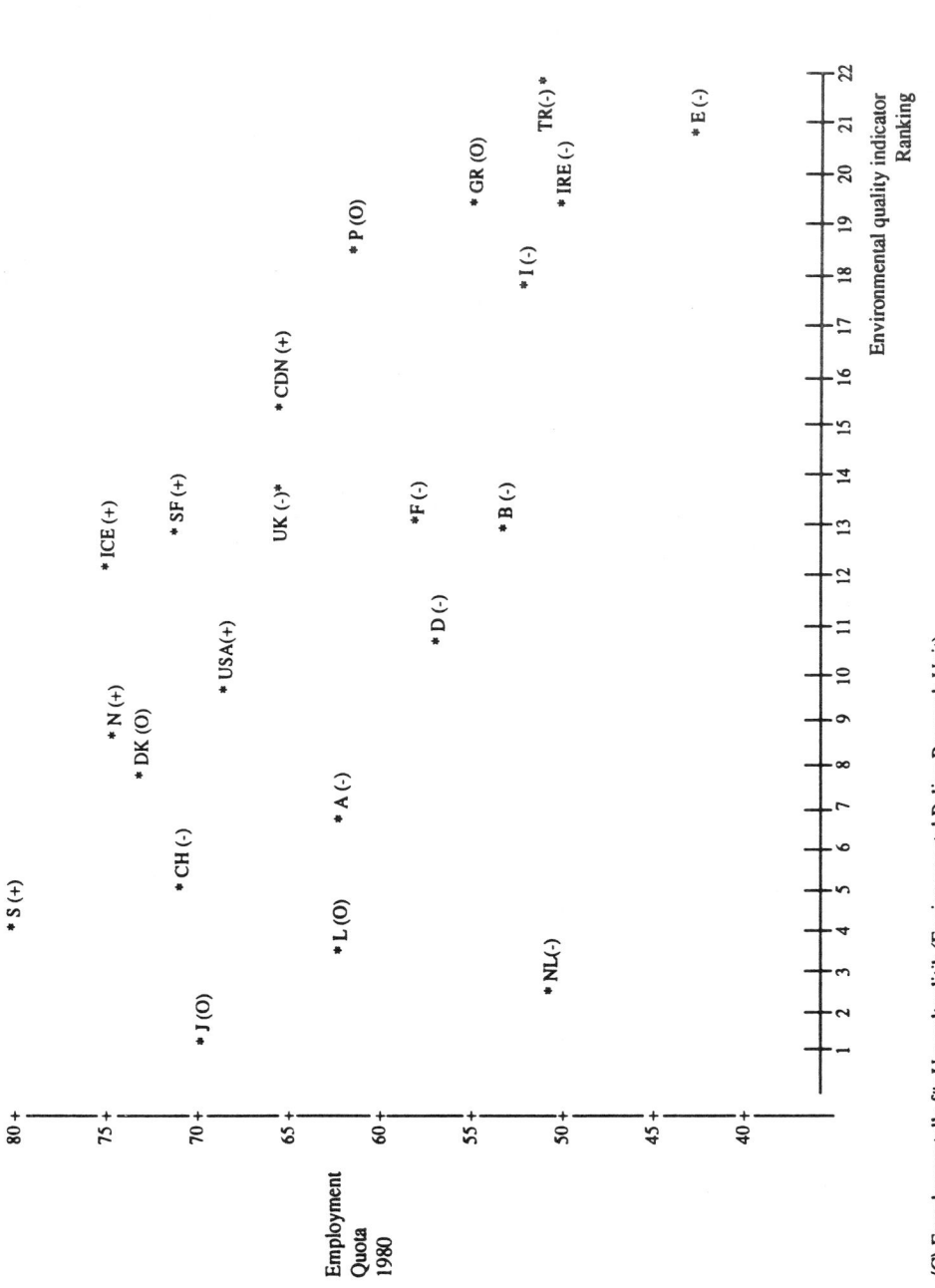

⟨C⟩ Forschungsstelle für Umweltpolitik (Environmental Policy Research Unit)

(1) Explanation: see Figure 2
(2) Persons employed as % of potential labour force; trend 1970 – 1985 in brackets

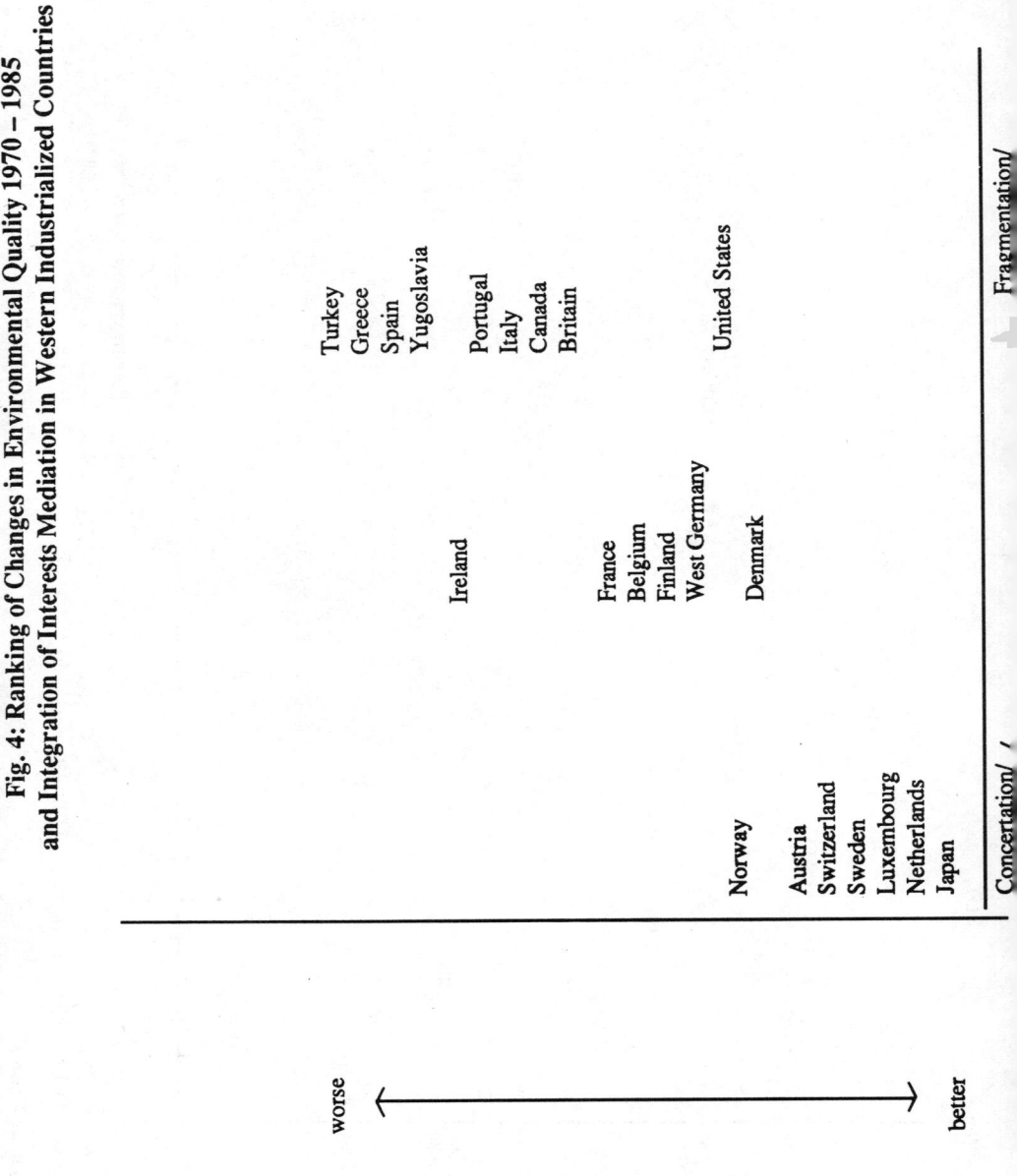

Fig. 4: Ranking of Changes in Environmental Quality 1970 – 1985 and Integration of Interests Mediation in Western Industrialized Countries

```
Ranking of
changes in
environmental
quality

worse
↑
|                                                    Turkey
|                                                    Greece
|                                                    Spain
|                                                    Yugoslavia
|
|                                                    Portugal
|                                                    Italy
|                                                    Canada
|                                                    Britain
|
|                        Ireland
|
|                                     United States
|                                France
|                                Belgium
|                                Finland
|                                West Germany
|                                Denmark
|
|   Norway
|   Austria
|   Switzerland
|   Sweden
|   Luxembourg
|   Netherlands
|   Japan
↓
better
     Concertation/                              Fragmentation/
```

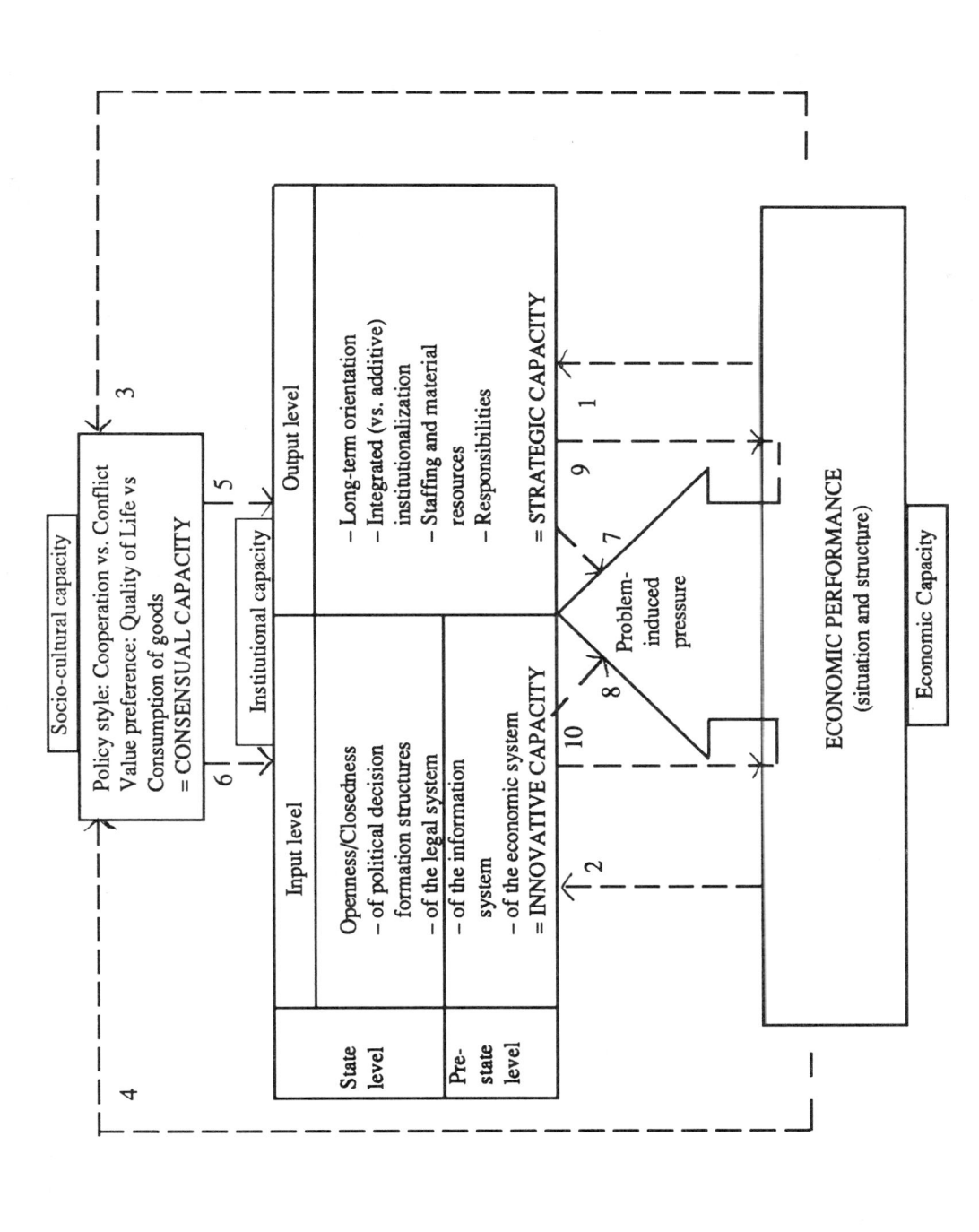

		Output level	— Long-term orientation — Integrated (vs. additive) institutionalization — Staffing and material resources — Responsibilities = STRATEGIC CAPACITY
State level		Input level	Openness/Closedness — of political decision formation structures — of the legal system — of the information system — of the economic system = INNOVATIVE CAPACITY
Pre-state level			

Socio-cultural capacity

Policy style: Cooperation vs. Conflict
Value preference: Quality of Life vs Consumption of goods
= CONSENSUAL CAPACITY

Institutional capacity

Problem-induced pressure

ECONOMIC PERFORMANCE
(situation and structure)

Economic Capacity

Environmental Cooperation Between the Nordic Countries and Eastern Europe

John STORM PEDERSEN and Troels NORUP PANILD

1. Introduction

When trying to reduce pollution in the region of the Baltic Sea, the Nordic countries now face a situation in which it is better to spend money on reducing the border-crossing pollution from Eastern Europe than on reducing the domestic pollution in the Nordic countries themselves. This is not to deny that there are still serious environmental problems in the Nordic countries, as for example the problem of nitrate pollution generated by the Danish farmers, which have to be solved in the Nordic countries within a short time. Nevertheless, roughly estimated, the environmental situation in the Nordic countries can be improved with the same result by using 1 Danish Krona to reduce the transborder pollution in Eastern Europe compared with using 10 Danish Krona to reduce the pollution in the Nordic Countries. This relationship makes it reasonable to give some kind of environmental aid to Eastern Europe and to generate cooperation for ecological and industrial modernization in the region of the Baltic Sea.

Besides, one faces a situation where great political will is expressed to support the reform processes in Eastern Europe. Support is given in order to stabilize more democratic regimes as well as to introduce a more market-oriented economy. Seen in this perspective, a situation in which the Eastern Europeans "import" the environmental problems associated with the Western post-war model for economic and social development must be avoided. Furthermore, the Eastern countries cannot use the post-war model of the

Western countries in general. If the Eastern countries "import" this post-war model they will within a few years be in a situation where they have an old fashioned or out-dated model for economic, social and ecological development, and thus be in a poor situation both from the point of view of international competition and of national welfare: a situation which could have disastrous consequences for the long-term development of Eastern Europe.

Finally, one faces a complex institutional situation in the region of the Baltic Sea when trying to make environmental aid-programmes and to establish cooperation for economic and ecological modernization. Of the Nordic countries (Denmark, Sweden, Finland, Norway and Iceland) only Denmark is a member of the EC, while the other countries are members of EFTA. Furthermore, Denmark, Norway and Iceland are members of NATO, whereas Sweden and Finland are neutral. Finally, Iceland and to some extent Norway are geographically rather far from the Baltic Sea.

The Eastern countries, which were all members of COMECON and the Warsaw-alliance, have now dissolved these organizations and are discussing whether in the long run to join the EC, to leave the USSR, to join the Western countries, etc. This situation makes it rather complex when talking of generating aid-programmes for Eastern Europe and cooperation for development.

In spite of the complex situation, some initiatives have been taken in a short time, and others are under consideration. The problem is to combine and balance the initiatives to form general strategies if improvements are to be made in the environmental situation and support for the reform processes is to be given in a rational way.

In this paper we will start with the debate on environmental aid-programmes from the Nordic countries to Eastern Europe and cooperation between the Nordic countries and Eastern Europe when handling transborder pollution. Then we will proceed to discuss economic and ecological modernization in a wider perspective – both empirically and theoretically.

2. The Rationale of Giving Aid and Cooperating

The first, and probably the most important reason for giving environmental aid to the Eastern European countries and for establishing cooperation between Eastern Europe and the Nordic countries to improve the environmental situation is the fact mentioned in the previous section: transborder pollution is a major source of degradation of the environment in the Nordic countries.

The air-borne transborder pollution from Eastern Europe generates more sulphur in the air than the Nordic countries generate themselves, although it is only 3.5% of the total amount of the sulphur in the air of Eastern Europe which reaches the Nordic countries. It is estimated that 22% of the sulphur in the air in Denmark, 40% in Finland, 5% in Iceland, 23% in Norway and 34% in Sweden comes from Eastern Europe. It is almost the same situation with regard to nitrogen[1].

There are of course big differences in the allocation of transborder air-borne pollution within the individual countries. In the southern part of Sweden, for example, the situation is critical. The problem cannot be solved within Sweden even if much money is spent. The transborder pollution from Eastern Europe must be reduced to avoid a collapse in the ecological system in parts of southern Sweden. The transborder pollution from Eastern Europe can partly be explained by the fact that Eastern Europe uses twice as much energy as the OECD countries per produced unit and the resources used for energy production are much "poorer" (brown coal) than in the Western countries, which means much more pollution per produced unit of energy. Furthermore, in Eastern Europe there is a large waste of energy. Just in GDR, it is estimated that as much energy is wasted as is used per year in Denmark[2].

---

[1] From Norges Meterologiske Institut: An appendix in the background notes from the Danish Ministry of Environment in relation to the decision making process when establishing the Nordic Environment Finance Corporation.

[2] See for example Nuti (1984) and *Information* 9 January 90 (*Information* is one of the "sober" newspapers in Denmark).

Though the data on water pollution in the Baltic Sea is not as good as the data on air-borne pollution, it can be estimated that Eastern Europe generates 60% of the phosphor pollution as well as some other sources of pollution. Further, large amounts of heavy metals are discharged into the Baltic Sea by, for example, some big chemical plants in the USSR. Seen from an economic point of view, it is at present cheaper for the Nordic countries to reduce the water pollution in the Baltic Sea by spending money in Eastern Europe – due to the low level of pollution control when handling waste water, etc.[3].

To sum up: it is necessary to reduce the transborder pollution from Eastern Europe to the Nordic countries if the environmental situation is to be improved significantly, and this can at this stage be done most "profitably" by environmental investments in Eastern Europe. But even if there exists a large degree of political will, as well as popular support to help Eastern Europe, some degree of guarantee that this will lead to improved environmental standards is needed. And one will expect, in the long run, mechanisms for dealing with ecological problems built on economic policies and instruments such as, for example, the polluter-pays-principle.

The second kind of reasons for establishing cooperation are the political ones. Environmental aid can be seen as a way of stabilizing the relatively fragile democratic governments of Eastern Europe. Also, efforts especially in the environmental field, can support the "greener" part of Eastern European societies and help to break up the old power coalition which has been built around the party, heavy industry and the security apparatus[4].

In a period when environmental questions are placed high on the agenda in the West, and where there has been strong public support for the changes in the East, such a move may also prove popular in domestic politics.

---

[3] Background notes from the Danish Ministry of Environment in relation to the decision-making process when establishing the Nordic Environment Finance Corporation.

[4] How strong this old coalition is still remains to be seen. Even though the Communist parties and the security apparatus have been considerably weakened, at least heavy industry may still pose some defensive power to block or slow down changes.

The third reason for aid and cooperation is that it can be used as a way to strengthen the Nordic countries' own environmental industries by giving them new and larger markets to sell to[5]. If environmental awareness continues to grow world wide as has been the tendency over the last five years, the environmental industry will be important in the future. The Nordic countries can have an important role to play, if they continue to develop the relatively strong position which their environmental industry has today as a result of their relatively strict legislation and the modern production system with its high economic performance. When the general economic reconstruction gets under way, Eastern Europe could be a very important market for Nordic companies due to their relative geographical proximity.

Fourthly, however, a Nordic aid programme will depend on the amount of economic resources the countries are willing to put into it. There has been an increasing political will to give many resources to the environmental field, but it remains an open question as to the amount of extra resources that can be found – without taking from other regions, such as, for example, many countries in the Third World, which also need support to improve their environment.

3. The Rationale of Receiving Aid and Cooperating

The Eastern European countries may be interested in receiving environmental aid and cooperating for various reasons.

Firstly, environmental awareness has been increasing in Eastern Europe; the environmental field was one of the first areas where the Communist governments were met by the emerging opposition. The environmental problems formed an important part of the opposition's political agenda in countries like Czechoslovakia, East Germany and the Baltic States. We may then assume that many of the governments that have come to power, after the elections in 1990,

---

[5] How much this will actually benefit the Nordic environmental industries remains to be seen. It will also depend on what kind of aid the Nordic countries decide to give. See the discussion later in the paper.

will be more concerned with ecological problems than the previous Communist governments.

Secondly, since environmental problems have normally been outside the political agenda of the Communist parties, a close international cooperation in this field will probably not be met with such strong resistance from the former power elites, especially in heavy industry, as may be expected in other fields.

Thirdly, environmental aid and cooperation can be a way of getting access to some Western technologies which would otherwise be very expensive, if affordable at all, in a situation where most of the Eastern European countries suffer from debt and balance of payment problems, and where the hard currency constraint places severe limits on which new technologies and investment goods can be bought from Western countries.

However, one may not expect that improvement of the environment will have the highest priority for the newly elected governments. They will face demands for more consumer goods from the population, and in general, the whole question of a restructuring of the economy will have a high priority on the political agenda. This fact stresses the need for environmental policies which can be integrated into different kinds of restructuring policies in the economic field.

One should be aware of the tension that exists between generating a free market system, which now seems to be characteristic of the whole of Eastern Europe[6], and improvement in the quality of the environment: a tension which seems to call for some state intervention in the production sphere. This shall be discussed in the last section of this article.

---

[6] The future form of the economy is still rather unclear in countries like in Romania and Bulgaria, whereas Poland has taken some rather drastic steps in liberalizing the economy.

4. Rationale for Using the Nordic Forum

In this section we shall discuss the possibilities and limitations in using the Nordic Council[7] as a forum. For the Nordic countries an interest can be perceived in showing that the Nordic countries can still act together. In the last years there have been attempts to strengthen the role of the Nordic Council to balance the new dynamism of the European Communities. As part of these ideas, stress has been placed on the importance of what are seen as specific Nordic values, such as the Welfare State and environmental and consumer protection.

Secondly, by using the Nordic forum instead of the individual Nordic countries offering bilateral help, the risk of investment is spread, and it should be possible to increase both information about Eastern Europe as well as the influence which the Nordic countries can expect.

Thirdly, there may be an Eastern European interest in not being so dependent on the EC and especially on Germany, and therefore the Nordic countries may provide some kind of alternative – not in an absolute sense, since they all participate in the G-24[8] and since their resources are limited compared to those of the whole EC, but rather in a relative sense, for example, as a way of introducing qualitatively different forms of cooperation and aid.

Fourthly, however, it may be assumed that space for a joint Nordic effort will be relatively limited. Both Sweden and in particular Finland have their own special relations with Eastern Europe and the Soviet Union, and it is likely that they will still continue to develop these bilateral contacts. For Denmark, its EC membership gives access to what is regarded as an important forum for contacts with Eastern Europe.

---

[7] The Nordic Council was formed in 1955 and has played a key role in the fields in which the Nordic Countries cooperate, although the grand plans for Nordic cooperation, such as the Scandinavian defence alliance and Nordic Economic Community, never came into being. Less ambitious goals have been realized, such as the Nordic Labour Market and the abolishment of using passports when crossing inter-Nordic borders.

[8] The group within the OECD which coordinates policies towards Eastern Europe.

5. A Typology of Various Forms of Aid

In this part of the paper the different types of environmental problems are outlined which have to be taken into consideration when giving aid, establishing cooperation and forming environmental policies. Environmental policy can, broadly speaking, be defined as a policy which regulates the ways in which man interferes with nature for the purpose of achieving a certain quality of nature.

Man interacts with nature mainly through the use of natural resources, both renewable and non-renewable, for production; through the way in which the production process in the widest sense[9] emits pollution; and finally by the disposal of the various waste products.

Environmental policy, therefore, must deal with at least three different areas: resource management, process management and product management[10]. It must include a policy for the use of natural resources, focusing on how to economize the use of non-renewable ones. Secondly, it must deal with the pollution coming from the production processes. This can be done either by cleaning the waste products from these processes or by reusing the products. Finally, it must deal with the different waste products of human activity, either by purifying them to such a degree that they can be returned to nature, or by recycling them for other purposes.

What happens in most forms of waste disposal is that the product is transformed from one substance to other substances, which are clean enough to be recycled back into nature, with a remaining smaller portion which have to be dealt with in another way. This is, for example, the case of waste water from factories and cities. The purified water is fed into the sea, while the toxic particles which are caught in the purifying system are disposed of in another fashion.

It is characteristic that technology plays a major role in the above-mentioned main areas of environmental policy. It will be especially important to influence the development of new technol-

---

[9] Also including transport of goods and people.

[10] Cleaning of areas that have previously been spoiled by pollution could also be included.

ogies so that environmental considerations will be embodied in them.

Since it is the purpose of environmental policy to attain a certain quality of nature, it must also include a systematic monitoring of the state of nature as well as research into how different human activities affect it. As in other areas, laws and regulations are often used as instruments to carry out environmental policies[11]. To carry out policies, a state needs an environmental administration which has both the necessary technical, as well as administrative, expertise. The success of policy will also depend on the extent to which it is supported by the citizens or at least not opposed by them. Therefore, there may also be a need for a general environmental education to increase people's awareness of the problems.

5.1 Eastern Europe and Aid Programmes

We may now consider how the general elements of environmental policy mentioned can be used in an aid programme for the Eastern European countries.

Possible aid can be divided into two main categories. Firstly, the type that in itself should create a better environment. This consists mainly of different techniques and technologies either in the form of knowledge export or of investment goods where the technology is embodied in the good itself. Secondly, there are the auxiliary functions for an environmental policy, where the different systems that have been created to carry out the policy may be used as models or sources of inspiration.

The first main category can be subdivided into five main groups:

Firstly, the export of purifying systems to be installed into existing factories, or to replace inefficient cleaning of the waste water from big cities. This could be in the interest of the Nordic countries since in the short run, it is probably the most efficient way of reducing the crossborder pollution. Also there should be enough Nordic firms with expertise in this field to start the export, although a po-

---

[11] This does not imply, however, that all environmental policies will have to be strictly legalistic: Economic means can in many cases be as if not more, useful as the traditional ones. But they too need a legal framework to be established and enforced.

tential problem is that a rather large amount of money is invested in the field in the Nordic countries at the moment, which may create some short term capacity problems.

The second main group would be technical assistance to improve the use of existing technologies. That is, the same output can be made by a lower input of raw materials, energy consumption and waste products[12]. How large the possibilities for such a strategy are remains to be seen. But experiences in the West after the first oil crisis show that relatively positive results could be achieved with relatively minor changes in the existing technologies. This kind of aid will mainly have to consist of experts, for example, consulting engineers, going through factories to suggest where improvements can be made[13].

The third main group is the export of new investment goods that have environmental considerations embodied in them. This is naturally linked closely to the general restructuring of the economies of Eastern Europe. Agreement exists among the majority of observers that most of the Eastern European industry is not of a standard to produce goods which can compete on the world market. Therefore, a general improvement in the economic situation of the Eastern European countries will partly have to be reached by a rather large import of investment goods from the West. From an environmental point of view, it is important that when decisions are made on which kinds of new production equipment the countries shall buy, their effects on the environment are taken into consideration. As most of the Eastern European countries face a rather strong hard currency constraint, environmental aid could take the form of the Nordic governments agreeing to pay part of the extra price of the investment goods that are safer for the environment.

---

[12] Much research points to the fact that to obtain a certain output, the Eastern European countries need a much larger input than in the same industries in the Western countries. This is especially critical in the case of energy consumption. As has been pointed out by, for example, the Brundtland report, many of the major worldwide ecological problems are related to energy consumption.

[13] Changes in the economic system could strengthen these attempts. If the firms realized that they could go bankrupt the incentives to decrease costs should be larger. This tendency will be more pronounced if the firms have to pay what is closer to the (world) market price for their inputs.

The fourth main group tries to deal with the hard currency constraint, by exporting factories which can produce environmental goods such as purifying systems, instruments to measure pollution, investment goods that are less damaging to the environment, etc. The factories may even be able to re-export to the Western countries, due to relatively low labour and raw material costs, and may therefore be able to regain the foreign capital which will be needed to be invested in the beginning.

This may also be important in a situation where rising unemployment could be a threat to the legitimacy of many of the new democratic regimes, and where there is some fear of a communist backlash[14].

The fifth main group is the export of the recycling systems which have been developed in the Nordic countries. The advantages of these systems are that they reduce the need for raw materials, diminish waste materials and create jobs for the people employed in the system. A "famous" case is the Danish bottle recycling system, which owes some claim to international fame due to the fact that Denmark won a case in the European Court when it was found that the system was not created to protect Danish breweries against competition but rather as a legitimate way of protecting the environment. Export of recycling systems will involve some transfer of technical machinery, but the main part will be education of the people who will run the systems in the Eastern European countries.

Looking at auxiliary functions for an environmental policy, the experiences of twenty years of administration in the field may be important for the countries which are about to strengthen their own administration. However, one has to be aware that it is not possible just to take the administrative system from one country and simply transfer it to another country. It will have to be adapted to the particular circumstances of the specific country. Nevertheless, parts of the environmental administrative systems, such as the environmental laws, could indeed be a necessary part of the strengthening of

---

[14] This may be mixed with a populist nationalism. Such a mixture can already be found in the communist trade unions in Poland that are still stronger than Solidarnosc in terms of membership.

the administration in the East[15]. Here, the fact that the Nordic countries were among the first to adopt comprehensive environmental legislation is of importance.

Another important factor is to ensure that the Eastern European countries have enough experts with knowledge in the field. Since development runs rather fast, aid could consist of programmes to further educate people already working in the environmental field in Eastern Europe, as well as to give students in the environment field the possibility of taking part of their studies at a university or other institutions of higher education in the Nordic countries with expenses paid by the Nordic governments. Another part of the "software" aid could be to share the experiences of environmental education of the general public, for example, with regard to recycling systems, which in many cases such as garbage handling depend on large-scale cooperation from the general public.

Seen from the perspective of Eastern Europe, it must be an advantage to receive aid from and establish cooperation with the Nordic countries because the Nordic countries have – to a great extent – been able to integrate the handling of many of the mentioned types of environmental problems into the economic system as a whole without decreasing economic performance[16]. This is a very important phenomenon when both the economic performance and the environmental situation have to be considerably improved, as is the case in Eastern Europe. In this connection, attention must be paid to the fact that this in general requires a certain balance between the state (the political system) and the private sector (the market system); that is institutions should be generated which can balance environmental policies and business activities in appropriate ways. This issue will be discussed later on in this article.

---

[15] The laws are important since much of the legal tradition was suppressed during the Communist era, when the laws were viewed as being totally subordinated to the will of the Communist party.

[16] This is not to deny that there are big environmental problems in the Nordic countries. But it seems very important to be able to keep up a high economic performance at the same time as one tries to handle environmental problems. That is, it seems easier to handle environmental problems within a modern production system with a high economic performance, and such a system also produces in general fewer environmental problems.

6. Initiatives towards Cooperation between the Nordic Countries and Eastern European Countries

In this section of the article we shall give a short description of initiatives taken by the Nordic Council of Ministers and some of the single Nordic countries to give aid to and to generate cooperation between the Nordic countries and Eastern European countries. In this part of the article we will only describe quite new initiatives in spite of the fact that some old ones exist to handle and reduce the environmental problems in the region of the Baltic Sea[17]. Further, we will not discuss the support from the Nordic countries for Eastern Europe through, for example, the EC, the IMF and the World Bank.

Some new initiatives have been taken but they are so new that they are not yet in force or have only been in force for a very short period. Further, it appears that many of the initiatives are uncoordinated. Many have a strong ad-hoc character, and are not placed within an overall framework for dealing with environmental problems. Some of the initiatives seem to have been taken mainly to show that governments, public and private organizations are doing something in favour of Eastern Europe. For private firms most of the interest is based on attempts to generate markets for the future and they need, in this phase, some public arrangements to do this[18] – especially regarding the risk and slow turnover which business activities in Eastern Europe involve.

The Nordic Council of Ministers has, in consideration of the present situation, taken an initiative to establish a Nordic Environment Finance Corporation (*Selskabet for Nordiske miljøinvesteringer*).

---

[17] For example agreements such as UN agreements to avoid pollution in relation to ships (MARPOL), the Geneva Convention on air-pollution (1979), the Helsinki Convention on water-pollution (1974). Further, there exist some agreements between countries on environmental problems, such as for example Denmark and USSR (1975), Bulgaria (1988).

[18] Telephone intreviews with some major consultant firms in Denmark (end of 1990). Here it was said that money is needed from the state in relation to business projects if markets in Eastern Europe are to be generated at this stage.

The aim of this corporation is to support environmental projects in Eastern Europe – Poland, USSR, Czechoslovakia and Hungary – that have positive effects on the environment in the Nordic countries. The projects will be based on cooperation between firms in the Nordic countries and firms in Eastern Europe. The cooperation can and is widely expected to be based on joint-venture or similar business arrangements. In such cases the Environment Finance Corporation can support projects by financial means. The Environment Finance Corporation has 342 mill. D. Kr. for investments in projects[19]. It is expected that this sum of money will be able to support 20-30 projects or 4-8 projects in each Eastern European country mentioned. In cases where more projects apply for money than is available the criteria for support will be among others, a) the benefit to the environment in the Nordic countries, and b) traditional business criteria. Projects that are based on normal business criteria can also apply for support – in competition with other commercial projects – from other financial institutions within the Nordic Council of Ministers.

With the experiences we so far have from existing, planned and expected projects, it is thought that the projects will fall into the following categories:
– Transfer of know-how;
– Equipment for handling environmental problems: standardized as well as individually fitted equipment for end-of-pipe solutions;
– Some turn-key systems/plants.

The projects are generally expected to take place in the fields of energy, purification of waste water, etc. and consultancy jobs on broader issues.

One good example to be followed: in Poland a Swedish firm is cooperating with a Polish firm to improve the purification of waste water in such a way that waste material can be transformed into material to be exported as input in production systems abroad.

As can be seen, the initiatives taken by the Nordic Council of Ministers do not fit very well into the earlier discussed typology for

---

[19] 1 ECU is about 8 D. Kr.

environmental policies in the sense that they tend to focus very narrowly on only one of the possible strategies. The basic strategy is to support projects generated in (mostly) private firms which benefit the environmental situation in the Nordic countries. This is not to argue that this is without advantages. For example, major benefits are that the Eastern European countries and the individual firms within these countries will get some urgently needed know-how on how to run private firms and how to cooperate, and through this they will get know-how which can both improve economic efficiency and the environment. However, the problem with this strategy is that it does not employ an overall framework which can help create a solution to environmental problems in the region of the Baltic Sea. Furthermore, the present strategy tends to focus on projects which from the beginning are most interesting from the economic perspective of the single firms. According to the experiences in the West, this generates many problems when dealing with environmental problems, for example, great difficulties in employing long-term rather than short-term goals.

Some other initiatives have been taken. A short description of the newest initiatives in the Scandinavian countries (Denmark, Sweden and Norway) shall be given.

In Denmark the Parliament has decided (8 February 1990) to establish an arrangement for supporting environmental improvements in the Eastern European countries. One will support environmental projects and cooperation agreements with 100 mill. D. Kr. per year over a five-year period. This arrangement was put into force on 1 January 1991. A committee comprising ministries, the Green movement and traditional interest groups decides which kind of projects and cooperation arrangements are to be established.

In addition to this, within a special programme for supporting the reform processes in Eastern Europe the government has decided to use 300 million D. Kr. for projects and cooperation arrangements in Poland, Hungary, the Baltic States and Czechoslovakia. The money is to be used within two arrangements as follows:

1. The Pool for the Eastern European Countries (*Øst-lande-puljen*). This pool will support projects in the fields of agriculture, education, energy, fishing and occupational environment if the projects

are based on cooperation arrangements and stimulate the reform processes towards market systems.

2. The Fund for Investment in the Eastern European Countries (*IØ-fonden*). The money in this fund will be used to stimulate commercial development in Eastern Europe. It is not a condition that supported projects shall improve or even take the environmental aspect into consideration.

The money will be used and managed by a fund, which also manages projects and money in underdeveloped countries of the Third World.

Finally an arrangement to guarantee investments made by Danish firms in Eastern Europe has been established by the state.

If one looks at Norway and Sweden, similar arrangements as in Denmark have been established or are under way. It must be said that Poland has a high priority in Denmark and Sweden compared with other Eastern European countries.

In addition to the official initiatives mentioned here, many initiatives are taken in all the Nordic countries by both private and public institutions, organizations and firms; that is, for example establishing cooperation between universities, commercial schools, private health organizations, etc. Furthermore, in the field of occupational environment, which in general has a weak position in the field of the environment – as well as in the aid-programmes and cooperation agreements – public institutions in Denmark and Sweden dealing with occupational environmental problems compete in attempts to get cooperation agreements with the USSR. The Danish and Swedish institutions mentioned will export "systems" to the USSR to solve occupational environmental problems and will import commodities to be sold in Western Europe by these public institutions.

To sum up: some initiatives have been decided and others are under consideration. But the initiatives have been – until now – very uncoordinated and no overall strategies are employed. Poland and Hungary and now the Baltic States seem to have a higher priority than other Eastern European countries in arrangements developed to support both the environmental situation and the reform processes in general.

Besides the problem that – until now – no overall strategies have been employed when dealing with environmental problems in the region of the Baltic Sea, yet another problem exists, namely: how to create a framework for cooperation in the region of the Baltic Sea among the many states and regions hoping to become national states. A framework for cooperation is the basic condition if overall strategies are to be established at all in the field of environmental protection. Seen in this perspective, the Nordic model for cooperation on environmental protection might be of some interest.

6.1 The Nordic Model for Cooperation on Environmental Protection: A Model for Cooperation in the Region of the Baltic Sea?

The Nordic cooperation on environmental protection is based on the Helsinki Treaty of 1962 to which three articles were added in 1974. Due to this:
- the Nordic countries shall as far as possible equate the other countries' environmental interests with their own (article 30);
- the Nordic countries shall also seek to harmonize their rules for environmental protection (article 31);
- the Nordic countries shall coordinate the establishment of nature reserves and outdoor areas and the rules for these (article 32).

In practice, attempts to realize the intentions of the Helsinki Treaty are made by five-year cooperation programmes for Nordic Environmental Protection created within the Nordic Council of Ministers. The Nordic Council of Ministers submits proposals to and follows up recommendations from the Nordic Council. The Nordic Council (established in 1952) consists of 87 parliamentarians and government representatives from the Nordic countries. The Nordic Council of Ministers has a total budget of 611 million D. Kr. and uses 18.5 million D. Kr. for environmental cooperation. The present five-year programme for Nordic Environmental Protection (from 1988, Elsinore/Helsingør) is in principle based on the Brundtland Commission's report "Our Common Future" which stresses that attention must be focussed on interdisciplinary cooperation, long-term goals and looking upon environmental issues in an international perspective.

Furthermore, some working groups in relation to the five-year cooperation programme for Nordic Environmental Protection have been established within the Nordic Council of Ministers to analyze certain environmental issues and to make proposals for instruments and policies to deal with these issues. Working groups on knowledge and information about environmental problems, on air, water and soil pollution and on instruments and policies to handle different types of pollution, exist and work together with other groups.

The way the Nordic Council of Ministers and the Nordic Council functions, and hence the Nordic cooperation on environmental issues, must be stressed. The Nordic Council of Ministers and the Nordic Council are not supranational bodies. That is, these bodies cannot on their own decide on behalf of the single Nordic states. Decisions made by the Nordic Council of Ministers are not binding for the Nordic states. Decisions in the Nordic Council of Ministers have to be ratified in each member state to come into force. This could be looked upon as a very weak and ineffective type of cooperation, but in fact it has been effective in the Nordic case.

In Scandinavia, an "Internal Market" has already been created in several important respects through the mentioned way of Nordic cooperation. A common labour market exists; there is a reciprocal recognition of the different countries' educational degrees; the same privileges are given to citizens no matter which country they are living in; passports are not needed when crossing borders, etc. In the field of environmental protection, an effective cooperation also takes place. Cooperation among the Nordic countries has, so to speak, developed from the "bottom up" over a long period of time. Therefore, there has been no demand nor a strong need for supranational bodies to create and keep up cooperation (Storm Pedersen, 1990c). There has been a demand and a need for bodies which could be places for free discussions and for coordination of cooperation. The Nordic Council of Ministers and the Nordic Council reflect this situation to a great extent.

The model for Nordic Environmental Protection might be of some inspiration when thinking of a framework for cooperation on environmental protection which could establish over time the conditions for overall workable strategies in the region of the Baltic Sea. It is obvious that major problems will arise as discussed in the first section of this article when the many states (belonging to different international organizations and different European regions) and regions hoping to become national states, as is the case in the region of the Baltic States, have to cooperate. In such a complex situation it is impossible to create supranational bodies which can generate and employ overall strategies in the field of environmental problems in the region of the Baltic Sea. But if some progress is to be made some places must exist where free discussions can be held, declarations made, proposals for overall strategies to be employed can be submitted, etc. regarding environmental problems.

Over time cooperation and policies regarding environmental problems in the region of the Baltic Sea will evolve and be workable in practice if places such as those which exist in the Nordic model for cooperation are established. This already seems to be the case. By using the model for Nordic cooperation used by the Nordic Council it was possible to gather almost all the countries and regions in the region of the Baltic Sea at a conference on environmental problems in Sweden (Rönneby) in September 1990 (*Information*, 30 September 1990).

One major issue is still to be discussed: what types of overall strategies are possible to employ when dealing with environmental problems in societies based on a market system?

7. Some Lessons for Eastern Europe from Market-Based Societies for Handling Environmental Problems

In this section we shall discuss some lessons from market-based societies when dealing with environmental problems and industrial development as it is obvious that the Eastern European countries will use some kind of liberal model in the future. Also, in this part of the article some lessons from the Scandinavian countries will be taken into consideration.

7.1 Institutions in Market-Based Societies

Support of the reform processes in Eastern Europe, in general, means supporting the dismantling of centrally planned economic systems and supporting the creation of more liberal or market-oriented societies. If support for the reform processes is not to generate explosive conflicts between economic and ecological and hence social development, then this support must also favour establishing instruments and institutions which can regulate market systems in agreement with an ecological and hence a social point of view. Why is this so?

If a market society is analyzed by means of the classical socio-economists such as Smith (1980), Schumpeter, (1976), and Polanyi (1971a and 1971b) among others, then one can trace a certain agreement on the fact that a market system can be characterized by a unique combination of socio-economic efficiency, developmental dynamics *and* socio-economic and ecological destruction as the "cost" of economic development (Storm Pedersen 1988).

The socio-economic efficiency and the developmental dynamics in a market-based society are attractive elements. From these two elements come many (and a still increasing amount of) consumer goods, high productivity, attractive jobs, possibilities to generate many kinds of lifestyles, social positions, etc. But on the other hand the "costs" of the system are that existing jobs, life styles, social positions, etc. are often undermined through economic development. Seen from an individual point of view, the system becomes both "good" and "bad" at the same time. The individuals want the "benefits" from the system and aim at avoiding the "costs". From a historical point of view, a central theme in market societies has then become how to balance "benefits" and "costs" of the system in the most appropriate ways. This central theme has been analyzed at best by Polanyi (1971a and 1971b) and Kapp (1978). These writers show that there is a correlation between the diffusion of the market system and the creation of institutions and instruments that are formed to attempt to control the "costs" of the system: that is, to balance the "benefits" and "costs" of the market system. Polanyi writes (1944, quoted from Swaney and Evers 1989: 76):

"While on the one hand markets spread all over the face of the globe and the amount of goods involved grew to unbelievable proportions, on the other hand a network of measures and policies was integrated into powerful institutions designed to check the action of the market relative to labor, land and money."

In other words: creating institutions in market societies has been a way to balance "benefits" and "costs" seen from a developmental point of view, including, for example, policies to deal with unemployment and environmental problems. The creation of institutions and instruments to balance "benefits" and "costs" in a market-based society has of course been a centre for political, social, etc. conflicts from a historical point of view. Therefore, the design and functioning of the institutions influence the combination of the three central elements of a market system mentioned above and then the direction of the development of society. Furthermore, the design and functioning of institutions influence the distribution of "costs" and "benefits" of the system among social groups, different types of firms, individuals, etc. to a great extent. This fact means that the design and functioning of institutions will always be a centre for conflicts.

Seen in the above perspective, Eastern Europe, in creating more market-dominated economies, has a big task in front of it when creating institutions; that is, to "import" or generate institutions themselves which can balance and distribute the "benefits" and the "costs" of a market society in appropriate and fair ways in oder to, among other things, limit the risks for political and social "counter-revolutions" against the reform processes.

7.2 The "Scandinavian Model"

In the above-mentioned analysis of Polanyi and Kapp, the Welfare State in general is considered as an institution which has been created to balance and distribute the "benefits" and "costs" in various forms of a market system in appropriate and fair ways. Within the framework of the "Scandinavian Model" this can in short be expressed in the concept of equality among the citizens without losing a high economic performance in the market-based parts of society. This concept of the Welfare State has evolved in a long historical process; that is, as reaction to negative consequences of a market system based on the formation of interest groups within a democratic framework. One result of this process has also been that the Scandinavian countries (Denmark, Sweden and Norway) must be characterized as strongly organized societies in the sense that almost all social groups are organized. This phenomenon has, within the framework of the "Scandinavian Model", created a situation where conflicts and struggles between the interest groups within a democratic framework over time meant that institutions were developed which were designed to work out effective and functional compromises between the interest groups while taking the concept of the "Scandinavian Model" into account.

Furthermore, this results in societies which according to Klippe (1982) have been able to incorporate a number of different allocative rationales, including economic, social, political, environmental and resource ones. An allocative system which is based on a form of mixed administrative and negotiatory economy (Hernes 1978) or on a kind of game theory principle (Johansen 1977) has been created. To be workable this type of "Scandinavian Post-war Model" needs a high rate of economic growth. This fundamental condition has now become the major weakness of the model.

All major interest groups have agreed that the only way to handle major conflicts between the interest groups and to fulfil the concept of the "Scandinavian Model" (that is, to gain a high standard of living, have a fair distribution of the "costs" and the "benefits" of the market system and keep up socio-economic development at a rather high level) is through a modern economic system with a very high socio-economic performance (Storm Pedersen 1988, Storm Pedersen/Bevort 1989).

On the one hand, such an economic system in general is in itself a big advantage for the ecological system. That is, an economic system with modern production systems and a high economic performance leads in general to fewer environmental problems and less damage to the ecological systems (Jänicke et al. 1988) and has the possibility to adjust rapidly to new conditions, including environmental concerns (Christie 1988).

On the other hand, however, major problems now occur at the ecological and the political level. The Western post-war economic model has, as is well known, now generated and accumulated so many "costs" in terms of environmental problems, through circular, cumulative causation (Kapp 1978) that these begin to undermine the "benefits" of this model: a general and great improvement in the standard of living, a rather fair distribution of "costs" and "benefits" and a modern economic system with high economic performance (Storm Pedersen 1988 and 1990b; Storm Pedersen/Bevort 1989). This topic has to a large extent been summarized in reports such as "Our Common Future" (Brundtland-Commission 1987) and "*Betænkning om miljøregulering og vækst*" (Kampmannudvalget 1988). The reports conclude that the end-of-pipe solutions (taller chimneys, cleaning and filtration of waste water, regulation of traffic, etc.) are no longer able to handle the environmental problems in appropriate ways. A new model for economic, social and ecological development needs to be generated if a fair balance between and distribution of "benefits" and "costs" in relation to markets is to be re-established. That is to say, fundamental structural changes must take place.

7.3 Structural Changes and the "Scandinavian Model"

Strongly organized societies become a disadvantage when structural changes have to take place. Major interest groups stick to the existing model because they know the names and the rules of the games belonging to that model and because their political, economic, etc. positions are related to it. This means that societies become rather slow and less flexible in adapting to new conditions when major structural changes are needed and interest groups play a decisive role in the decision-making processes. The road to a new model for economic and social development is a process of long duration and paved with major economic, social, etc. conflicts. And the more strongly the interest groups are organized the greater these conflicts will be.

Furthermore, the environmental costs of the post-war economic model are a threat to the Welfare State. The "Scandinavian Model" has only to a very limited degree been designed to deal with environmental problems created by the post-war economic model. One of the reasons for this is that environmental problems have played no major role in the concerns of the major interest groups, nor therefore in the formation of consensus about what are the important issues in society, how they are to be handled and in what ways. This phenomenon is due to the fact that protection of the environment is a very complex issue and an issue which is often in conflict with the interests of traditional interest groups such as unions demanding more employment, the Socialist parties demanding further economic growth to generate an "economic surplus" to be used to reduce social problems, etc. This means that it is very difficult to create major interest groups dealing with protection of the environment which play a major role in the formation of consensus on the major issues the society has to deal with.

Therefore, protection of the environment has not become a central issue built into the concept of the "Scandinavian Model" from the very beginning. The result is that environmental issues are dealt with by relatively weak institutions and interest groups. The case today is that when the environmental costs of the post-war model increase so too does public spending and, therefore, taxes. In practice, the Welfare State has been designed in such a way that it has to pay the environmental costs of the post-war model: costs which have now become unacceptable for the majority of people in the Scandinavian countries. This fact is now expressed in polls[20].

To sum up: also the "Scandinavian Model" now faces a critical situation due to the environmental costs of the post-war economic model. A high rate of economic growth cannot be expected for the future and economic growth cannot be used as a general indicator of success. A new model for economic and hence social and ecological development has to be created. Furthermore, the Welfare State has to be redesigned to be able to handle the environmental problems in more appropriate ways. Finally, the interest groups must realize that environmental issues must play a major role in the decision-making system both within the interest groups themselves and in reaching consensus on what are the major issues in society

---

[20] *Politiken* (The biggest of the "sober" newspapers in Denmark) 2 May 1989 on polls from "Institut for Konjunkturanalyser".

and how to deal with them. The interest groups must also understand that they have to give up the existing model for development and participate in creating a new and better one.

If one looks at the present situation in a perspective of Kondratieff's theory of "Long Waves" (Kondratieff 1979), one will say that a shift from an old or out-dated "Long Wave" to a new one creating the conditions for a new period of development is taking place in these years. Kondratieff's theory is an attempt to describe long-term economic development and hence the development of societies through long-lasting "ups and downs" containing structural changes or crisis. One "up and down" will take about 50-100 years. This theory has been developed in detail by many as a way to describe a certain pattern of economic development and hence the development of societies (Marx 1972; Mandel 1973 and 1982; Schumpeter 1961a and 1961b; Barr 1979; Storm Pedersen 1988). In this article we shall not discuss such a comprehensive theme as a shift from one "Long Wave" to another or major structural changes in the "Scandinavian Model" due to a shift from one "Long Wave" to another. We will stick to the main issue: lessons to be learned from the Western countries and the "Scandinavian Model" concerning ways of dealing with environmental problems.

This means that it suffices to state that for some years it has been argued that state intervention and the size of the Welfare State have increased too much. The consequence of this should be that market mechanisms are damaged. This leads to an inefficiency in the allocation of resources and to a society which in general will be less flexible. The phrase "Eurosclerosis" used by the OECD, economists in the EC and Emerson (1988) expresses this (doubtful) argument, which has led to political demand all over Europe for more use of market systems and less use of state intervention and public institutions in the allocation of resources. This is an attempt to re-establish the flexibility of society as a strategy for creating economic growth. This is, for example, the basic idea behind the project of the Internal Market in the EC (Storm Pedersen 1990a). Seen in this perspective, environmental problems more or less have to be dealt with within the framework of a market system. Within such a framework, the polluter-pays-principle (PPP) is regarded as the major instrument by traditional or so-called neo-classic economists and has been recommended by, for example, the OECD for many years when dealing with environmental problems.

Therefore, the question of whether the PPP is an appropriate instrument in dealing with environmental problems or not shall be examined in the next section.

7.4 Market Versus State

The theoretical background for the PPP is to be found in the old debate on externalities. This debate originated with Marshall and Pigou in 1890 and 1920 respectively and has been a major economic issue since the turn of the century. We face externalities when (Baumol 1972: 392):

> "Members of the economy do things which benefit others in such a way that they can receive no payment in return, or where their actions are detrimental to others and involve no commensurate costs to themselves."

Or externalities occur whenever a decision variable of one economic agent enters into the utility function or production function of some other agent. More simply: when costs or benefits are not allocated correctly in a market system we face externalities. When externalities occur the neo-classic theoretical solution is very simple in principle: find the externalities and then find out who has generated them. Then make account of the externalities and place costs and benefits due to them in the right places in the market system. This can, for example, be done by taxes and subsidy as the traditional Pigouvian solution recommends. This model as a framework for handling externalities has been debated as mentioned for many years and there are many issues involved. The trend in the debate among neo-classics is, however, that externalities can be handled in the framework of the model mentioned, at least at the theoretical level. And it is within the model mentioned that the polluter-pays-principle has its origin. If one causes costs to other persons the model says that one has to pay. In practice it can be very difficult to realize the PPP. Take for example the case of air pollution: who has generated the air pollution, who is affected and how much, what is the price of air pollution? This is hard or almost impossible to find out in a complex and modern society and thus generates major problems in society.

If the PPP is to be an appropriate instrument for dealing with environmental problems, it must be possible to administer the PPP correctly because, if this does not happen, then as discussed above, the Welfare State has to pay. That is to say, the PPP is transformed into a tax-payer-principle in many cases which creates a major problem with public expenditures and hence political and social conflicts regarding the size of the Welfare State. And this is, in fact, what has been happening in recent years because it is impossible in practice to administer the PPP strictly.

Furthermore, new research summed up by, among others, Schot (1989), and Cramer et al., (1989), and Kemp and Soete (1989) shows clearly that the PPP must be handled *very strictly* if it is to be able to generate new technology, which is necessary if the environmental problems are to be handled in appropriate ways. The PPP must also be supported by flexible state regulations, grass-roots movements, etc. if major positive effects are to be achieved. And the best results are reached when solutions to environmental problems are related to general improvement and development of technologies from the very beginning: that is, in connection with the so-called "technology-nexus", the processes where new types of technologies and products are generated and selected in very complex processes with many actors (interest groups) involved over a long period (Schot 1989). But even this is problematic. As Kemp and Soete (1989) show, development of technologies which can handle environmental problems in appropriate ways is rather difficult to generate in firms in market-based societies. Until now firms consider handling environmental problems as "costs" even though it is not true in many cases when seen in a longer time perspective (Storm Pedersen 1988). Furthermore, the linkages between those who produce and use environmental equipment and technologies are much weaker than in normal user-producer linkages, which create some problems when generating new technology that deals with environmental problems in appropriate ways.

Finally, small and medium-sized firms lack the capacity to pick up information about how to handle environmental problems and how to use new technologies which can reduce environmental problems. And on top of this, many firms find that they are in a very insecure situation regarding changes in state-regulated norms, standards and legislation.

All this amounts to the fact that it is very difficult to integrate the handling of environmental problems into the processes of a market system and it is obvious that the PPP is too weak and general an instrument for handling environmental problems in appropriate ways.

Seen from this perspective, changes in the way firms handle environmental problems have to come to a great extent from outside until new routines, procedures, etc. for handling environmental problems have been established within the firms.

Here, interest groups and the creation of institutions play an important role. Unfortunately, as mentioned above, interest groups related to industry, to the agricultural sector, the fishing sector, etc. and to workers have stuck to the old post-war model and therefore not created institutions or instruments which could put pressure on firms to change ways of handling environmental problems.

The situation, however, is now changing slowly because the long-lasting crisis has now kept the major interest groups under political and economic pressure for so long that they have to change their attitude towards economic and social development and even towards environmental problems. Besides, more and more individual firms, farmers, etc. are trying to develop new types of methods of production, new types of consumer goods, etc. because they find it profitable. And such changes are now on a small scale supported by both public and private organizations and institutions. Even the trade unions now accept that handling environmental problems might create some unemployment for a period of time. Nevertheless, the creation of a new model for development involves new formations of consensus and the setting of new rules of the games between interest groups. It also involves a new division of labour between the private and public sector in terms of generating new institutions, new legislation, etc. to balance the "benefits" and the "costs" of a market system. It involves generating new patterns in production systems, new consumer behaviour, etc. Furthermore, it means that a whole range of new linkages between users and producers, private firms and public institutions, educational and research programmes, etc. are to be established. The creation and implementation of a new model is such a big task that one may wonder how it is possible at all with so many actors involved. Seen in this perspective, institutions in society which can generate consensus among interest groups regarding the central goals, strategies, etc. are very important, even when the "price" may be some loss of flexibility compared to a "pure" market society. And it is urgent that Eastern Europe generate new institutions to make a developing market system stable and to limit the conflicts which have existed in Western societies between economic, social and environmental development in order to avoid having to go through all the phases which Western countries have gone through in attempts to balance "benefits" and "costs" of a market system in the post-war period (end-of-pipe solutions, small changes in technologies, major changes in production systems, etc.; Strübel 1989a and 1989b).

8. Concluding Remarks

What kind of lessons can be summed up and learned in relation to Eastern Europe when supporting the handling of environmental problems and the reform processes in general? We find the following lessons important:

1. Support for the handling of environmental problems and support for the reform processes in general must be backed up by support for the creation of new institutions which can balance "benefits" and "costs" in a market-based society; that is, support for the creation of a complex model of society.

   Furthermore, regarding environmental problems, support must be given to institutions which can employ all the categories necessary for handling environmental problems, as discussed in section 5 of this article.

   Finally, the Nordic countries might be of some help, stimulating the creation of a fair balance between market and state as seen from the viewpoint of economic and social development and dealing with environmental issues at the same time.

2. Support must be given to the establishment of different interest groups so that all interests can be made clear and so that interest groups can participate in handling problems in Eastern countries in a dynamic and constructive way within a democratic framework, and thereby support the development mentioned in the previous paragraph.
3. Eastern Europe should not simply "import" the Western postwar model because it is or will soon become too "costly" in terms of environmental problems even though it will reduce the now existing problems in Eastern Europe considerably. Eastern Europe must try to avoid repeating all the phases that the Western countries have gone through in handling environmental problems. Eastern Europe must participate in generating a new global model for economic and ecological development. The alternative can be that Eastern Europe will remain in a poor situation in the world market for some years, namely as sub-supplier to the Western countries due to cheap labour costs, backward industries, etc. In such a situation the Eastern countries will be forced to stick to the Western post-war model for development for many years to come. This is not an appropriate way to handle the environmental nor the industrial problems in Eastern Europe.

Bibliography

BAUMOLL, W. J., 1972. Economic Theory and Operation Analysis, Englewood Cliffs: Prentice Hall.

BARR, KENNETH, 1979. Long Waves: A Selective Annotated Bibliography, in *Review II*, 4 Spring: pp. 675-718.

BRUNDTLAND-COMMISSION, 1987. Our Common Future, Oxford: Oxford University Press.

CHISTIE, IAN, 1988. Cleaning Up a Continent. Environment Policy in Eastern and Western Europe, in *Policy Studies*, August 1988 – Policy Studies Institute.

CRAMER, J. et al., 1989. Stimulating Cleaner Technologies Through Economic Instruments, Possibilities and Constraints, Hague: Discussion-paper for the EEC seminar "Economic Implications of Low Waste Technology, 16-19 October 1989.

EMERSON, M., 1988. What Model for Europe? Cambrigde MA: MIT Press.

HERNES, G. (ed.), 1978. Forhandlingsøkonomi og blandingsadministration, Bergen: Universitetsforlaget.

JÄNICKE, MARTIN et al., 1988. Structural Change and Environmental Impact. Empirical Evidence on Thirty-one Countries in East and West, Berlin: Wissenschaftszentrum Berlin für Sozialforschung, FS II-88-402.

JOHANSEN, LEIF, 1978. Forhandlingssamfundet in *Socialøkonomen no. 8,* Oslo.

KAMPMANN-UDVALGET, 1988. Betænkning om miljøregulering og økonomisk vækst, Hvidovre: Metals Miljøudvalg.

KAPP, K. W., 1978. The Social Costs of Business Enterprise, Nottingham: Spokesman.

KEMP and SOETE, 1989. Inside the "Green Box". On the Economics of Technological Change and the Environment. Merit, Maastricht Economic Research Institute on Innovation and Technology.

KLIPPE, PER, 1982. Den nordiske modellen, Olso: Paper to the Nordic Workerkonference – 1982.

KONDRATIEFF, N. D., 1979. The Long Waves in Economic Life in *Review II,* 4 Spring pp. 512-562.

MANDEL, ERNEST, 1982. Långa våger i den kapitalistiske utvicklingen, Göteborg: Rode Bokforlaget.

MANDEL, ERNEST, 1973. Der Spätkapitalismus, Frankfurt am Main: Suhrkamp Verlag.

MARX, KARL, 1972. Das Kapital, Band I-III, Berlin: Dietz Verlag.

MILJØ-INTERN, 1990. Storstilet Østhjælp er på vej in *Miljø-intern*, February 1990.

THE MINISTRY OF ENVIRONMENT, 1990. Answers from the Minister of the Environment to questions in Parliament; The Ministry of Environment, 22 January 1990.

THE MINISTRY OF ENVIRONMENT, 1989/90. Some Background Notes from the Ministry of Environment in relation to the decision-making process when establishing the Nordic Environment Finance Corporation.

NUTI, MARIO D., 1984. Economic Crisis in Eastern Europe: Prospects and Repercussions, European University Institute Florence: EUI Working Paper No. 26.

POLANYI, KARL, 1971a. The Great Transformation, Boston: Beacon Press.

POLANYI, KARL, 1971b. Primitive, Arcaic and Modern Economics, Essays of Karl Polanyi, edited by G. Dalton, Boston: Beacon Press.

SCHOT, JOHAN, 1989. Constructive Technology Assessment and Technology Dynamics: Opportunities for the Control of Technology – The Case of Clean Technologies, Appeldorn, TNO Centre for Technology and Policy Studies.

SCHUMPETER, J. A., 1961a. The Theory of Economic Development, London: Oxford University Press.

SCHUMPETER, J. A., 1961b. Konjunkturzyklen, I-II, Göttingen: Vandenhoeck & Ruprecht.

SCHUMPETER, J. A., 1976. Capitalism, Socialism and Democracy, New York: Harper & Brothers.

SMITH, ADAM, 1980. The Wealth of Nations, Middlesex: Penguin.

STORM PEDERSEN, 1988. The Contemporary Society with Mixed Economy, Roskilde University Centre, Denmark – Ph.D. thesis (Only Summary in English).

STORM PEDERSEN and BEVORT, 1989. The Challenge of Economic Integration in Europe in the 90's. Paper given at a conference in Keswick, UK 20-22 September 1989.

STORM PEDERSEN, 1990a. European Integration – Prospects and Challenge to the Scandinavian Model in *Macroeconomic Theories and Policies for the 1990's*. Forthcoming at MacMillan, 1990.

STORM PEDERSEN, 1990b. Externalities and the Social Dimension: Florence. A Departmental Lecture at EUI, Department of Economics, 30 November 1989. Working Paper no. 2, 1990, Roskilde University Center.

STORM PEDERSEN, 1990c. The Internal Market as an Opportunity for and Challenge to the Scandinavian Countries and the "Scandinavian Model" in *Lise Lyck (ed.)*; The Nordic Countries and the Internal Market in the EEC, København: Handelshøjskolens Forlag – Nyt Nodisk.

STRÜBEL, MICHAEL, 1989a. Technologietransfer und grenzüberschreitende Umweltpolitik in Europa in *Ulrich Albrecht (ed.)*; Technikkontrolle und Internationale Politik, Opladen: Westdeutscher Verlag.

STRÜBEL, MICHAEL, 1989b. Umweltregime in Europa in *Beate Kohler-Koch (ed.)*; Regime in den Internationalen Beziehungen, Nomos: Baden-Baden.

SWANEY and EVERS, 1989. The Social Cost Concepts of K. William Kapp and Karl Polanyi. in *Journal of Economic Issues*, No. 1, March 1989.

UDENRIGSMINISTERIET, 1990. Finansieringskilder og økonomiske støtteordninger i forbindelse med reformprocessen i Østeuropa. Udenrigsministeriet, København, Marts 1990.

ØSTLANDE-PULJEN, 1990. Notat om retningslinier for administrationen af "Øst-lande-Puljen".

Economic Development and Ecological Crisis in the Former GDR: Opportunities Offered by Change

Peter PICHL and Uwe SCHMIDT

The parliamentary elections in the GDR held on 18 March 1990 marked the end of a broad popular debate which also centred on new ways in environmental policy. It was the pending environmental problems with their multiple social consequences which motivated many people to act for a change in social conditions. Within a historically short period the now democratically legitimated political structures will lead to a far-reaching adjustment of the overall economic and political conditions on the territory of the former GDR to the structures prevailing in the Federal Republic of Germany. This process is accelerated by German unification. Those new macro-social conditions will provide the possibilities for and set the limits to changes in the living and working conditions. In this context, a basic process of change in the economic structure of the former GDR will be indispensable for several reasons. As the current changes rule out the maintenance of previous structures of production and performance of the GDR economy, society's relationship with nature will necessarily have to be a new one. If the government wishes to play a politically effective role, it has to encourage processes that orient the change of national economic structures towards a higher environmental compatibility of production. The following reflections relate to ways for solving this problem.

1. The Initial Situation: The Interaction between Structural Crisis and Ecological Crisis

In the national economic process of production, materials extracted from nature are transformed by human labour into material and non-material goods. According to the natural laws, the materials extracted from nature cannot all be transformed. They are discharged into the natural environment as waste. This very general conception may also be applied to the total sum of the individual processes taking place in the national economy. As in the individual process, so too in the national economy as a whole the result produced, seen in relation to the input of materials, indicates the efficiency of the totality of that process. International comparisons clearly show that this efficiency may differ considerably from country to country. If all conditions are equal, the efficiency of the processes of labour and value formation is determined by the structure of the productive processes and their interaction through the division of labour. Developed national economies are characterized by the fact that certain overall conditions have to be heeded under conditions of high national economic output and that factors like the emission of contaminants have to meet well-defined conditions of balance to avoid a deterioration of living conditions and welfare. The example of the GDR shows that any neglect of those overall conditions and arbitrary structural decisions result in a major loss of efficiency and in a noticeable fall in the quality of life.

If one makes the attempt to characterize the arbitrary changes in the GDR's historically developed structure of production, one will notice that the contradiction between the kind of endowment of nature and the kind of use of nature has developed with comparable acuteness in practically none of the other European countries. This contradiction can be proved, for example, on the basis of emissions per unit of output,[1] of energy consumption per unit of output and of the high dynamics in the damage done to ecosystems, especially to forests (see Table 1).

---

[1] With a unit energy consumption of 233 Gigajoule/inhabitant, the GDR, after the United States and Canada, has the third highest unit consumption in the world (based on unpublished data of the Roundtable, January 1990).

Table 1

Proportion of damaged forests on the GDR's territory

Year	1983	1984	1985	1986	1987	1988	1989
Proportion	12%	13%	19%	29%	37%	44%	50%

Source: Institut für Umweltschutz 1990, p. 28.

It is the structure of the national economy which underlies the flows of materials and energy on which blame has to be laid for the ecologically harmful effects of production in the first place. In the following, we shall deal with some problems which stand for many of the multiplicity of structural defects in production and consumption and in the social organization of attendant processes.

2. Ecological Consequences of Relative Overindustrialization

Theoretical statements of Leninism, the Soviet Unions's practical experience and the politically competitive situation with regard to the dynamically evolving economic system in the Federal Republic of Germany have for decades made gross output a key criterion for the success of social development in the GDR. The misplaced allocations thus caused by the centrally controlled investment policy express themselves, on the macro level, in trends that are also noticeable in other Eastern European countries: the preference given to commodity-producing industry over the other sectors and, moreover, the preference given to industry over agriculture and the service sector. In 1985, for example, the share of the goods-producing industry in the GDR's gross national product was some 67 per cent and that of the service sector some 15 per cent, while the respective figures for those two sectors in the Federal Republic of Germany were about 41 percent each (see Table 2).

Table 2

Contributions made by the different economic sectors to the 1985 GDP in percentages

	FRG	GDR
Goods-producing industry	41	67
Services (incl. government)	41	15
Agriculture and forestry	2	7
Trade, transport, communications	16	11

Source: Bundestag 1987: 345.

Compared with the international average, there was an overemployment of about two million people (with regard to its level of development) in the former GDR, and an underemployment in the service sector (Pichl/Schmidt 1989:12).

The oversize of the goods-producing sector can be traced to the doctrine of productive labour which has so far been dominant in East European countries and which states that only labour that creates material values produces national income and national wealth. Therefore, in cases of doubt the planning authorities have always redistributed scarce resources to the detriment of what they understood as non-productive sectors. A visible result of this policy is the depressing situation in the health service in East Germany, the deplorable state of streets and highways as well as of the railway system and the heavily damaged housing stock.

Given this situation, it is possible to point out the specific causes underlying the oversize of the industrial sector: the insufficient integration of this country in the international division of labour and the stagnating or even regressive development of the division of labour within the national economy. While the former process is largely caused by political factors, the latter process necessarily results from laws that are inherent in an economy of scarcity.

The efforts to concentrate the control of economic processes in one hand only again and again expressed itself – especially in periods of increased external economic pressure – in strategies aimed at autarky and self-supply, which became apparent in slogans such as "self-sufficiency" and "import substitution". The latest processes of this kind and those with the most serious consequences were the large-scale application of microelectronics from 1977 on, which made excessive demands on the GDR's investment capacity without producing internationally marketable products on a major scale, and the large-scale replacement of energy imports with the domestic lignite in the eighties. The replacement of fuel-oil alone required an additional amount of 50 million tons of raw lignite to be mined. Concentration on lignite as an energy resource[2] not only required over 30 per cent of the total investment in the industrial field annually, but it is the main problem in the environmental sector. The use of lignite accounts for the greatest part of air pollution through sulphur dioxide (SO_2), nitrogen oxides (NO_x), carbon monoxide (CO), dusts and organic compounds (CH). The mining of lignite by the open-cast method destroys nature and urban settlement areas. Carbon-based chemistry, which uses lignite, is one of the main factors in the deterioration of the waters because of its tar wastes. In 1984, the GDR undertook a commitment to reduce its emissions of sulphur dioxide by 30 per cent by 1993. In reality, emissions increased by 20 percent by 1989 (see Table 3).

---

[2] In 1988, the GDR accounted for 26.2 per cent of world production with 311 million tons, on the basis of which it produced more than 70 per cent of its primary energy.

Table 3

Reduction of sulphur dioxide emissions in selected countries in the period from 1980 to 1985

Country	Emissions of sulphur dioxide (in 1 000 tons)		Reduction of emissions (in per cent)
	1980	1985	
Finland	584	375	− 35.8
France	3 558	1 845	− 48.2
FRG	3 200	2 640	− 17.5
Netherlands	445	230	− 48.3
United Kingdom	4 670	3 580	− 23.3
GDR	5 000	6 000[a]	+ 20.0

[a] In 1989.

Sources: OECD 1987: 23; unpublished new data for the GDR.

The sulphur dioxide emissions in the GDR were more than 60 per cent above those of the FRG; if the figures are related to area and inhabitants, the GDR has values which are nearly ten times as high, and the pollutant intensity of the gross national product for sulphur dioxide is thirteen times as high as that of the FRG. In regard to nitrous oxides, the situation is comparatively good; here, the pollutant intensity of the gross national product is only about twice as high[3].

3. Ecological Consequences of Microstructural Change

On the microstructural level, international comparisons are naturally more difficult in view of the multitude of problems of classification and evaluation and, if the national specifics of the separate

---

[3] Statistical Yearbook 1989: 155.

countries are taken into account, they are also less indicative. Nevertheless, a comparison between structural development in the former GDR and that in other countries points to further problems: particularly in the past 20 years the production of high energy and environment-intensive products has been increasing at a rapid pace (see Table 4).

Table 4

Development of the production of selected goods in the GDR from 1970 – 1987

	1970	1975	1980	1985	1987
electric energy	100	124.9	146.1	168.2	168.0
town gas	100	120.4	145.3	182.2	190.0
raw lignite	100	94.3	98.7	119.4	118.2
lignite briquettes	100	85.7	87.1	88.8	86.7
petrol	100	131.2	149.1	192.4	209.3
diesel-oil	100	134.1	169.1	175.5	176.3
sulphur	100	91.1	87.1	80.3	78.9
potash fertilizer	100	124.8	141.4	143.2	145.0
nitrogen fertilizer	100	136.2	238.7	272.6	333.4
phosphate fertilizer	100	99.5	86.1	69.7	67.8
plastics/synthetic resins	100	163.3	232.6	283.0	286.6
synthetic fibres	100	236.4	293.2	333.4	340.8
crude steel	100	128.4	144.6	155.5	163.2
rolled steel	100	125.7	150.5	165.5	172.8
ore for concrete	100	129.3	148.7	152.9	148.9
cement	100	133.5	155.8	145.4	155.7
paper	100	110.5	117.0	119.4	126.1
meat	100	136.4	147.3	165.1	167.5
butter	100	126.6	129.9	146.4	143.7
white sugar	100	135.2	135.7	168.7	165.7
beer	100	122.5	142.0	145.9	145.0

Source: Statistical Yearbook 1989: 24-30.

Table 5

Specific (area-related) output of selected products in various countries in 1985 (indicated in t/km^2)

Country	Wood felling/ ha of areas	Spun rayon	Artificial silk	Paper	Lignite	Electric energy GWh/ km^2	Town gas TJ/m^2	Petrol	Crude Iron	Cement	Sodium	NaOH	H$_2$SO$_4$	Nitrate fertilizer	Potassium fertilizer	Phosphate fertilizer
GDR	3.6	1.13	0.23	8.2	2.87	1.06	1.04	45	25	111	9.1	5.9	8.2	11.6	32.2	2.8
FRG	4.2	0.65	—	31.7	0.46	1.60	0.74	77	118	—	5.8	14.6	16.5	4.2	8.7	1.6
Austria	3.8	1.13	—	21.3	0.04	0.47	—	24	39	55	—	—	—	2.9	—	—
CSSR	4.1	—	—	7.5	0.79	0.66	1.07	—	75	81	1.0	2.6	10.2	4.8	—	2.4
Poland	2.0	—	0.05	3.5	0.22	0.45	—	12	33	51	3.4	1.4	9.5	4.6	—	3.0
Netherlands	—	—	0.9	—	—	1.8	0.67	335	123	83	—	—	38.8	44.2	—	9.7
Belgium	—	—	0.12	—	—	1.76	1.36	148	245	175	—	—	59.2	22.7	—	10.9
France	2.2	0.03	0.01	9.4	0.004	0.6	0.13	3	26	41	2.8	2.8	7.2	3.1	3.1	1.9
UK	2.0	0.33	0.07	13.0	—	1.23	0.28	96	40	55	—	—	9.5	5.0	—	1.2
Sweden	1.9	0.07	—	15.6	—	0.3	—	67	6	5	—	0.9	2.1	0.4	—	0.3
Yugoslavia	1.3	0.7	0.27	49.3	—	1.47	2.23	67	15	189	2.8	8.1	16.0	2.8	—	1.7

Source: Statistical Yearbook 1989: 44-56, own calculations.

The dash (—) indicates that there are no data available.

A look at the production of selected products per area of national territory will clearly show the ecological dimension of that structural development (see Table 5). The contradiction appearing here between the structurally conditioned high intensity of the use of nature and the average capability of nature to assimilate pollution goes undoubtedly beyond the limits of ecological compatibility.

The situation has been made even more difficult by the fact that the structure of the GDR economy has been "escalating", as it were: structural change has principally taken place through starting new productions. The preference given to new branches in investment distribution by the government has hardly been capable of ensuring simple reproduction in the traditional sectors so that a major part of the output has been produced on the basis of antiquated and often extremely polluting technologies. A case in point is the real average age of fixed assets (see Table 6).

The results to be found there are even better than they actually are given the artificial system of evaluation. The share of machinery and equipment which at the end of 1986 belonged to the fixed asset (capital stock) of the industrial enterprises, although they were more than 20 years old, was on average 19.2 per cent of the national economy, oscillating between some 10 per cent (domestic trade, geology, forestry) and over 30 per cent (coal and energy, posts and telecommunications).

Table 6

Real average age of productive fixed assets according to GDR ministries (date of registry: 31 December 1986)

Sector	Average age (years)
Coal and energy	17
Ore mining, metal-working, potash	13
Chemical industry	14
Electrical engineering, electronics	10
Heavy machinery and plant construction	13
Machine tool, general machine and farm machinery building	11
Light industry	13
Foodstuff and regionally administered industry	13

Source: Unpublished data from GDR Central Office of Statistics.

4. Structural Problems of the Regional Division of Labour and Their Ecological Consequences

As a result of the general concentration of centrally controlled processes of industrialization on already existing centres, the traditional distribution of industry, which was frequently based on certain natural conditions, has not been developed qualitatively, but has been expanded quantitatively. Industrial areas which had their basis in the cost-efficient availability of raw lignite as the primary material of the processing industry and as a source of energy for energy-intensive processes of production were especially badly affected by this development. The productions that had historically developed in these areas were not being diversified further but were multiplied in their frequency. The labour needed for it was often settled there through a systematic housing policy and other supportive measures.

For the natural environment and the living conditions of the people this policy led to a regionally highly accentuated division into areas with a high output of pollutants through the concentration of certain non-diversified processes of production with very complicated living conditions, and regions which processed and consumed those products with a low output of pollutants. This regional structure created a considerable potential of conflict and hampered an ecologically-oriented structural policy which could include the necessary closing down of especially polluting productions.

Of special consequence was the connection between highly energy-intensive processes of lignite-based chemistry and the equally lignite-based generation of power in the Leipzig area, as the environment has been damaged there in a twofold manner.

A generally known example of this is the district of Borna with the factories at Böhlen and Espenhain. In this district and in the adjacent areas south of Leipzig there is one gas generation plant and 15 briquetting plants. The concentration of coal-processing processes in the area is characterized by the fact that the following sectors of the GDR's productive capacity operated there:
- 19.1 per cent of raw lignite mining;
- 35.0 per cent of briquetting;
- 8.3 per cent of electric energy generation;
- 6.5 per cent of municipal gas generation;
- 84.8 per cent of lignite low temperature carbonization (2 700 000 tons);
- 31.3 per cent of lignite pulverized fuel production (679 800 tons);
- 80 to 90 per cent of carbochemical production, including 497 000 tons of raw tar based on lignite and 142 100 tons of middle and light oils as well as 256 700 tons of gasoline (6.0 per cent of GDR production) and 474 900 kt of diesel fuel (7.5 per cent of GDR production)[4].

As the GDR's lignite carbonization capacity was concentrated in this area, the carbonization processes annually accounted for the following emissions:

---

[4] Data based on unpublished material of the GDR Central Office of Statistics.

- 5.04 million tons of dust;
- 4.2 million tons of dry and damp vapours, including:
  - 1 000 million cubic metres of exhaust air;
  - 24 600 tons of SO_2;
  - 3 600 tons of H_2S;
  - 2.5 tons of mercaptans;
  - 7 600 tons of organic vapours;
- 24.6 million cubic metres of waste water including 6.9 million tons of water from the main processes of production[5].

The acceptance of such massive emissions on a relatively restricted area proves that environmental compatibility has been totally neglected.

At the moment, environmental compatibilities are being revealed in the microeconomic and regional field following the pressure from the newly emergent political forces in the former GDR and in particular after German unification. This is leading to the closure of plants not only in the Böhlen and Espenhain areas, but also at Pirna (artificial silk factory), Schkopau (carbide production), Ilsenburg (copper mill) and in other areas.

The social cost there manifests itself in its broadest sense as:
- unusability of social wealth;
- dismissal of workers on a large scale (for instance up to 12 000 workers in the Böhlen–Espenhain area);
- high expenditure to dismantle dangerous plants and to recover the areas and create new employment.

These consequences go far beyond the costs described in the literature. They make especially clear the social dimension of ecological change caused by the dismissal of workers, which points to the contradictory connection between the ecological and social compatibility of environmental policy.

In the former GDR, this connection will have to be the basis to start from in defining an environmental policy.

---

[5] Own calculations based on Mohry 1986.

5. Ways of Effecting Future Structural Change in Terms of Economic Policy

What has been said so far clearly shows that the complicated interaction between economic efficiency, ecological compatibility and social stability in the GDR has largely been upset. With productivity in the former GDR being less than half of that of the FRG, the national economy has for years been developed to the detriment of the natural environment and of future development (neglect of investment) to keep up in some way with the living standards and the consumption level in Western European countries. Although any future economic policy will have to be geared under all circumstances to the three aims of:
a) increasing the efficiency of economic activity,
b) enhancing environmental compatibility, and
c) ensuring the necessary stability,

these three pillars are related to one another in a very contradictory manner. This contradiction is *per se* not specific to the GDR, but in the economy of the GDR (just as in those of other Eastern European countries) the distance between these pillars is especially great. Any overemphasis on one of these three aspects must necessarily affect the other two: a unilateral economic policy aimed at adapting the GDR's level of productivity to that of the FRG must necessarily be to the detriment of the environment and of social concerns; any priority given to ecological recovery must result in grave economic and social consequences (on account of the resultant increases in cost and the closing down of polluting factories). On the other hand, if too much stress were laid on social concerns, then efficiency levels and environmental recovery would suffer.

The re-establishment of Germany's statehood is not likely to be able to cut that Gordian knot in the short run. Coping simultaneously with all of these three important tasks is an aim which is making high demands on economic performance and capability and on the conduct of economic policy.

With the transition to a market economy, the overall political conditions for a structural development based on efficiency criteria will noticeably improve: as a result of the elimination of directive planning and (central) resource allocation and price control, prices will reflect the scarcity of commodities and thus force industrial enterprises to gear their production to the consumers' preferences and to production costs. In the long run, these economic mechanisms will enable the economy operating on the former GDR's territory to specialize in terms of the comparative advantages available to it. Today we can only speculate as to the specific directions of that structural change as the present situation does not permit us to make well-founded statements on the competitivity of the separate branches and industrial enterprises.

But it goes without saying that in order to improve the ecological situation especially in the energy and fuel sectors, and in the chemical and metal-working industries, major structural changes and the closing down of factories will be inevitable[6]. Such changes can only be socially acceptable if they are backed up by governmental retraining programmes for released labour and by programmes for the development of new industries. This applies in particular to the industrial area of Halle-Leipzig-Bitterfeld, the attractiveness of which as an industrial centre is greatly impaired in view of the heavy pollution created there so far.

International cooperation could go a long way towards considerably improving the conditions for coping with the ecological problems outlined above in accordance with economic and ecological requirements. In the face of the global dimension of the ecological problems (which, as far as SO_2 emissions in the former GDR are concerned, is borne out by Table 7) the prerequisites for such cooperation should be seen as good. The questions which will be given priority in this connection will be elucidated on the basis of an extremely important series of problems facing the GDR: winning acceptance of a decentralized and ecologically compatible generation of energy.

---

[6] These three branches alone accounted for over 90 per cent of the sulfur dioxide emitted in 1988.

Table 7

Transboundary sulphur dioxide flows for the GDR in 1988

Country	Export from GDR	Import to GDR
	(in 1 000 tons)	
Norway Sweden Finland	128	0
Poland	486	36
CSFR	232	112
FRG	188	82

Source: Institut für Umweltschutz 1990, p. 13.

6. The Development of Decentralized Energy Supply Systems as a Task of Structural Policy

With more than 5 million tons of sulphur dioxide emitted and 2.2 million tons of dust, the energy industry on the territory of the former GDR is an economic sector with low environmental compatibility. Additionally, major devastations of the surface (4 000 ha annually), water pumpages on a large scale (over 5 cubic metres per ton of coal)[7] and the multiple costs of mining, conversion, processing and application of raw lignite heavily impinge on the goods supply efficiency as major quantities of labour have to be spent on the elimination of damage done or on additional costs resulting from damage.

Another aspect of the emission of noxious material connected with processes of energy supply has to be seen in the context of the

---

[7] Data from Energiestatistik DDR, Leipzig, Institut für Energetik (unpublished).

spatial distribution, the number and the frequency of energy and conversion processes.

While there are some large detached power plants whose high chimneys cause the spreading of noxious materials over wide areas, there are in urban agglomerations a great number of small and mini-sized emitters of noxious materials which, given the low height of their chimneys and sub-optimal combustion, stress the people living in these conurbations and the plants, buildings and equipment necessary for the functioning of life processes. In the city of Leipzig, for example, domestic stove heating emissions account for 50 per cent of the total emissions of sulphur dioxide during the six months of winter[8]. This is why an environment-related structural change in the energy sector will also have to be concerned with decentralized forms of energy supply if the ecological and social compatibility of the energy supply is to be improved. This includes a consistent use of the new general conditions and of the organizational principles underlying them.

The post-war period in the GDR saw a rigid hierarchical and centrally run structure of energy supply aimed primarily at ensuring the energy needed for the processes of industrialization. In the seventies, the supply of district heat and hot water to the people living in new residential areas became an important task. In the field of energy supply, the spatial and temporal control of energy and the minimization of macroeconomic expenditure – in terms of minimum input of fuel per unit of process energy – became criteria of optimal use. Under the conditions of relatively extensive domestic raw lignite deposits and the exclusion of energy magnitudes from estimates of economy, the demand for energy at fixed real cost prices, which only contained the conversion-related final or process energy prices, was able to develop in an uncontrolled way. In order to minimize the price-effective cost, full use was made of the conditions to exploit the effects of economies of scale. As a result of these processes there developed nation-wide, internationally linkable, hierarchically structured systems in the supply of electric energy and gas. They were composed of:

---

[8] Data from the Bezirkshygieneinstitut Leipzig, 1987 (unpublished).

- the spatially nearly identical system of extraction and transformation (open lignite mines and adjacent condensating power plants of a large size) to reduce the transport of unprocessed energy to a minimum;
- the nation-wide system of distribution of upgraded energy in various hierarchical levels to reduce losses to a minimum; and
- the decentralized consumers.

With regard to district heat, the supply system was similar, but did not go beyond the municipal or at most the regional level.

Given this system and the underlying general conditions (such as constant energy prices with accompanying major subsidies, budgeting requirement and allocation of energy, neglect of social cost, absolute priority given to domestic raw lignite as the "cheapest primary energy" and the resulting low level of diversification of the different forms of energy), the *supply* rather than the *use* of energy became the principal purpose of the energy sector's policy.

Under such conditions the GDR, following the structure-forming processes in the energy sector and in connection with the development of energy consumption by industry and domestic users, became a country with maximum values in the *generation* of energy per unit of output. Simultaneously, the GDR had a consumption of energy that was often twice as high as the international average with regard to many energy use processes in industry and consumption.

Since the mid-seventies attempts have been made to make the secondary use of released energy a source for budgeting by the government. This shows that there has been awareness of the fact that this system has exhausted its quantitative margin and that a new quality of energy use processes has become necessary.

The attempt to include new energy use processes into the previous budgeting system etc. results in contradictions which can only be solved under different social and economic conditions, of interaction between scarcity and prices, and on the market, with the government fixing the general conditions. In this way, it will be possible to give a new meaning and content to energy supply which consists in rationalizing the *use* of energy in such a way that macroeconomic conservation becomes possible, which could be reflected as costs and price advantages on the market.

Since the beginning of the eighties there have been in many highly industrialized countries changes in electric supply companies for which the concept of "passage to the utility company for the service of electric power" has been used. This concept comprises a new strategy of supply which makes *collective energy use* rather than *terminal energy use* the subject of energy supply. On the one hand, the attempt is made to decrease demand through various energy economy measures and, on the other hand, to reduce the quantity of energy needed for the supply through full use of the energy potential, viz. the potential of the energy released to perform work. Basically the aim is to maximize the use of energy once it is released and to approximate for this purpose the energy transformation processes as closely as possible to the use with a view to exhausting all components of the energy potential, especially the multiple possibilities of coupling. This requires a decentralization of energy transformation processes, which includes the coupling of power-heat, power-cold, power-pressurized air, heat-cold, heat-heat, etc.

The use of energy potential coming directly from the environment and of previous waste materials also belongs to this category. The economic interest of electric supply companies is no longer directed towards selling the greatest possible amount of energy for utility purposes, but towards maximizing energy conservation and fully or partially profiting from the resultant benefit.

On account of the above-mentioned energy, economic and ecological problems of the central energy supply that has been in existence in the GDR so far, the establishment of utility companies has to be seen as a structural change that is equivalent to the change of the national economic branch structure. The general social conditions required for it greatly differ from those based on the supply and sale of energy for utility purposes.

In the following, we shall try to deal with the most important of the conditions to be created for an environmentally compatible change in the energy sector.

7. Necessary General Social Conditions for a Decentralized Energy Supply in the Former GDR

The most important general condition influencing the demand for energy is the *pricing of the form of energy on the basis of its scarcity*. This includes material control of a broad spectrum of different forms of energy and their scarcity, which has to be measured in market terms. This is made impossible by a one-sided governmentally decreed orientation towards one kind of primary energy resource, accompanied by steadily increasing subsidies, viz. cost factors that do not have any bearing on prices. It is the most important function of scarcity to allow the recognition and the use of thresholds of substitution of collectible energy on the basis of different primary energy sources.

A second important condition is the *re-establishment of municipal and local property rights* over the power generation and distribution installations necessary for the towns and villages, which in the post-war period were abrogated. They guarantee both a great interest of towns and villages in a good supply and also the necessary income to ensure investments in buildings and installations. This purpose is served by the money that comes in through licences given to supra-regional energy supply installations with which there is cooperation and by income from services to supply the inhabitants, the local industry and commerce.

The third important condition for a decentralized and environmentally compatible energy use is the *access to the capital market*. Many towns and villages, upon taking over their proprietary rights, will have an increasing demand for investment that cannot be met by local finance sources. It will primarily serve the purpose of lowering the demand for energy and making greater use of the energy potential offered by the existing installations. As an example, with price conditions changing, it will be profitable in terms of economy and energy to convert the district heat supply installations in towns to heat-power coupling. Such capital-intensive processes can only be fully used if the necessary major credits are provided in advance, including the possibility of paying back the credits with money earned by energy conservation.

The fourth and most important condition is the *new role of the state* which, mostly by exerting indirect influence, will proceed from the central control of the most important processes to mediating between the interests of the different centralized and decentralized electric supply companies, the towns and villages and the citizens, and which will fix the general conditions for all those affected by energy supply. Such a function would be, for example, the fixing of emission limits for all electric supply companies or the elaboration of energy supply programmes for towns and villages, and many other things. In many towns and villages, for example in the former FRG, these and other general conditions not mentioned here have resulted in the development of energetically, economically and ecologically efficient energy supply systems.

Under the concrete conditions of Eastern European countries (less so for the GDR after reunification) it may be assumed that even if the necessary general conditions mentioned here are established, the development of advanced and environmentally compatible decentralized energy supply systems in short periods of time will only be possible if substantial resources are provided by Western European countries. This applies both to direct financial aid to investment processes through appropriate measures of promotion and to making available urgently needed know-how for advanced technologies. With its high pollution intensity, the energy sector of former East Germany, even after reunification, constitutes a considerable strain and load on the environment of major parts of Europe. Giving aid to its restructuring is therefore both in our own interest and in the interest of all: it is a sort of ensurance of the future of this continent.

Bibliography

BUNDESTAG, 1987: Materialien zum Bericht zur Lage der Nation im geteilten Deutschland, Deutscher Bundestag, Drucksache 11/11 of 18. 2. 1987.

INSTITUT FÜR UMWELTSCHUTZ, 1990: Umweltbericht der DDR. Informationen zur Analyse der Umweltbedingungen in der DDR und zu weiteren Maßnahmen (Berlin: Verlag "visuell").

MOHRY, HERBERT, 1986: Zum Problem der Schaffung abproduktfreier Territorien im Bereich der Energiewirtschaft der DDR, Ph.D. thesis, Magdeburg.

OECD, 1987: OECD Data Compendium 1987, Paris.

PICHL, PETER/UWE SCHMIDT, 1989: Entwicklung der Produktivkräfte, Zukunftssicherung und internationaler Vergleich, Berlin, typescript.

STATISTICAL YEARBOOK OF THE GDR, 1989, (Berlin: Staatsverlag der DDR).

East European Countries Facing Ecological Cooperation in Europe

Marek PIETRAS

Ecological problems determine political, social and industrial development processes of the modern world, both internally and within international affairs[1]. International relations are influenced by global ecological interdependencies. On the one hand, ecological problems broaden the sphere of discrepancies and conflicts. On the other, they function as the crucial element of cooperation among countries and nations. They also bring about an alteration in the notion of international security, international ecological security being its integral item.

Europe is one of the most industrialized regions of the world and the scale of industrialization and transportation means that the ecological threat is approaching a critical point. The solution of the problem in question has become internationalized, which, in turn, imposes the need for a new ecological order in Europe. In confronting the unity of Europe's ecosystem and its reaching a turning point, not only does an all-European cooperation become indispensable, but also, above all, a new ecological awareness on the part of both statesmen and communities as well as qualitatively new processes of coexistence are absolutely essential. The present stand of East European countries on ecological problems and ecological cooperation in Europe requires analyses and conclusions.

---

[1] Our Common Future 1987; Pietras 1989; Timoszenko 1986.

1. Factors

The involvement of East European countries in ecological cooperation in Europe has been conditioned by three factors: the degradation of Europe's ecological environment, the international ecological debate and the process of the Conference on Security and Cooperation in Europe.

1.1. Degradation of Europe's Ecological Environment

The high level of industrialization, urbanization and density of the population in Europe causes a constant threat regarding degradation of the natural environment. Especially dangerous is air pollution, which causes further degradation of waters, soils, fauna, and flora.

Air pollution is mostly caused by excessive emissions of nitrogen oxides and sulphur dioxide. As the atmosphere does not respect state borders, polluted air shifts long distances. Italy exports it, for instance, to Austria, Switzerland and Yugoslavia; Great Britain mostly to Scandinavian states and Germany. Germany emits polluted air to East European countries; they, in turn, to neighbouring countries and Scandinavian states. The results of environmental degradation in one country may be perceptible in another, far from its place of origin. Exceptionally dangerous threats for the European ecosystem are caused by acid rains, leading since the beginning of the 1980s to the dying off of forests. Europe is facing one of the most serious ecological disasters in modern times. Other elements of the European ecosystem are also being degraded. Increasing water consumption in the process of industrial production causes underground water resources to be used up, leading to barrenness in many regions in Europe; pollution of soils and waters is progressive. Excessive emissions of carbon oxides contribute – through the increasing "greenhouse effect" – to climatic warming[2]. Seas surrounding Europe are also subjected to systematic degradation. There has been a constant accumulation of toxic substances, especially originating from petroleum.

---

[2] Brown 1989.

Ecological threats also afflict East European countries. Regarding the situation in Czechoslovakia, Poland and the Soviet Union, these states are treated as the ecological degradation centre in Europe. British and Scandinavian scientists, researching the causes of acid rains in Europe, came to the conclusion that air is mostly polluted by Czechoslovakia, Poland and the former GDR. Also for this reason, Eastern Europe is treated as Europe's "ecological sewer". Here, mechanisms regulating the regenerating ability of nature, the ability to maintain the ecosystem's homoeostasis, is disordered. As pointed out by A. Peccei, the world is not able to oppose the mass invasion of industrial civilization's waste, nor does it have the power to restore all the destruction brought about by man. L. Brown and S. Pestel in "The Report on the State of the World, 1987" stressed that the counterpoise of environmental threshold barriers resisting pollution was violated. This, in turn, leads to the presumption that as so many elements of the ecosystem are losing their stabilitiy, unexpected impetuous alterations of a discontinuous character may become common.

Ecological threats acquire crucial meaning in the ongoing process of internationalization. As the ecosphere is uniform and indivisible, this frames ecological interdependencies among states. The process leads not only to an internationalizing of differing aspects of the international ecological state of affairs in different countries, but also causes their increasing adaptability to external impulses and compelling forces that are extremely difficult to forecast and control. The process in question has influenced the evolution of the East European countries' stand regarding international ecological cooperation.

1.2. The International Ecological Debate

Another factor of consequence for the East European countries' involvement in ecological cooperation in Europe was the broad international debate on the preservation of the natural environment. The debate was essentially inspired by the U Thant Report, published in 1969. It is stressed that for the first time in the history of mankind, there has been a world-wide crisis affecting both developed and developing countries, and concerning the attitude of man towards the environment.[3] It is also emphasized that if the process in question continues, future life on Earth may be threatened. It is, then, necessary to consider ecological problems and undertake preventive actions. The Report also presents the world's main ecological problems and evaluates the existing procedures for averting disaster.

Significant impulses for international ecological cooperation were created by the Stockholm Conference in 1972, inspired in considerable measure by the U Thant Report. The Conference confirmed the urgent need for joint action and common rules inspiring nations to protect and improve their natural resources. Its Final Declaration expressed twenty-six rules connected with the preservation of the environment. It also pointed out the present decisive moment in history, in which there would be an inevitable need to adjust human activities all over the world to their outcome on the environment. It seems that the most significant achievement of the Stockholm Conference consists in the lasting introduction of ecological affairs into international relations, with both statesmen and public opinion being aware of their importance. Although East European countries – because the Cold War prevented the GDR's participation – did not participate in the Conference, they took ecological issues seriously. Moreover, before the Conference, they initiated an all-European cooperation at the forum of the United Nations' Economic Commission for Europe. This led, in turn, to organizing the Prague Symposium (1971) which considered ecological threats. It was stated that Europe is threatened by the serious consequences of environmental pollution and it was agreed that Europe should form an ecological unity[4].

The U Thant Report and the Stockholm Conference stimulated international debate and the organization of numerous ecological conferences during the 1970s and 1980s.

In the 1970s, conferences were mainly organized by the UN agencies[5], whereas in the 1980s, in turn, an international ecological de-

---

[3] U Thant 1969: 121.

[4] Michajlow 1976: 26.

[5] Mencke-Glückert 1985: 211; Wajda 1989: 70.

bate developed resulting in thirty international conferences of a wide range (in the first half of 1989, nine were organized). Many a time, East European countries inspired participants and organizers; at other times they refused to participate.

1.3. The Process of the Conference on Security and Cooperation in Europe

After the Stockholm Conference, significant impulses for an all-European ecological cooperation were created in the process of CSCE. In this respect, its Final Act combined three elements: the will to strengthen security and cooperation, conceding the claim for an unpolluted environment as one of the fundamental rights of man and making the rule of environmental preservation one of the most significant elements in international relations in Europe. This approach goes further than the one adopted by the Stockholm Conference. The Stockholm Final Declaration led to a consensus as regards international ecological cooperation. The process of CSCE, however, does not only mean making declarations: it also stimulates actions in order to solve regional ecological problems. The Conference conditioned the development of ecological cooperation in Europe, creating thus unquestionable possibilities of action for East European countries. At the first stage of CSCE in 1973, Hungarian and GDR delegations presented a joint declaration considering the development of cooperation in the field of economy, trade, science and technology, and preservation of the environment[6]. The document called for developing all-European cooperation, both bi- and multilateral, as regards ecology. It also indicated fields and forms of realizing cooperation (joint research programmes, joint conferences, exchanges of scientists and information).

Ecological issues became a permanent element of the process of CSCE, this being confirmed by conferences in Belgrade, Madrid and Vienna. The Final Document of the Vienna conference stressed to an exceptional degree the need to strengthen ecological cooperation aimed at maintaining and restoring ecological balance in

[6] CSCE 1983: 58.

the air, water and on the earth[7]. The most important event was the Sofia meeting organized in the fall of 1989, entirely given over to ecological affairs. It resulted in recommending a set of guiding rules concerning further means and cooperation in new fields of environmental preservation.

While evaluating the effects of these factors exerted on the form and content of the East European countries' involvement in ecological cooperation in Europe, one should emphasize that it was the process of CSCE and the international ecological debate that held basic importance. The problem of the progressive degradation of the environment was not fully comprehended, influencing the actions of the countries in question only to a certain extent. This was confirmed by the declaratory character of most initiatives. The Eastern involvement in ecological cooperation in Europe was primarily the function of international factors, rather than of domestic desires resulting from the worsening state of natural resources. Significant revaluation came with the 1980s, when the process of environmental degradation also in Eastern Europe began to be comprehended to a considerable degree. This factor, in turn, promoted the East European countries' involvement in ecological cooperation in Europe.

2. Conception

With regard to ecological cooperation in Europe, East European countries aim at the preservation of the environment and counteraction against its degradation, as well as the development of ecological cooperation, understood as an element of the construction of an all-European infrastructure of security. At the beginning of the 1980s, Soviet studies stressed that ecological problems had not been sufficiently examined; their character being more global and universal than ever. I. Frolow notes that the ecological issue has become the most significant contemporary problem, trespassing over state borders. If men do not thoroughly alter their attitude towards nature, he says, "the ecological bomb" will cause inevitable dire

---

[7] CSCE 1989: 110.

straits[8]. In the GDR, it was indicated that vital interests of nations and states crucially depend on finding a way out of ecological threats, regardless of their political system[9]. In Poland it was stressed that the world-wide character of challenges and issues is the striking part of the present stage of civilization. Economic, ecological and other crises lead to increasing threats for the world and mankind. The growing ecological interdependence demands joint, complex and global solutions[10]. It was also admitted that close cooperation among all European nations is necessary in order to prevent the ecological catastrophy.

This stand has undergone a long and far-reaching process of evolution. In the 1950s and 1960s, the threat of environmental degradation was neglected, if not silenced. This was facilitated by a specific understanding of industrial development and the place of ecology in it. In economics, the natural environment was treated as the so-called "inexhaustible good", which created the stereotype of abundant and inexhaustible nature offering all necessary resources. The accepted model of industrialization, hinged on the development of heavy industry, made smoking factory chimneys a symbol of civilizational advance. Since the beginning of the process of straining industrialization, bureaucracies were not willing, or were hardly able, to regard postulates put forward by ecologists. Ecological action was confined to founding national parks. The idea of the external character of ecological threats was equally dominating: if there appeared evident cases of degradation of the environment that could not be concealed, they were explained as temporary results of imposed competition and relating economic and military necessities[11]. It was assumed that the problems in question were solvable within the framework of economic planning, which is not available in capitalist states. In international relations, the importance of ecological threats tended to be depreciated. They were

---

[8] Frolow 1982.

[9] Pancke 1982.

[10] Orzechowski 1987: 10.

[11] Heinemann et al. 1987: 114.

considered to be falsely exaggerated by different western movements. Such an approach to ecological problems meant that extending international ecological cooperation was hardly expected.

The 1970s brought new elements to the attitude of East European countries to the problems of ecology. Firstly, a broad range of ecological problems were treated as a significant element of ideological struggle. Making no mention of the progressing degradation of the domestic natural environment, efforts were made to prove the superiority of the socialist economy over capitalist management. It was stressed that the socialist economy is able to create a natural balance between industrial processes and the preservation of the biosphere, as the nature of socialism excludes the antagonism between industrial targets and maintenance of the qualities of the natural environment. It was assumed that socialism, with the means of production owned by state or public bodies, its planning programmes and a humanist system of social goals, creates the best relations with the natural environment. It was taken for granted that antagonistic systems, such as capitalism, do not favour the natural environment. Progressive systems, in turn, create the premises, hinged on scientific and planning bases, to influence nature[12]. Considering social and political factors, the western approaches, which explained the causes of the degradation of the natural environment in terms of scientific and technological progress pertaining to any state regardless of political structure, were totally rejected[13]. This turned out to be the accepted way of dealing with the issue in question, although the degradation of the natural environment in East European countries was progressing at an alarming rate in consequence of the mania of gigantic industrial structures which emphasized only the immediate economic benefits but neglected the long-term ecological damage.

Secondly, under the influence of the broad international debate and actions that followed, East European countries were in favour of international cooperation on the ecological plane, especially within the framework of the United Nations' Economic Commission for Europe and the process of CSCE.

---

[12] Problema okruzajuszczej 1976.

[13] Wasiljew/Pisarjew/Chozin.

Considering the rule of consensus, the Final Act of CSCE can be treated as an expression of the East European countries' stand with regard to numerous fields of all-European cooperation. In the sphere of ecological activity, they declared the need for such targets as ecological threat research, increasing the effectiveness of local and international means to preserve the natural environment, developing the production of waste treatment facilities, unifying and harmonizing national policies concerning ecology. It was also emphasized that the preservation of nature is of consequence to present and future generations and that it is significant as regards the welfare and economic development of all states.

The inspiring role of CSCE was reflected in the Soviet proposal, announced in December 1975, to hold all-European conferences concerning the preservation of the natural environment, transportation and power industry. In the note of the government of the USSR (March 1977), defining the idea of the top-level talks on these issues, it was pointed out that the proposed issues are not solvable either at a national or subregional level, all-European cooperation being absolutely essential. The note included a list of questions to be discussed. Those concerning the preservation of the natural environment were the following: 1. long-distance transborder shift of polluted air, 2. activities in favour of the preservation of the maritime environment, 3. projects and application of technology eliminating waste products, 4. agricultural production and natural environment protection. The Soviet stand met the approval of European states, this being confirmed by the all-European conference regarding the preservation of the environment, organized in Geneva in 1979.

In the 1970s, East European countries exhibited a dual attitude toward environmental policy. On the one hand, they accepted the need for broad international cooperation while, on the other, they concealed their internal ecological problems. This lack of coherence created an essential obstacle as regards broad involvement in ecological cooperation in Europe.

Further revaluation of the East European countries' stand concerning ecological issues was brought about in the 1980s. In this period, the status of ecological cooperation was raised to become one of the main guiding lines of international activity of this group of countries and there was a simultaneous change of attitude towards internal ecological issues. In Poland, a major breakthrough occurred in 1980. Since then, ecological problems have been univocally recognized in the mass media, in scientific publications and in official documents. In the USSR, new impulses focusing an interest on ecological issues were created by the plenary session of the Central Committee of the Soviet Union Communist Party in 1985. Essential were, however, the proceedings of the 27th Congress of the Communist Party. According to M. Gorbachev, global contradictions connected with the basis of existence of civilization include, first of all, pollution of the natural environment, atmosphere and oceans, and exhaustion of natural resources. He claimed that there was a distinct need to introduce effective international mechanisms and procedures that would guarantee the treatment of national resources as a good common to mankind. It was also pointed out that one country or a group of countries are not able to solve global problems, and that there is an indispensable need for world-wide cooperation. Further, this need was treated as the categorical requirement of the times we live in. It was also emphasized that relations between countries with different social systems require new ways of political and ecological thinking.

The process was of particular importance when these countries started facing the ecological restructuring of their economic systems. A common question has been raised – and not only within this group of countries – of how to reconcile the preservation of the environment with taking decisions concerning economic development. Undoubtedly, one has to evaluate as positive the development of the conviction that the preservation of nature is an inseparable part of social and economic development of these countries. Similarly positive is a strengthening of the conviction that relations between the natural environment and the economy are not a zero-sum game.

The changes in question caused a similarity of postulates and claims put forward in both East and West European countries. In the GDR, for instance, arguments were put forward for production without ignoring the need for an ecological revival of industrial society. This concurrence of viewpoints and interests created the basis for developing cooperation. East European countries, besides cooperating in science and technology and actions taken to create "international ecological law", started to attach more and more importance to cooperation in production. This was seen in a Polish proposal, presented at the United Nations but addressed mainly to European countries and set forth by President W. Jaruzelski, concerning an unconstrained flow of experience, licences and technology, to be used in the preservation of the natural environment. Following the Chernobyl disaster, cooperation in nuclear plant safety began.

The end of the 1980s, in connection with the advancement of democracy and internal reforms, brought about a unique international effort exerted by East European countries in the field of ecology. The suggestions originating here and actions taken by these countries are more and more significant contributions in the European and global ecological debate.

Among these activities, the conference of peasants' parties, organized in 1988 in Warsaw, is particularly important, the Polish standpoint being presented at the proceedings. It was indicated that the preservation of the environment should be treated as the all-important issue, ranking with nuclear disarmament. It was also stressed the conviction that the soil, air and water are a common heritage of mankind that may be protected from eventual degradation by a joint effort. The proposal was addressed to the Secretary General of the United Nations, and concerned the declaration of rights and duties of countries in the field of ecology. This would be a code of procedure for states and nations that could guarantee – when complied with – the ecological ability of the world to preserve the human race.

During the 43rd Session of the United Nations, the Polish minister of foreign affairs stated that safe ecological development may for some countries turn out to be an unobtainable luxury due to the lack of funds and technology. Thus, there is a need for international bodies, including the United Nations, to identify "the areas of emergency", where international aid should be supplied to realize norms relating to the preservation of the environment[14]. This postulate means that for many countries, it is not the political will that matters, but rather the shortage of funds is the fundamental reason for

---

[14] Cf. Rzeczpospolita, September 29th, 1988.

increasing ecological threats. As the ecosystem is a global one, it generates an urgent need to overcome national and state egoism and to supply ecological aid to areas in danger of degradation. Taking into account ecological interdependencies, supplying aid also means aid for the very supplier.

A significant stage in the process of evolution connected with the East European countries' attitude towards ecological cooperation in Europe refers to the declaration of the Warsaw pact countries entitled: "The consequence of the arms race for the natural environment and other aspects of ecological security", adopted in July 1988. The document, stressing military aspects of ecological threats, makes actions of member countries in support of all-European co-operation in the field of the preservation of the natural environment the top-ranking political issue. It also emphasizes that application of measures which would let Europe become an example of ecological cooperation corresponds in the full sense with the idea of an indivisible Europe. In order to put the idea into practice, the member countries of the Warsaw Pact put forward in the document a set of proposals aimed at assuring the preservation of the environment in Europe. They made declarations in favour of an unconstrained exchange of ecological data, free access to modern ecological technology, and building up a system of precise information including actions taken up by countries in the field of ecology and ecological accidents. Aiming to expand existing ecological cooperation in Europe, it was proposed to summon an all-European meeting of ministers responsible for ecological issues, and to work out a programme concerning collective actions.

The initiation by the USSR, in the spring of 1989, of a unique campaign for the preservation of the natural environment became a new phenomenon within the East European countries' stand towards ecological issues. This resulted in introducing a new term to the diplomatic language of the CSCE: "the fifth basket", meaning the whole complex of ecological problems. The Soviet Union joined the existing international conventions concerning ecological problems, announcing simultaneously the priority of its international commitment over domestic legislation. In connection with the 1992 UN Conference on Environment and Development, the USSR was in favour of working out a code of procedure for states in the field of ecology and concluding a convention on the most burning ecological questions, including a settlement of the question of universal use of ecological technology, setting up an international ecological fund and creating, within the framework of the UN, an ecological security council with political capacity[15].

This unique "ecological offensive" has received, however, a relatively cool welcome by West European countries – a consequence of a negative evaluation of the Eastern actions up to the present regarding solving ecological problems. This activity led time and again to the initiation of progressive declarations and conventions of international scope, while the international ecological situation worsened. Moreover, the West negatively evaluates the fact that East European countries did not join numerous conventions controlling ecological issues, nor did they introduce many international standards. Furthermore, with Eastern economies facing a profound crisis, with their outdated systems consuming large quantities of natural resources and energy, and with their restricted financial abilities, it seems dubious whether East European countries have anything to offer in the sphere of ecology beside their intellectual potential[16].

In general, the above opinions and doubts do not depreciate the contribution of East European countries to ecological cooperation in Europe. However, taking into consideration efforts to overcome division and create the symbolic "common house", this situation is a serious challenge, and is all the more essential as in some East European countries – after the political transformations in 1989 – there exists the conviction that the ecological barrier could become an obstacle on the way to Europe. In order to surmount the obstacle in question, these countries have to set in motion the processes of adaptation to ecological norms and standards used in Western Europe. Realization of this goal requires, however, not only their own efforts, but also broad and multiform international cooperation.

---

[15] Nowe Czasy, vol. 39, 1989.

[16] Pierielet 1988: 96.

3. Actions

The forms of East European activity promoting the preservation of the natural environment have evolved from subregional activities, mainly within the Council for Mutual Economic Assistance (CMEA), through all-European cooperation, especially on the plane of the UN Economic Commission for Europe (ECE), to bilateral cooperation with capitalist countries.

The subregional activities encompass both bilateral and multilateral undertakings. Considering the unity of the natural environment within the European ecosystem, these activities are an essential contribution to its preservation. Bilateral cooperation is most often controlled by appropriate agreements. Initially, Poland entered into agreements relating to the conservation of frontier water with Czechoslovakia (1958), the USSR (1964), and the GDR (1965). Then, in 1973, Poland signed a complex agreement with the GDR concerning the preservation and formation of the environment, and with Czechoslovakia in 1974, an agreement on air pollution control.

The multilateral cooperation of CMEA countries in the fields of environment preservation reaches back to the early 1960s. It comprises both cooperation in science and technology, and in production, initiated in the second half of the 1970s. In the 1970s, the preservation of the environment was accepted as one of the top priorities of joint technological research in the complex programme of integration of CMEA countries.

The first programme, realized in 1971-1975, included only six research issues: hygienic aspects of the preservation of nature, conservation of ecosystems, social, economic, legal and educational aspects of the preservation of nature, protection of water resources, liquidation and utilization of municipal and industrial waste. The cooperation in question turned out not to be complex, as it did not deal with every branch of industry responsible for environmental pollution. Therefore, the programme to be realized in 1976-1980 comprised eleven issues and it took it for granted that the research results were liable to be converted into a fact within the economic system of member countries with utmost haste. In practice, ecological problems were removed to the background, which meant that the results in question did not come up to expectations. They left out of account the issues connected with environmental preservation on the international level, e.g. economic aspects of transboundary air pollution, or influence of ecological undertakings on international relations. The programmes to be realized in 1981-1985 and 1986-1990, were, to a high degree, a continuation of the former. They, however, included several new elements, such as technology for eliminating waste products or ecological information services. This was probably due to the Geneva conference of 1979, which had addressed precisely these issues.

In the 1970s, the first attempts to cooperate in the production of cleaning facilities were started. Efforts to create the basis for cooperation did, however, not reach beyond the starting point. The crucial obstacle sprang from the lack of conception of an international division of labour within the framework of CMEA regarding the production in question. The results obtained by "Interwodooczistka", an international joint-stock company founded in 1977, were not optimistic enough. It aimed to satisfy the needs of CMEA countries for cleaning and water treatment facilities. The resulting effects were, both in this field and in relation to cooperation in the scope of science and technology, still insufficient, regarding the CMEA countries' demands and potential to contribute to an all-European cooperation.

The growing awareness of ecological threats and increasing international and domestic pressures created premises to start negotiations (March 1988) and sign, on July 1st 1989, in Wroclaw, a trilateral agreement on ecological cooperation between Poland, Czechoslovakia, and the GDR. These long and tough negotiations were initiated by Poland. The agreement controls in a complex way the problems of environmental preservation and the rational use of natural resources in the signatory countries. It establishes the obligation of stopping the degradation of the natural environment, especially as regards frontier regions. It also makes stipulations on cooperation in the scope of a reduction of water and air pollution. It compromises cooperation in science and technology, and acting together as regards monitoring and production of facilities for environmental preservation. It also contains legal regulations concerning arbitration of matters in dispute resulting from extreme pollution, including ecological disasters. However, the agreement lacks regulations regarding claims for damages in case of the disasters in question, as the GDR and Czechoslovakia eluded liability for extreme transborder pollution of the environment as stipulated by international law. The wording that concerns gas emissions is insufficient. In spite of Polish suggestions to make it precise, it was only agreed that signatory countries will try to reduce gas emissions, especially of sulphur and nitrogen oxides affecting frontier areas, to the best of their abilities. Realization of resolutions included in the agreement is to be supervised by a committee consisting of persons having the power to act on behalf of governments of countries entering it.

Other instances of subregional activities, exceeding, however, the framework of CMEA, are the involvement of these countries in co-operation in support of the protection of the Baltic Sea and its resources. The basis for further actions are the Gdansk Convention on the Preservation of Living Resources in the Baltic Sea and its Straits (1973), and the Helsinki Convention on the Preservation of the Baltic Maritime Environment (1974). The GDR, Poland and the USSR are, among others, parties to these conventions. The former was initiated by Poland, with the resulting cooperation being carried out within the International Fishing Committee of the Baltic Sea. With reference to the development of navigation and the progress of urbanization and industrialization of sea-board states, the latter convention points at the roots of maritime environmental pollution and labels the substances that are forbidden or strictly limited as regards the Baltic environment. Bringing the convention aims to fruition is supervised by the Committee of Preservation of the Baltic Maritime Environment (HELCOM).

Subregional activities of East European countries also concern other areas. On the initiative of Bulgaria, the United Nations Environment Programme decided to include the Black Sea area in the programme aiming at the preservation of inland seas and help in solving the most burning problems. In 1987, representatives of Bulgaria, Roumania and the USSR agreed on the text of a future convention concerning the preservation of the maritime environment of the Black Sea. In December 1987, in Sofia, a meeting was concluded of the Balkan states experts concerning the preservation of the natural environment of the Peninsula. The meeting was also attended by representatives of Albania, Bulgaria, Greece, Yugoslavia and Roumania. Roumania was the initiator of the declaration concerning preservation of the Danube waters, signed in Bucharest, in 1985 by all the Danubian states, whereas in 1988, Czechoslovakia came up with a proposal to develop ecological cooperation with six neighbouring countries.

All-European cooperation in the field of the preservation of the natural environment is mainly realized within the framework of the ECE, its development being to a large extent promoted by East European countries. The ECE took up this field of interest on the initiative of Czechoslovakia, the country which in 1967 propounded the development of an ecological cooperation project. Due to the proposal, in accordance with the resolutions of the 24th Session of the ECE, the problems of environmental preservation became one of the top priorities of its proceedings. It was assumed that the organization is to be responsible for the general framework of all-European cooperation in environmental preservation, information and consulting services, working out ecological standards and advice for national ecological policies. The organizational structure was shaped to carry into effect the assigned tasks, the Board of State Senior Advisers dealing with ecological issues being created.

Within the process of CSCE, East European countries declared new initiatives concerning ecological issues. The Soviet Union proposed calling an all-European conference dealing with the preservation of the natural environment. This conference was held in Geneva in November 1979. The staple of its proceedings was connected with long-range transboundary air pollution and technology eliminating waste products. The convention on long-distance transborder air pollution, which came into force in 1983, is very important. Its resolutions created the conditions to form, at the conference in Munich in 1984, the "30-per cent club", i.e. a group of countries which accepted to reduce by 30% by 1993 sulphur dioxide emissions, taking 1980 as the base year. From among East European countries, the following joined the Club: Bulgaria, Czechoslovakia, the GDR, Hungary and the USSR[17]. Poland and Roumania backed

---

[17] But see for the results the contribution of Pichl and Schmidt in this volume.

out, with Poland explaining its refusal by reference to the lack of funds and technological abilities to carry on the project.

The Geneva conference also adopted a declaration regarding technology for eliminating waste products. This cooperation includes: implementation of improved industrial processes to reduce pollution, designing durable products, waste valorization, rationalization of resources and energy consumption and application of closed production cycles.

The Chernobyl disaster brought new elements to the all-European ecological cooperation. It contributed to an awareness – and not only in East European countries – of threats resulting from modern technology and led to progress as regards regulations concerning environmental preservation. In September 1986, the Vienna conventions on early information and aid in case of nuclear break downs and radiation threats were adopted. East European countries, including Poland with the proposal of a monitoring system connected with radiation protection, crucially contributed to their working out.

The second half of the 1980s brought a broadening of bilateral cooperation between East European and capitalist countries in the field of the preservation of the natural environment, based on agreements. Although a number of agreements were signed in the 1960s and 1970s, they only considered protection of frontier waters against pollution. Those signed in the second half of the 1980s, enlarged on these matters. Poland signed such agreements with Finland (January 1986), Sweden (October 1986), Holland (September 1987, its executive protocol being signed in September 1989), and with West Germany (November 1989). These agreements concern water conservation, preservation of water and air from pollution, rational waste disposal and mutual specific research. The agreement with Sweden stipulates for cooperation in the production of facilities and measuring apparatuses for environmental preservation, with joint ventures being established. The agreement with Holland deals with noise suppression and controls the involvement of both countries in creating an all-European system of monitoring relating to air pollution.

In the modern world, now facing increasing ecological threats, the state of the natural environment and attitudes towards it are an essential criterion as regards human culture. Correlations between economic and technological development and ecological culture are indispensable. In order to reach the aim, it is essential to restore the coherence between national and international activities in support of environmental preservation, and to accept universal ecological norms and standards. However, the involvement of East European countries in ecological cooperation in Europe is accompanied by a unique gap concerning the objective state of environmental degradation versus the ecological consciousness of decision making centres and societies, the gap between the awareness of threats and undertaken action, and the gap between consciousness and financial ability to take up joint actions.

Bibliography

BROWN, N., 1989: The "Greenhouse Effect": A Global Challenge, in *The World Today*, Vol. 4.

CSCE, 1983: Od Helsinek do Madrytu. Dokumenty KBWE (Warsaw).

CSCE, 1989: Dokument Koncowy Spotkania Wiedenskiego, in *Polska a realizacja uchwal KBWE* (Warsaw 1989).

FROLOW, I., 1982: Globale Probleme und Humanismus (Berlin/GDR).

HEINEMANN, G. ET AL., 1987: Es gibt kein Zurück. Gorbatschows Reformen – Chancen für Europa (Bonn).

MENCKE-GLÜCKERT, P., 1985: Weltökologische Probleme, in *K. Kaiser/H.-P. Schwarz (eds.)*, Weltpolitik. Strukturen – Akteure – Perspektiven (Bonn), pp. 209-219.

MICHAJLOW, W., 1976: Srodowisko i polityka (Wroclaw/Warsaw/Kraków/Gdansk).

ORZECHOWSKI, M, 1987: Polska a nowe koncepcje bezpieczenstwa miedzynarodowego, in *Sprawy Miedzynarodowe*, Vol. 7-8, p. 10.

OUR COMMON FUTURE, 1987: Our Common Future. Report of the World Commission on Environment and Development (Oxford).

PANCKE, H., 1982: Globale Probleme und Menschheitsfortschritt (Berlin/GDR).

PIERIELET, R., 1988: Ekologiczeskaja diplomatija, in *Miezdunarodnaja Zyzn*, Vol. 10, pp. 96 seq.

PIETRAS, M., 1989: Problemy ekologiczne jako zmienna spolecznosci miedzynarodowej, in *Spolecznosc miedzynarodowa wobec problemów globalnych* (Warsaw/Lublin).

PROBLEMA OKRUZAJUSZCZEJ SRIEDY W MIROWOJ EKONOMIKIE I MIEZDUNARODNYCH OTNOSZENIJACH, 1976 (Moscow).

TIMOSZENKO, A. C., 1986: Formirowanije i razwitije miezdunarodnogo prawa okruzajaszczej sriedy (Moscow).

U THANT, 1969: Czlowiek i jego srodowisko. Raport Sekretarza Generalnego ONZ U Thanta z 26 maja 1969, in *L. Ochocki*: Ochrona srodowiska. Problemy – refleksje – dokumenty (Warsaw), pp. 121 seq.

WAJDA, S., 1989: Zagadnienia ekologii jako plaszcyzna wspólpracy Wschód-Zachód w Europie. Przeglad Stosunków Miedzynarodowych, Vol. 1.

WASILJEW, W./PISARJEW, W./CHOZIN, G.: Ekologija i miezdunarodnyje otnoszenija.

Part III

Perspectives of an All-European Environmental Policy

Geographical Aspects of East-West Environmental Policy

Frank W. CARTER

> "Lets talk of graves, of worms, and epitaphs;
> Make dust our paper, and with rainy eyes
> Write sorrow on the bosom of the earth".
>
> *The Tragedy of King Richard the Second*
> Act III, Sc. II
> W. Shakespeare

Introduction

Awareness of the fragility of nature in Shakespeare's many metaphors still rings true in the contemporary scene. To "Yield stinging nettles to mine enemies" confronts us with a situation reminiscent of today's pollution problems which have to be grasped if we are to live in a better, healthier world. Nowhere is this more applicable than to our European continent now suffering from the ravages of intensive economic exploitation and environmental mismanagement.

This paper will examine the spatial implications of this process against the background of Europe's more than thirty countries in which the long-range transboundary transport of pollutants is obviously a problem of international concern. In recent decades efforts to foster environmental cooperation between industrialized capitalist and socialist nations have had to overcome not only the barrier of dealing with the complex East-West hostilities that until recently characterized the modern world, but also the problem of raising the level of ecological awareness within the European continent[1].

Geography and the Environment

The role of geography and geographers in problems relating to the environment is linked to a spatial appreciation of differences in pollution levels and their analysis. Suggestions are made in the hope of providing a means of accounting for the reciprocity of interactions between Man and the environment. This demands a methodology which provides for synthesis and at the same time allows for analysis, quantification and prediction, and hence a way of providing practical assistance in the formation of new problems and research topics and as far as possible proving capable of presenting new insights. Traditional regional monographs often neglected to take account of the contemporary development and practical achievements of ecologists, whilst studies from the mid-1960s sometimes utilized the rather loosely defined unit of natural community as a focus of geographical study. Perhaps the critical unresolved factor at this time was whether to consider Man and Society as the central pivot of the ecosystem, or whether to advocate the primary definition of a "physical" environment first and subsequently place Man within the ecosystem so defined.

Certainly, much of the anthropological research and cultural ecology which is couched in ecosystem terms first sees Man and Society as the focus of interest so that the environment of the ecosystem is defined in terms of the arena in which humans operate. Conversely, ecological studies have been largely based upon the recognition of natural and semi-natural ecosystems, which is primarily defined in terms of vegetational or habitat characteristics. Apparently the main contribution ecologists can make to geography is in providing a methodology which is consistent with a systems approach,

---

[1] D.R. Kelly, "East-West Environmental Cooperation", *Environment*, Vol. 22, No. 9, Washington D. C. 1980, p. 29.

as in human and urban ecology. Resource use and conservation, though associated with the ecosystem approach, have received increasing attention from geographers. Ecologists have primarily concerned themselves with natural communities in which Man plays a relatively subordinate role, but it is increasingly evident that Man's influence in the functioning of these ecosystems is of equal merit as a focus of study. In this case, studies of pollution need to be considered within geographical as well as ecological and sociological criteria. Clearly, within the European context a knowledge of supply and demand situations, of human behavioural traits and social values, together with an understanding of ecological processes, can provide a rational basis for future management proposals and resources utilization. It is evident therefore that a geographical approach to the environment would appear to elevate Man to a more dominant role than is the case of his ecological counterparts.

Geographers are also becoming increasingly interested in environmental aesthetics[2], a topic located within the sphere of environmental ethics. For example, here the environment includes all the observer's external world: the natural, cultural and the constructed environment. Buildings, gardens, sculptures, etc. are part of the environment and how Man perceives and experiences the world through attachment to place, home, district and milieu[3]. This leads to the all-important question of whether those living at present have the right to exploit the existing natural resources for themselves and also leave future generations with pollution that is difficult to eradicate[4].

Given this discursive background on the possible role of geography in studying environmental problems it is opportune to ask how this is applicable to an appraisal of East-West policy in Europe. This

---

[2] Y. Sepänmaa, *The Beauty of Environment: A General Model for Environmental Aesthetics*, (Suomalaisen Tudeakatemian Toiniituksia) Sarja - Ser. B Nide - Tome, 234, Helsinki, 1986, p. 17.

[3] Y.F. Tuan, *Topophilia. A Study of Environmental Perception, Attitudes and Values*, (Prentice Hall Inc.), Englewood Cliffs, 1974, p. 93.

[4] D.S. Mannison, M.A. McRobbie & R. Routley (eds.), *Environmental Philosophy*, (Monograph Series, No. 2) Dept. of Philosophy, Research School of Social Sciences, Australian National University, Canberra, 1980, 385 pp.

will be attempted within the framework of environmental degradation of air, water, soils and vegetation, noise and visual pollution.

Air Pollution

After two generations of abuse we are all aware that a deadly pall of sulphurous smoke hangs over Europe. Many may be familiar with the static picture often portrayed in maps of areas where major emissions occur, but this fails to illustrate that a lot of this sulphur is carried great geographical distances before finally settling sometimes in the most unspoilt areas of natural beauty. Therefore, given the large distances that acid-forming pollutants can travel through the atmosphere, it is clear that acid deposition is an international problem[5]. Acceptance of this problem was clearly admitted during the last decade; members of the "30 per cent Club" set themselves the target of cutting their sulphur emissions by that amount by 1993 in terms of 1980 levels. By 1987, total sulphur emissions in Europe had fallen by 18 per cent, but the spatial pattern was somewhat uneven. While some countries have already achieved reductions of over 30 per cent (e.g. Sweden, Austria, Switzerland) others such as Poland, Bulgaria and Turkey have recorded positive increases and are going to find it difficult to achieve their target[6]. Furthermore, poor response (only 10 of the 28 countries monitored by E.M.E.P. have confirmed emission levels) and questionable accuracy of data, particularly from Eastern bloc nations, brings the validity of the whole exercise into sharper focus.

The legacy of our polluted continent can partly be blamed on the divided policies adopted by the capitalist and socialist-communist states over the last four decades. The Eastern bloc countries never admitted to pollution problems during the first two decades of the post-World War II era. In spite of Stalinist and post-Stalinist heavy industrialization policies, pollution of any kind was, according

---

[5] A. Rosencranz, "The Problem of Transboundary Pollution", *Environment*, Vol. 22, No. 5, Washington D. C. 1980, p. 15.

[6] H. Alm, "Emissions are Falling: but is it Enough?", *Acid Magazine*, No. 8, Sept. 1989, Stockholm, p. 5.

to their propaganda, only to be found in the West where the capitalist profit motive was the cause of their environmental degradation problems. Yet in Western Europe, the control of air pollutant emissions from the combustion of fossil fuels at stationary sources (power plants, industrial centres, etc.), has long been an integral part of environmental control policies. The earliest emission control requirements of the 1960s were concerned with the removal of particular emissions (fly ash) from coal combustion. During the 1980s legislation on SO_2 and NO_x emissions from existing, as well as new stationary sources, was either adopted or under consideration in many Western countries. For example, some of the most stringent emission regulations in the world are found in West Germany[7].

Unfortunately, West Germany's proximity to the Eastern bloc countries and the problem of transboundary pollution, tended to nullify some of these stricter controls. Emphasis on heavy industrial production initiated by Stalin as a means of catching up with the West and supplying arms to the Soviet military machine, meant that the East European satellite countries tended to ignore the perils of air and other anti-pollutant laws (Czechoslovakia already had 350 by the early 1970s)[8], and in reality major significance was given to production norms and the fulfilling of plan targets. Factory managers even budgeted for state pollution fines in their enterprise accounts; thus fines became a mere transfer of money from one state coffer to another without any financial harm being felt by state employees.

The results of this policy are becoming increasingly clear to Western nations with the break-up of Communist Eastern European regimes in 1989. Only now is the rest of Europe able to comprehend the environmental degradation suffered by the Eastern satellites, yet so often denied by the Communist party hierarchies. The disappearance of the so-called "Iron Curtain" in a concentrated political move has exposed environmental devastation on a scale much greater than ever feared; areas with some of the heaviest known

---

[7] O.E.C.D., *Energy and Cleaner Air: Costs of Reducing Emissions*, Paris, 1987, p. 35.

[8] F.W. Carter, "Pollution Problems in Post-War Czechoslovakia", *Transactions: Institute of British Geographers*, (new Series) Vol. 10, No. 1, 1985, pp. 17-44.

global concentrations of pollution have been revealed in spite of attempts to hide such knowledge over the past forty years.

Much of the problem has been associated with the dearth of high quality fuels in Eastern Europe and the abundance of lignite, a soft brown low calorific coal found and used in abundance in most satellite countries. Cutbacks in Soviet oil and gas supplies have encouraged the use of lignite for domestic energy needs, particularly as a fuel for thermal electricity power stations and as a raw material for the chemical industry. In some states like East Germany, Czechoslovakia and Bulgaria, lignite is used because there are few alternative fuels, although it is costly to transport and less efficient than almost any other conventional hydrocarbon energy source. The resultant burn off produces considerable waste, largely in the form of pungent ash and deadly SO_2. Thus, for example, in East Germany, 6 million tonnes of SO_2 are emitted into the atmosphere annually, a figure three times that of West Germany, yet a country double its size[9]. Life expectancy in Leipzig is six years below the national average, whilst 80 per cent of its children under seven years develop either chronic bronchitis or heart problems, victims of the 400,000 tonnes of SO_2 falling annually on the city. Bitterfeld has obtained the dubious title of being the most polluted city in Europe[10]. Similarly, air pollution remains a very serious problem in Czechoslovakia (North Bohemia, Bratislava, Brno and North Moravia), parts of Poland such as Silesia, in Bulgaria (Sofia, Pernik) etc.

Compared with Czechoslovakia and East Germany, Poland does not emit as much SO_2 – 8.8 tonnes per km^2 as against 35 and 22.6 tonnes respectively[11]. However, the concentrated nature of industry and the transfer of pollution from other countries means that some areas do suffer chronic air pollution. An estimated 50 per cent of total SO_2 deposition in Poland is imported from neighbouring coun-

---

[9] A. Bridge, "The Environmental Nightmare in East Germany", *Independent*, (24.11.1989).

[10] A. McElvey, "Disease Rife in Bitterfeld the Most Polluted City in Europe", *Times* (20.1.1990).

[11] F.W. Carter, *Post-war Pollution Problems in Poland*, Paper presented at the Institute of British Geographers, British/Polish Seminar, London, 1986. 56 pp.

tries[12]. The worst affected area is the Upper Silesian Industrial District which accounts for a third of all generated SO_2 and two thirds of all solid waste[13]. Maximum deposition of air pollution occurs in Chorzow, where 4,075 tonnes per km are dumped on the land annually. In Cracow, concentrations of SO_2 in the atmosphere regularly exceed legal norms by 700-800 per cent. The city also contains the notorious Nowa Huta Steel Mill built in the 1950s reputedly to intimidate the city's intellectual life; the city experiences 135 days of smog annually, which in turn has had a damaging effect on the beautiful Renaissance architecture now suffering from constant attack by acid rain and airborne hydrocarbons[14]. Health problems are also numerous; in Katowice residents of this city have a 15 per cent higher incidence of circulatory diseases and a 47 per cent higher occurrence of respiratory ailments. Cracow suffers the country's highest infant mortality rate at 258/100,000 compared with the national average of 184/100,000[15].

Much of this environmental neglect is worsened by use of worn-out heavy industrial plants in urgent need of modernization, rationalization and investment. Car ownership, though lower than in Western Europe, is troubled by poor quality and high gaseous emissions. Varieties such as the Wartburg, Trabant, Skoda, etc. have poor exhaust facilities. In contrast, an increasing number of Western European cars have been subject to public sensitivity from an ecological viewpoint. Some cars get the ecological hard sell, especially new German models, which not only run on unleaded petrol, but are equipped with catalytic converters. Certainly, differentials in the price of unleaded and four-star petrol in Western Europe vary considerably (e.g. highest in Denmark, lowest in Portugal); similarly, there is encouragement in the use of diesel and the European

---

[12] J. Rostowski, "Environmental Deterioration in Poland", *Radio Free Europe Research*, Vol. 9, No. 37, München, (14.9.1984).

[13] E. Pudlis, "Once there was a Queen...", *Earthwatch*, No. 36, 1989, pp. 3-4.

[14] M.L. Hanley, "The Battle to Save Cracow", *World Development*, Vol. 3, No. 2, March 1990, pp. 8-10.

[15] D. Hinrichsen, "Poland's Chemical Cauldron", *Amicus Journal*, Spring 1988, pp. 3-7.

Community, as part of its harmonization proposals, is recommending a noticeable differential in favour of diesel by 1993[16]. Further, the European Community has proposed stricter limits on lorry emissions to curb pollution and improve trade links across the Alps. Austria's restrictions on trans-Alpine routes was initiated in the belief that 90 per cent of all carbon dioxide, (the main gas responsible for greenhouse global warming), and half of all hydrocarbons and nitrogen oxide emission, were produced by road traffic. The European Commission wants to persuade Spain, Portugal, Greece, Denmark, the UK and Ireland to switch to alternative transport modes (e.g. rail, waterways), where at present 90 per cent of all goods are carried by road. New European environment standards for lorries after 1992 and cars after 1996, may help limit air pollution, just as limits for dust and particles which should come into force at the end of 1994[17].

Water Pollution

As with air pollution, water mismanagement is another serious European problem. Only now is the full extent of East Europe's ecological disaster becoming more apparent and its damage is far more awesome than anything in Western Europe; rivers and other bodies of water do not respect international political boundaries. Rivers originating in Eastern Europe carry their affluence to the seas of Northern (Baltic, North Seas) and Southern (Mediterranean, Black Seas) Europe. Green parties in Western Europe have attracted our attention to the abuse of such rivers as the Danube, but electorally they have not had the support that is probably deserved. Nevertheless, parliamentary representation in eleven European countries (including West Germany, Sweden, Italy, Belgium, Luxembourg and Austria) augers well for future development.

Acidification of groundwater used for drinking purposes has been noted in several European countries. Occurrence has been greatest

---

[16] Anon, "Major misses a chance with 'eco-friendly' diesel", *Times* (23.3.1990).

[17] L. Walker, "Lorry emission cuts to aid Alpine trade", *The European*, (4-6.5.1990).

at local levels where soil and rocks lack sufficient quantities of carbonate to reduce the impact; whilst acidification in industrial areas is largely due to atmospheric deposition, agricultural regions suffer from increased application of ammonia fertilizers[18].

Acidification by atmospheric acid deposition has been found throughout Europe. Scandinavia has been particularly hard pressed by this problem; in southern Norway considerable acidification has taken place (pH 4.3-4.5) of surface waters, which accounts for most of the region's public water supplies. Similar processes are at work in Sweden, where attempts at liming are seen mainly as a "holding" operation. In Finland, acid deposition is lower than the previously mentioned countries, but snow, an important element of groundwater recharge, has contained pH values of 4.5-5.0 over the last ten years. Further south in West Germany, examples of acidification in areas of shallow groundwater (e.g. Taunus region) have been located in non-agricultural areas, whilst the Harz Mountains have provided evidence of high levels of many heavy metals (e.g. cadmium)[19].

Some of these harmful chemicals have travelled from points of origin in Eastern Europe. The intense industrialization programme in East Germany has had its inevitable spin-off on river pollution. From Bitterfeld various industrial wastes are dumped untreated directly into the Mulde River, and recent studies have found dioxin and other poisonous chemicals present there. The nearby Elbe River, en route from Czechoslovakia, has mercury levels 250 times higher than European Community limits, with fish washed up dead on its banks[20]. In Poland, water pollution is a serious ecological problem, resulting from industrial waste, agricultural chemical fertilizers and most importantly untreated sewage. Half of Poland's urban centres have no sewage works, with raw effluent ejected straight into the river network. Only about 40 per cent of the mechanical sewer

---

[18] J. Farsland, "Acidification of Rain and Groundwater in Relation to Land Use (in Denmark)", *International Conference on Acid Precipitation - Water Control and Human Health*, Uppsala, Sweden, 1985, pp. 1-9.

[19] U. von Brömssen, "Acidification of Drinking Water around Europe", *Acid Magazine*, No. 6, March 1988, Stockholm, p. 35.

[20] A. Bridge, *op cit*, p. 10.

processing plants are efficient, whilst biochemical plants are rare. Fifty per cent of the country's rivers are classified as unfit for industrial or agricultural use (IV) with less than a fifth considered suitable for human consumption (I and II)[21]. In 1982, Poland's longest river, the Vistula, contained no water fit for human consumption and 56 per cent was in the Class IV category[22]. Every river in the Katowice province is completely polluted, whilst at Cracow, the Vistula River has a higher sodium chloride (salt) concentration than in the Baltic Sea[23]. The transport of such waste eventually reaches the seas of our continent. The northward flow of Poland's rivers puts severe pollution pressure on the Baltic Sea. Even pollution originating near the Czechoslovakian border flows into this sea. The International Council for Monitoring the Cleanliness of the Sea recently stated that the Baltic is probably the most contaminated body of water in the world. It is nearly an inland lake and natural conditions such as low average depth, minimal exchange of water with the North Sea, and low vertical mixing, make it particularly sensitive to pollution. All waterborne sewage, industrial effluents and agricultural chemical waste ends up in this sea, of which the Vistula River alone contributes 34 km^3 of liquid effluent annually[24]. Agricultural run-off from Poland's heavily fertilized farmlands amounts to 91,400 tonnes of nitrogen per annum, constituting over two thirds of the total nitrogen entering the Baltic. It is the dumping ground for industrial waste not only from Poland, but also from East Germany and Lithuania, as well as the Scandinavian countries. Fishing catches are declining dramatically and even summer bathing on its beaches is jeopardized[25]. The entire ecosystem of the Bay of Gdansk is under

---

[21] J. Rostowski, *op cit*

[22] K. Rawluk, *The State of the Environment in Poland*, (Uniwersytet Jagiellonski), Kraków, 1982, p. 32.

[23] A. Perlowski, "Budgets to Fight Pollution in Poland, 1980-1985", *Environmental Policy Review*, Vol. 1, No. 1, Jan. 1987, Jerusalem, pp. 38-43.

[24] E. Pudlis, *op cit*, pp. 3-4.

[25] C. Booth, J. Borrell & R. Schoenthal, "Darkness at Noon", *Time International*, No. 15 (9.4.1990), p. 26.

threat because pollution is killing the phytoplankton and rockweed which form the base of the food chain; on many parts of Poland's Baltic coast swimming is no longer allowed because of contamination.

The adjacent North Sea also presents a disturbing picture. The steady poisoning of the North Sea and one of its main rivers, the Rhine (the "Sewer of Europe"), has been recently highlighted at the Third North Sea Conference at the Hague (March 1990). Agreements were concluded to phase out completely the high toxic chemicals polychlorinated biphenyls (PCB's) by 1999, together with 18 pesticides by 1992, and to bring about a 70 per cent reduction in mercury, cadmium, dioxins and lead. It is also considered that the seabed of the North Sea was unsuitable for nuclear waste disposal[26].

Whilst the North Sea is surrounded by wealthy nations, at present all charged with a high-level of environmental commitment, the Mediterranean basin is in a more advanced state of deterioration. The state of the North Sea's deterioration is marked, but not beyond repair; conversely, the Mediterranean is seriously degraded both by coastal erosion and by extensive air and water pollution. The countries bordering its coasts are predominantly poor and striving for greater economic well-being, and its future may lie as much in the responsibility of the wealthy as the impoverished. The existence of the Mediterranean Blue Plan, promoted by the United Nations Environment Programme and a number of regional economic commissions, has created a community of interest and the establishment of a data base.

Geographical analysis has revealed that 85 per cent of the pollution flowing into the Mediterranean comes from land-based sources, the bulk carried by rivers. An estimated 90 tons of DDT and other pesticides flow into the sea annually as well as quantities of lubricating oil, heavy metals (e.g. mercury, cadmium) industrial waste and untreated sewage. Furthermore, pollution poses a serious health hazard to about 100 million tourists who visit the basin each year[27].

[26] M. McCarthy, "Patten serves criticism and pledges wholesome North Sea", *Times*, (10.3.1990), London.

[27] I. Guest, "Mediterranean States Agree on Treaty to Control Land-Based Pollution", *Ambio*, Vol. 9, Nos. 3-4, Stockholm, 1980, p. 194.

One arm of the Mediterranean basin, the Adriatic Sea, has become intricately linked to this conflict situation. Tourism, a significant economic factor for both Italy and Yugoslavia, must not be discouraged as a result of environmental degradation. As Italian experts claim that algae are already proliferating all around the northern Adriatic, one is reminded that in 1989 the fear that algae were some type of noxious substance kept thousands of tourists away from the northern and central Adriatic. Guidelines for action include an Italian governmental stimulus for scientific research on the problem and a master-plan for the Adriatic which will take account of the current sea situation[28].

Furthermore, in Venice, the issue of the Adriatic Sea has received serious consideration and the Veneto Regional Government has applied to Rome for special funds to protect the tourist industry, a factor critical in the area's economic life[29]. In Yugoslavia, the Dalmation coast is also under pollution threat for its tourists, but here there is less governmental money forthcoming due to the country's serious economic situation. A recent study on the conflict situation between tourism, conservation and the environment on Hvar Island has revealed the need for stricter controls on such factors as water pollution[30].

Meanwhile, pollution and over-exploitation by the fishing industry have reduced fish yields in the Mediterranean, according to a report from the European Investment Bank and the World Bank[31]. It states that stocks in some areas are now down a fifth of their normal levels, and the environmental deterioration in the Mediterranean

---

[28] S. Faccin, "Quell' Adriatico tutto da scoprire", *Marco Polo*, No. 75, April, 1990, Venice, p. 19.

[29] R. Carrain, "Il Turismo a Venezia: Problemi e prospettive", *La Rivista Veneta*, No. 34, (Venezia verso il XXI secolo), Marsilio Editori, November, 1988, pp. 97-100.

[30] F.W. Carter, "Development and the Environment: A Case Study of Hvar Island, Yugoslavia", Paper presented at the Meeting on Development and Environment in the Mediterranean, 3-4 November 1989, Valletta, Malta (EADI) Mediterranean Cooperation Working Group, 25 pp.

[31] Anon, "Fish yields suffer big drop in the Med", *The European*, (4-6.5.1990), London.

basin is worsening by the day so that in certain areas, degradation could become irreversible.

Finally, the Black Sea is also on the verge of a catastrophe. Reports from Bulgaria's Institute of Ecology suggest that the situation is so bad that all life could disappear from the Black Sea and the chemicals poisoning it could begin polluting the atmosphere. The Black Sea is particularly vulnerable to pollution as it collects ten times more water per square metre of surface area than other oceans or seas. Much of the pollution comes in from major European rivers of which the Danube is the worst culprit, having flowed through eight highly industrialized nations which also have intensive chemical agriculture. Furthermore, the problem has been compounded by the construction of dams and irrigation projects which has reduced the influx of fresh water by 50 km^3 annually, reducing the thickness of the oxygenized surface layer to only 80-100 metres. Further prevention of such acts is urgently needed and a Bulgarian-Soviet proposal to launch a research and monitoring programme involving international organizations (e.g. United Nations Development Programme) is now under consideration[32].

Soil and Vegetation Pollution

Environmental disruption in Europe created by air and water pollution has affected parts of the continent's soil and vegetation cover. A direct consequence of air and waterborne pollution is the contamination of the land and forests through the deposition of sulphuric compounds. This causes severe soil acidification, making the soil less fertile and reducing productivity. More serious is the deposition of heavy metals which enter the food chain.

Moreover, farming, although suffering from air pollution, is at the same time one of the main water polluters through the use of pesticides and fertilizers in attempts to increase productivity. For example, so much manure has been used as fertilizer by Dutch farmers, that environmentalists claim that the country floats on it. Another problem relates to the disposal of industrial waste; whether this is

---

[32] M.L. Hanley, "Can the Black Sea be Saved?", *Acid Magazine*, No. 1, 1987, p. 16.

disposed of through incineration, burial, land fill or other methods, some of the residue gets leaked into the water table and hence into drinking water supplies.

Acidification from fertilization of farmlands and forests continues to be a pollution threat. Nutrient-poor soils with naturally low resistance to acid deposition can only tolerate annual sulphur deposition of no more than 2-7 kg./ha. In Sweden, for example, the south-West region has amounts totalling 20-30 kg./ha., whilst in parts of central Europe this reaches 30-50 kg./ha.[33]. In Denmark, a recent report suggested that less than 5 per cent of total acid deposition was attributable to acid rain and the rest was blamed on agricultural practice. It was found that in parts of the country only 30 per cent of the required lime dosage of 1,300 kg./ha. was being applied[34]. Similarly in the Netherlands less than a fifth of the acid load is due to atmospheric deposition, farming methods being responsible for the remainder, resulting in severe acidification of water in the country[35]. Approximately half of Czechoslovakia's water pollution is caused by agricultural activity. In a country where there is less than half a hectare of agricultural land per person, protection of this resource should be of paramount concern. Unfortunately, this is not the case. Excessive use of pesticides and fertilizers is one of the main causes of surface and groundwater pollution. Improper disposal of liquid animal manure also contaminates streams and ground water aquifers as does accidental spillage[36]. In Poland, many industrial workers grow their own fruit and vegetables on allotments near their homes; in Katowice province they have revealed a lead content of 8.510 mg per kg.[37]. The accepted safe maximum is 20 mg and the lead content in fruit and vegetables in the area is ten times higher than the

---

[33] C. Agren, "Drastic Emission Cuts Essential", *Acid Magazine*, No. 8, September 1989, Stockholm, pp. 30-32.

[34] J. Farsland *op cit*, p. 5.

[35] U. von Brömssen, *op cit*, p. 35.

[36] F.W. Carter, "Czechoslovakia's Ecological Crisis", *Earthwatch*, No. 36, 1989, pp. 8-9.

[37] J. Marcinkiewicz, "SOS Poland", *Environment Now*, October/November, 1987, pp. 48-50.

permitted norm. Other metals present in food in large quantities are cadmium, copper and zinc and unofficial estimates by the Polish Ecological Club suggest that two thirds of food produced in the Cracow region is unfit for human consumption[38].

Clearly there is a need for reduction in all these levels as quickly as possible. Attempts should be made to drastically cut emission levels (e.g. 80% of 1980 levels by 1993) and create a code of practice for the use of pesticides and fertilizers with the employment of inspectors to see that rules are obeyed. Such a code could include user training and equipment, protection of wildlife, plants and public footpaths, prevention of spray drift, the correct disposal of chemical wastes and the keeping of accurate records of pesticide and fertilizer use[39]. A recent development has been made by the United Nations Development Programme; at present they are helping the Hungarian government to tackle a number of environmental problems that plague not only that country but other parts of Eastern Europe. Projects are underway for developing non-toxic pesticides, monitoring and improving air, water, soil, etc. quality. One of the most significant projects is enabling Hungary's scientific community to deal with toxic industrial wastes, many of which defy traditional disposal strategies. Detoxifying methods through adding peat to fly ash have been particularly successful[40].

One of the most visible signs of pollution is the destruction of forests. Vegetation, especially forests, suffer from increasing contamination by industrial waste emission and other pollutants. There is general increasing concern by forestry economists on the severe damage done to valuable softwood (firs) forests by industry, particularly thermal power stations, but also metal refining. The latter is usually only a localized phenomenon and of limited interest for long-range pollution studies, but can illustrate damage done through transboundary pollution. For example, damage to forests in northern Norway has been attributed to emissions from the Soviet mining

---

[38] *Guardian*, (19.1.1990).

[39] M. Hornsby, "Code for farmers using pesticides", *Times*, (9.5.1990), London.

[40] S. Kane, "Finding a Use for Industrial Waste", *World Development*, Vol. 3, No. 2, March 1990, p. 11.

town of Nikel on the Kola peninsula; here SO_2 and other metal emissions from nickel production have affected Eastern Finnmark with SO_2 deposition of about one tonne/km^2 annually[41]. Much farther to the south of our continent there has been widespread forest destruction in the so-called "acid rain belt" of Central and Eastern Europe.

The situation of the forests in Eastern Europe is particularly serious[42]. Poland's forested area covers 28 per cent of the country's total surface area (i.e. 0.23 ha./per capita). Nearly half of the country's trees are less than forty years old, but only 14 per cent are over eighty years – suggesting a low level of climax vegetation[43]. An estimated two thirds of those stands are at risk from pollution[44], with damage most evident around Katowice where 150,000 ha. of conifers have been devastated. Sulphur dioxide and heavy metal pollution renders conifers more susceptible to attacks from insects such as the Bud Larch Moth and to fungal diseases. Nevertheless, over the last few years the wooded area in the country has slightly increased from 8,622 (1980) to 8,672 (1988) million hectares[45]. Together with this, there was an increase in the forest area located in regions of industrial pollution – from 14 per cent of all forests in 1985 to 17.4 per cent in 1988[46].

In Czechoslovakia, a third of the forests are dying and a further fifth are said to have suffered some degree of damage. The first instances of trees damaged by air pollution were observed in North Bohemia in 1947, and at the beginning of the 1960s the first large-

---

[41] T. Samstag, "Big Polluters on the Kola Peninsula", *Acid Magazine*, No. 8, September, 1989, Stockholm, pp. 30-32.

[42] D. Turnock, *The Human Geography of Eastern Europe*, (Routledge), London & New York, 1989, p. 286.

[43] K.R. Mazurski "Industrial Pollution: The Threat to Polish Forests", *Ambio*, Vol. 19, No. 2, April 1990, p. 70.

[44] J. Marcinkiewicz, *op cit*, p. 49.

[45] *Rocznik Statystyczny 1989*, (Clówny urzad Statystyczny), Warszawa, 1989, p. 12.

[46] *Ibid*, p. 30

scale destruction of forests was reported in that country[47]. At present foresters are trying to replace the less resistant coniferous varieties with more "smoke resistant" stands (e.g. Pinus uncinatus rotundatis), but this may only postpone and not halt their destruction by acid rain[48]. The fear remains that many of the mountains forming the international boundaries between Czechoslovakia and East and West Germany and Poland could be completely bare by the end of this century.

Other Pollutants

At this juncture it is perhaps significant to mention two other forms of pollution that have increased with growth of the European economy since the Second World War, namely noise and visual disharmony. More generally, the European governments have encouraged schemes to combat noise disruption. State enterprises and heavy industrial concerns are being reconstructed to reduce excessive noise and vibration, while special studies on the effects of motor traffic on the environment are being made. Unfortunately, there is a growth of "noise terrorism" across the continent portrayed by modern rock groups bent on providing music that breaks the sound barrier. Producing a heavy-going industrial noise combined with a dance-floor stomp, such groups create conditions which could contribute to long-term problems[49]. High noise levels can cause many illnesses, including deafness.

Visual pollution is also a growing menace. Environments are extremely varied and may include nature in a natural state, the cultural environment or in extreme cases the completely artificial manmade environment. It is the latter, particularly as a result of the post-

---

[47] F. Pohl, "Environmental Deterioration in Czechoslovakia", *Soviet and East European Survey, 1983-1984*, V. Mastny (ed.), Duke University Press, Durham, 1985, p. 309.

[48] F.W. Carter, "Pollution Problems in Post-War Czechoslovakia", *op cit*, p. 31.

[49] M. Bray, "Menace of the noise terrorists", *The European*, (4-6.5.1990), London, p. 23.

World War II rural-to-urban migration process that has added to the problem. The building of large often ugly architectural edifices for residential, office and other purposes has polluted the visual presentation of many European urban centres. This is especially evident in the Eastern Bloc where socialist city planning has created monolithic concrete jungles leading to drab housing estates and uninteresting city centres[50], replacing old street patterns and housing from a pre-socialist era. Fortunately, some efforts are now being made to conserve what is left of the past[51] for without it we would lack any sense of historical identity and the present would make no sense[52].

Conclusions

In spite of all the difficulties, it is clear that East-West environmental cooperation in Europe has produced some positive results, especially in terms of better coordinated research and monitoring efforts, and some programmes for dealing with limited regional and water basin problems. The WICEM conference, which this author attended in the mid-1980s[53] clearly signalled the role of politics in environmental protection and attempted to show the caring face of industry towards the protection of nature. This helped to replace an earlier concept that sheer quantity was considered the best indication of a state's economic development, an idea taken to extremes

---

[50] F.W. Carter, "Prague and Sofia: An Analysis of Their Changing Internal City Structure", Ch. 15, in *The Socialist City*, R.A. French & F.E.I. Hamilton (eds.), (Wiley), London, 1979 pp. 425-460.

[51] F.W. Carter, "Historic Cities in Eastern Europe: Problems of Industrialisation, Pollution and Conservation", *Mazingira*, Vol. 6, No. 3, Oxford, 1982, pp. 62-76; R.A. French, "Conserving the Past in Soviet Cities", *Occasional Paper*, No. 235, (Kennan Institute for Advanced Russian Studies), The Wilson Center, Washington, D.C. 1990, 22 pp.

[52] D. Lowenthal, "The Past is a Foreign Country", (Cambridge University Press), Cambridge, 1985, 489 pp.

[53] L.H. Sallada & B.G. Doyle (eds.), "The Spirit of Versailles: The Business of Environmental Management", (World Industry Conference on Environmental Management), I.C.C. Publishing, Paris, 1986, 367 pp.

in Eastern Europe with the belief in "tonnage ideology"[54]. In the latter half of the decade catastrophes at Chernobyl and Bhopal together with the 'Spring of Nations' in Eastern Europe has created a more united continental approach towards policy making for environmental protection. Unfortunately, progress is slow.

Attempts at reducing atmospheric and other forms of pollution depend not only on technical and economic issues, but also on changes in attitudes and concepts. Industrialized countries have to recognize the need to make their socio-economic activities and life styles environmentally sound[55]. Unfortunately, Europe in a spatial sense is far from united in this approach. Eastern Europe consists of countries with unregulated industries and cheap sources of labour which can undercut more environmentally conscious West European competitors. This suggests a geographical need for regional standards of pollution control, which involves not just information data base compilation, or setting codes of conduct, but a disciplined European pollution inspectorate capable of enforcing the plethora of laws on the statute books. Time is of the essence, yet there will have to be some phasing introduced to allow for the seriously polluted environments of Eastern Europe to respond to these changing demands.

The results of new measurements made in the Swiss Alps provide stunning evidence that thinning of the ozone layer is increasing levels of harmful ultraviolet-B radiation in Europe[56]. Certainly decades of communism have wrought ecological havoc in East European states, and they are now desperate for West European expertise to clean up the mess. As a member of the "30 per cent Club", Czechoslovakia must also reduce its emissions of SO_2 to two thirds of its 1980 level by 1993 – a reduction of over 900,000 tons. By 2000

---

[54] M. Jänicke, H. Mönch, T. Ranneberg & U.E. Simonis, "Econmic Structure and Environmental Impact: A Survey of Thirty-One Countries", I.I.U.G. dp. 87-1 (WZB), Berlin, 1987, p. 1.

[55] P. Vellinga, "The Noordwijk Declaration on Climatic Change", (Ministerial Conference on Atmospheric Pollution & Climatic Change), Noordwijk, (6-7.11.1989), p. 5.

[56] D. Concar, "Fears for Europe's ozone", *Times*, (Science Report), (23.4.1990), London.

AD, Czechoslovakian officials proclaim that 1.3 million hectares of pollution-affected land will be under protection with technological measures in place to protect a further 732,000 ha.[57]. In the USSR, the decentralization and reform of the Soviet economy will be crucial for the recovery of the environment. Whole branches of industry, including those having influence on the environment (wood, chemical, metallurgical, etc.)[58] will have to adhere to the ecological aspects of reform if the long-term state of the Soviet environment is to improve[59]. Gorbachev himself has laid special emphasis on the importance of the environment.

Even the World Commission on Environment and Development has a very geographical motto – "Think globally – act locally". Today, anything is possible, and the options placed before the European continent are wider than ever as the demarcation line between the two blocs fades away. One concrete option is the provision of a Green Marshall Plan through a European aid package to all seven of East Europe's emerging democracies[60]. Such help would transcend political and national boundaries and hopefully make Europe a cleaner and healthier place to live.

---

[57] F.W. Carter, "Czechoslovakia's Ecological Crisis", *Earthwatch*, No. 36, London 1989, pp. 8-9.

[58] A first attempt was the Law of State Enterprises, adopted in June 1987, see *Pravda*, (20.6.1987), Moscow.

[59] Z. Wolfson, "Perestroika and Glasnost in Environmental Policy", *Environmental Policy Review*, Vol. 2, No. 1, Jan. 1988, Jerusalem, p. 17: See also G. Enyedi, A. J. Gijswit & B. Rhodes, *Environmental Policies in East and West*, (Taylor Graham), London 1988; J. de Bardeleben, *Environmental Problems in Europe*, (OUP), New York, 1990: D. Pearce, "Hot billions riding on warm air", *Times*, (18. 5. 1990), London.

[60] Anon, "Green Marshall Plan for the East", *Conservation Now*, Vol. 1, No. 1, March/April, 1990, p. 25.

The Principle of Spatial Responsibility: Understanding the Background of Cooperative Environmental Policies in Europe

Barbara RHODE

Introduction

With the opening of the East and the beginning of the process of political and economic integration, it became obvious that Eastern Europe would bring not only the burden of a highly damaged economy but also a physical environment which is highly polluted and which demands quick therapies. Eastern and Western Europe share the same continent, we are parts of the same physical systems, and we share as well the responsibility to care for our common surroundings and our common future. How can this recently gained perspective be transformed into international cooperative policies?

The consciousness of a commonly shared Europe did not develop until recently in peoples' minds because the iron curtain restricted any common actions, common policies and the necessary flow of information on essential facts and details which serves as the condition for action. After the first fascination and joy about the liberation of the Central and East European countries, very quick everyday policies have come back to the politicians and the people of the Western countries, not caring too much about the fate of our Eastern neighbours. The attitude of carelessness and indifference is predominant when help is requested.

The newly established governments in the East are overburdened with problems which have to be solved and it is evident that financial, technological and organizational help is needed. The Western European population sometimes seems to be reluctant to share problems as the difficult relation between the Eastern and Western population in the unified Germany shows.

The national environmental problems cannot be solved by the governments in Eastern Europe on their own. Why cooperation is needed, and why the responsibility for pollution sometimes lies more westerly than the Western countries regard the problem shall be explained in this contribution.

1. Revising Old European Environmental Policies

Even though knowledge of the conditions in the East was poor the environment as a topic of negotiation existed even during the time of the Cold War. But strangely enough, it seemed as if the environment had been developed as a topic of negotiation within the framework of the UN Economic Commission for Europe (ECE) not for its own sake, but rather it was more or less used as a platform for maintaining diplomatic contacts and staying in a common organization.

The topic of the environment was even picked up at a very early stage (in relation to the development of the theme) as a political issue between Eastern and Western Europe, i.e. when national governments were not yet equipped with environmental ministries and international organizations had not yet discovered the real importance of the issue.

The original goal of the ECE was dedicated to economic development. But this did not show as much progress as OECD or EC policies did. The ECE suffered very much from the political restrictions of cooperation between the two different political systems. Negotiations and collaboration on the environment became important for the ECE because all other direct economic cooperation had become more and more restricted and complicated during the Cold War period. Thus, the environment acted as a substitute for othere themes. At the time the environment emerged within ECE policies, it did not seem to be such a delicate and controversial political issue as it became in the second half of the eighties.

The instruments of cooperation being developed during the Cold War period had to be very vague and non-specific, the monitoring systems were poor and the correctness of the data could not really be queried. But under the conditions of the Cold War, the Convention on "Long-range Transboundary Air Pollution" in particular, was a clear success in exploiting the given unfavourable possibilities.

Moreover, this type of convention could well be taken as a successful model for finding a mutual starting point within an unclear situation: governments are not yet ready, or are not able for other reasons, but would like to start a public process, give moral support and involve themselves in the process according to their limited technical and financial options.

As the borders have now opened, other types of cooperation models must be developed. Stricter rules, better monitoring systems, better mutual information, exchange of the best solution technology and overall a concept of cooperative responsibility based on the geographical and financial conditions of the different regions is required.

The argument in this paper is a plea to politicians to better understand the historical background, the genesis of the European geography when applying more instruments on the international level, and to illustrate to politicians the reason why the environment is in the miserable condition it is in today. A greater variety of instruments must be established on the international level. Conditional for these new instruments is an understanding of the mechanisms which have until now operated on the surface, with the movements of the air, with the cycles of the waters and with the habits of the peoples.

This concerns on the one hand the instrumental side: the economic, legal and political incentives to change and regulate behaviour. On the other hand the environmental media: air, water, soil, etc. must be better related to reflections on future instruments. They operate in quite different types of interacting physical systems, the functioning of which has to be further investigated, including the interlinkages with other systems of natural or human-made origin.

Amongst the most important tasks of environmental research for the newly politically-shaped European landscape is a better understanding of the kind of impacts the distribution of the nation states have on the territory of the European peninsula, how countries influence each other and how the ecosystems interact with the policies of the national states. These interactions must be recognized and the national, regional and local positions must be reflected by these systems. Some countries are situated in places which give them more responsibility than others. This distribution must be understood for the new European idea of shared responsibilities and for a common future to work on the continent. Until now, the political separation has not allowed an honest look at these interlinkages.

When designing new models for cooperative policies in Europe, pitfalls and backsliding should be avoided as far as possible. Narrow-minded local solutions or solutions for single countries which help them to avoid certain problems but transfer the burden to another country are shortsighted and will only shift the problem instead of diminishing or solving it.

The very bad economic situation of the former socialist countries will attract many proposals for help and solutions which are inappropriate: e.g. the transfer of old but cheaper production technology which does not give the safest solution for the environment, the preferred investment into quickly established infrastructure which will repeat the mistakes made before in Western countries, the quick investment into new development projects before an overall plan and distribution system is developed, the sell-out of existing natural resources to commercial development projects, and many more possibilities.

Public planning is not an attractive issue for Eastern European countries at the moment as they have just abandoned the centrally planned economy and its heavy deficits. But the planning of a global framework must be the precondition for negotiations between private investors and the public authorities. Neglecting the necessities of these frameworks and stepping back into laissez-faire policies will definitely not produce optimal results concerning the environmental future. Public policies are caught in this phase of development between the necessity of giving quick leeway for serious investors and agreeing on necessary procedures of restrictions, monitoring and public control.

Before more closely investigating the issues of the European environmental systems, a short history of environmental consciousness and progress will be helpful to better show how environmental problems were able to occur and why they did not enter our minds earlier. But unfortunately there is no definite answer available as to whether it will be possible, even with those human mistakes in mind, to avoid some wrong developments in the future.

2. How Environmental Problems in Europe Developed

During the 18th and 19th centuries the Industrial Revolution changed the human environment dramatically. But the first reactions to these changes were of a social nature. The environment as a problem did not yet enter the people's consciousness, since the prosperity of industrialization and the thin layer of social improvement competing with the dangers of desperate poverty did not allow them to become aware of the environmental side of this rapid development. In the very long initial period the severe dangers of a polluted and destroyed environment were seen and often described, but mainly in fine arts and literature.

The contemporary answers to the newly acquired problems only pointed in the direction of technical, social and economic progress. Both the early capitalist as well as the socialist approaches agreed on the full support of further industrialization. It was the only driving and promoting factor for a better future. General developments showed that the 19th century was bringing about the worst environmental situation for living conditions in cities and in heavy industrial areas. But at the same time the technological progress made it possible for the city to be recognized as a system which could be redesigned in a more rational way and where new systems could be added to the old structures. Canals, water-pipes, gas and electricity, transportation systems, public waste collection and planned living quarters together with the new concept of garden cities showed that environmental problems could be faced and overcome with the achievements of industrialization.

Thus, for half a century the competition between ecology and economy was won by economic success. Both systems, the capitalist and the socialist, in struggling for ideological leadership, fully neglected the question of the environment and of the natural basis of humankind. Only the fascist ideology was able to touch upon the subconscious anxieties of rapid modernization and exploited the fear of losing roots in the changing human conditions of life.

With the new advances of a technical and social nature, it seemed that the environmental problems which derived from industrialization were governable, and all efforts to struggle for a better future were concentrated on economic progress. Economic prosperity quickly made the protection of nature an old-fashioned ideology. After a first phase of environmental awareness in the 20th century, progress until the late sixties was clearly defined in economic terms.

In the early post-war period the conception of "progress" was still quite similar both in the market economy world and in the socialist part of Europe. Doubts about the pure economic understanding of progress developed slowly in scientific circles during the fifties and sixties. The year 1972 signifies a change of paradigm in thought. It seemed to be the breakthrough in an understanding of environmental problems in Europe: it was the year of the Stockholm Conference on the Human Environment, of the publication of "The Limits to Growth" and of the first EEC directive on the environment. But still broad public support was not yet given to this scientific and political breakthrough.

Two years later, after the oil shock in 1973 in the Western industrialized world, the market economy went into recession, and most of the Western European governments invested intensively in nuclear energy in order to soften the economic consequences, totally forgetting about their endeavour in Stockholm. Caught in the choice between investment programmes in favour of economic improvements and ecological sustainability Western governments chose the improvement of the economy. Will the governments of the reform countries today make a better choice?

Instead of calming down public fears after the oil shock the huge investment programmes into nuclear power plants and giant technology frightened first a minor part of the population, thus slowly preparing the Green movement in Western Europe. Since then Western governments have had to learn that the decisions taken in Stockholm, and which soon afterwards were completely neglected, were now being taken up by a broadening part of the population.

But apart from the anti-nuclear movements of the seventies, it took another ten years, until the beginning of the eighties, before the general population became worried about other green issues. The pressure of the media quickly grew so strong that governments started to react. The pressure of the people, local initiatives, non-governmental organizations and the free media were important promoters of the environmental issue in the West.

The socialist countries, however, did not allow any democratic movement from the people. They never left behind the ideology of progress based on the deep belief in the type of first generation of heavy industries, the worker and the farmer as the protagonist of their politics. Pollution and the exploitation of resources were simply considered the normal side-effects of productiveness. What was economically successful had to cause environmental problems. Thus, the environmental problems were not regarded at all in a negative light. It was still commonly thought that air pollution even served as a silent indicator of industrialization and urbanization – and not only in the negative sense. It was even appreciated for a long time as something positive: smoke billowing from chimneys was still considered a symbol of productivity. It symbolised progress and wealth. Thus, many socialist countries chose to depict smoking chimneys and other environmental sins on their banknotes to show how their money was backed. Posters and paintings of smoking chimneys or mono-cultural agriculture were used for national propaganda to reassure the people's pride.

Barbara Rhode

Industrial Motives on Banknotes
50 Mark DDR and 50 Crowns CSSR

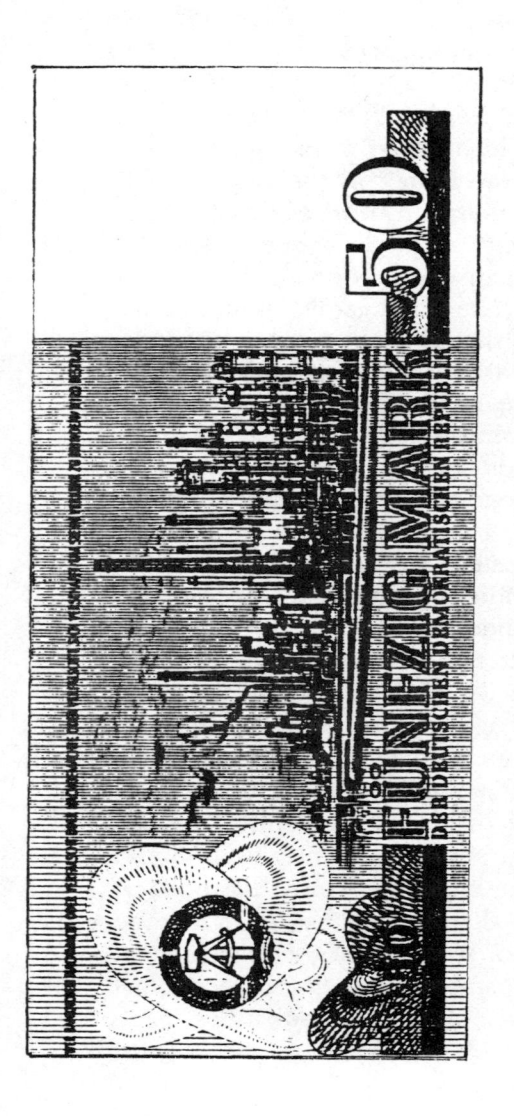

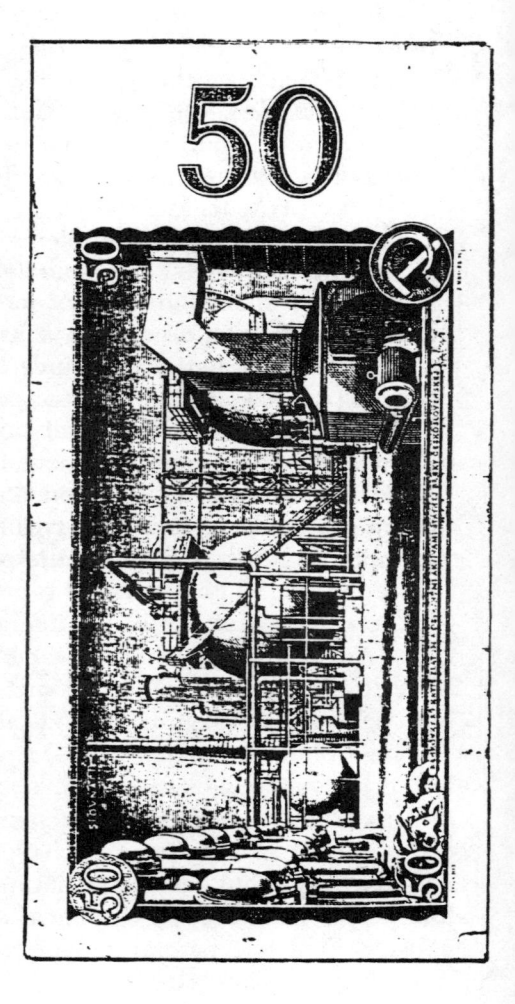

The green movement in the West, linking environmental problems to the capitalist system and the power of industries, could never understand why the socialist bureaucracies did not better handle the environmental issues. It was the task of the bureaucracies of central planning to fix values according to the needs of the people and the capacity of the countries. These bureaucracies, having absolute power in the state and run by the principles of the parties, related their power to the old type of industries. Obviously they were not able to transform the function of the industries into new patterns. The picture of modernity never moved. The images produced by the system reflected until the very end the visions of the 19th century.

3. European Variety

But it was not only the economic system which produced differences in the environmental conditions. The differences the past political system generated were only the very last to come and these differences will most probably vanish more or less within the next decade, as long as no new instability brings a new separation of environmental conditions.

In order to develop appropriate tools of application and cooperation the political system must understand that the shape of the European continent developed through a long history of formation, before mankind interfered in the process. Physical factors are operating on the surface and they interact with the natural and cultural basis. A convention giving the same options and the same responsibility to all countries is not optimal and closes its eyes to the existing distribution system of ecological interactions.

The political pattern today, only by accident, follows natural borderlines or relates to the physical shape. Human utilization and human history – in the sense of social history as well as the political development of neighbours – have changed the nature of Europe continuously. Thus, an explanation of the state of the environment today and the necessary political instruments to improve it must consider both the natural geography and the transformations made to it by the people. The Industrial Revolution as well as the political framework of nationally bound policies created quite differing structures, and will still create differing physical structures unless Europe forms a central decision-making agency, above the national governments. Whether a country will decide for nuclear or for renewable energy, whether it will support car traffic or rail, centralization or decentralization in living conditions, in industries, etc. will show typical structures in the physical environment after a while.

But before turning to the individual nations and their cooperative options for policies today it seems necessary to convey a feeling for the whole of Europe as a manifold and complex continent.

In the long history of formation between nature and culture the shape of the continent of Europe can be linked to very few major events: the Ice Age, the Neolithic Revolution, the Industrial Revolution and lastly the political post-war separation.

We started our reflections from the very last changes in Europe, that is with the economic and political separation which changed conditions during the last two decades. We briefly highlighted the changes of the Industrial Revolution and the framework of the modern national state operating with distinct distribution patterns and stimulation of policies.

From this late phase a brief jump back to the beginning of human productivity, which changed natural conditions in the period of the Neolithic Revolution, could give a glimpse of the enormous impact which the development of sedentary agriculture has had on the natural conditions of this continent. "Natural" conditions today are only to be found in artificially created and isolated conditions, as in national parks. The normal shape of today is of a purely cultured nature.

The natural geographical shape was given to the continent by the forces of the Ice Age. Physically, the fluctuations of the Ice Age determined the coastlines of Europe and, still more important, organized the drainage basins, the soil systems and the vegetative cover, which screened the animal life. Upon this background the climate operated and thus reinforced the natural conditions for the continent.

But what does this mean for finding the appropriate political tools of cooperation? It indicates the existing differences which cannot be changed but which distribute certain responsibilities as the geographical and climatic conditions of Eastern and Western Europe differ quite significantly. There are quite different timespans and energy patterns of material distribution operating which encourage or discourage certain effects and give policies distinct frameworks of functioning or not functioning. These operating systems must be understood in order to adequately organize conditions for effective policies.

Europe as a whole is shaped as a large peninsula of the much larger Asian continent. The size of the continent means that not much land is very far from the sea and the influence of the ocean is important with regard to wind directions, humidity and precipitation levels. There is an immediate environmental consequence which differentiates the landscapes in the West from the more land-locked states in the East.

In the West, the energy of the water cycle is much higher — there is a greater volume of precipitation, river length tends to be shorter, so rivers flow faster, erode more quickly, and carry more water into the sea.

The eastern type of drainage system is characterized by higher rates of deposition of sediment, lower hydrological energy and relatively less transfer of materials, whereas the countries in the West are regularly washed — with a certain peak in winter of course. In the Eastern countries the accumulation abilities of the air are by far higher. Air masses which are heated and cooled more slowly over the land-locked countries adjust their moisture without shedding too much water. The eastern system as well is also limited by a very low rate of seepage into the groundwater system because the layer of soils is much thicker and organicly richer. And, of course, there is much less seepage from the groundwater into the oceanic systems than in the Western countries.

This means in short, without following the necessary differentiations in detail, that the purifying capacities are more intensive in the Western countries, whereas the capacity of accumulation, with less deteriorating effects in the beginning (but probably with much worse effects later), is more likely to occur in the Eastern countries. Whereas the western landscapes recirculate more quickly materials which have been deposited, the eastern landscapes accumulate these materials for a longer period. In general, deposited materials in western lands or waters move more quickly onwards with the existing streams, currents or air movements, whereas these materials are less mobile in the East.

4. The Four Transportation Systems

Thus, the structure of this surface shows a specific distribution pattern of a varying capacity to digest pollution. Different transportation systems are operating on this uneven surface, dissipating unwanted materials, further dispersing them and thus spreading locally acquired pollution: the water system, the air system, the food chain and human trade.

4.1. Human Trade

The most flexible and independent transport system is human trade. It follows economic dominance patterns. Usable resources are brought to places of material wealth and possibly harmful waste materials are transported in the opposite directions. This transportation system is purely man-related and has no natural basis except for the natural place of gaining the resources by mining or drilling, cutting or catching, etc.

This is the only naturally fixed factor. All others depend only on the decisions of human activity and on the power structures between poor and wealthy countries.

Regulations and control of imports and exports could supervise and channel these movements if the international wish were not only expressed but also executed. In the case of trade, the responsibility lies more or less with the wealthier countries to agree on the protection of non-renewable resources of the less developed and poorer countries, such as rare species and their furs, woods from the rainforests, oil and other non-renewable resources.

Waste has no other origin than luxury consumption in the sense that some parts of the products were of no use at the place of consumption or in production. Waste takes the opposite route and travels further the more dangerous it is estimated to be. The pathway of waste may be controlled internationally by regulations and inspection.

The pattern of dominance has been heavily exploited, exporting raw materials (gas and coal) from the East to the West and vice versa for hazardous wastes. The famous dump site of Schönberg in the former GDR to which the Federal Republic of Germany frequently delivered great amounts of toxic materials now belongs after unification to one of the very problematic burdens of the past: the NIMBY (not in my backyard) principle did not work in the long run.

4.2. The Food Chain

The food chain is manifold and in its variety unpredictable. Today mother's milk can contain mercury from fishes contaminated on the opposite side of the world or DDT which was banned several years ago. Some substances are resistant, others are split up easily by gastric acids. This dissipation system can only vaguely be controlled by trying to control human food, i.e. by unpoisoned agriculture and animal breeding, by keeping the waters clean and the air unpolluted.

4.3. Air Movements

The most volatile system is the air, but it follows a strict natural pattern which cannot be changed by artificial control, even though it has now become clear that climatic changes are arising from the long-term changes of land use patterns and warming of the different layers of the atmosphere from constantly burning fuels. But an artificial control still seems to be out of reach.
In Europe a constant North-East drift exists, in winter more so than in summer. It was used by the high stack policies in the sixties, for instance in the German Ruhr-District (which was known under the famous but rather unsuccessful SPD slogan of that time: "Blue sky for the Ruhr-District"). A high stack policy was also established in the English Midlands in order to eliminate local pollution. This policy had a direct effect on the internationalization of the problem. It contributed to the acidification of the lakes in

Scandinavia and a little later to the acidification and the dying of the woods on the northern slopes and the northerly-opened valleys of the Alpine region. Measurements have shown that a dust or SO_2 load from England under certain conditions can take approximately 18 hours to reach the slopes of the Alps.

Dominant Direction of Wind in January (A) and July (B)

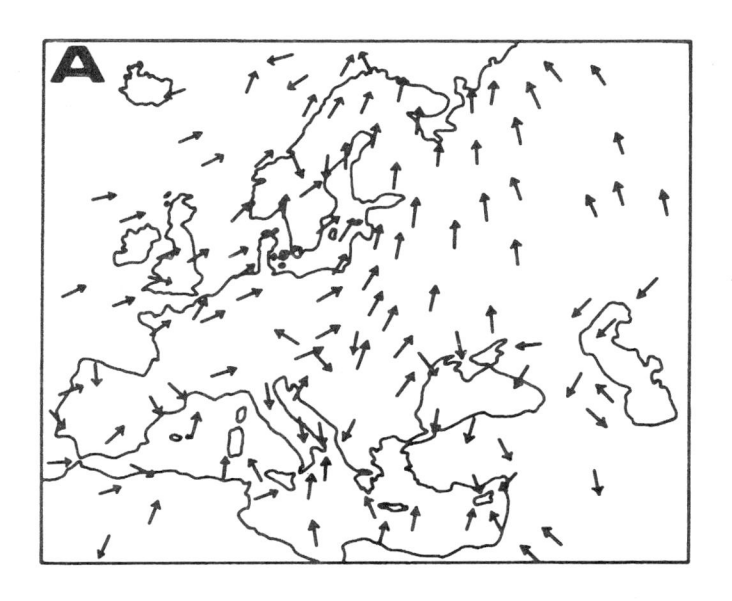

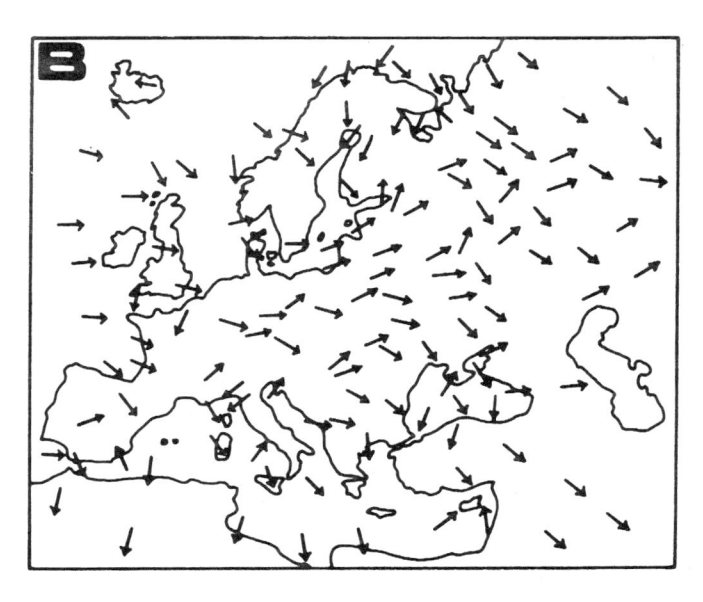

Thus, Western countries – though it has not been said in a political context – carry a greater responsibility for the European air conditions than Eastern countries, because Eastern countries are more affected by western emissions than Western countries by eastern emissions. Only on the global level the accumulation of all emissions together is playing a role again. This has not yet been fully scientifically proved as the Bergen conference has recently shown, but is thought to influence the climate.

It is quite clear that the real victims of pollution emissions from most European countries are the Scandinavians. For them an investment in filters and scrubbers in, for example, Czechoslovakia, Poland or in the region of the former GDR would pay off much more than the attempt to further reduce their own emissions, which could only be attained through very costly investments.

4.4. Water Cycles

The fourth transportation system is the circulation of water, which of course is again closely interconnected with the air and wind systems. Moisture and precipitation is a dissolved type of water transportation in the air and the evaporation power of the sun interlinks the drainage systems with the meteorological patterns of atmospheric circulation.

The main approach used for dividing the water systems in Europe are the eight major drainage basins. Again, keeping in mind what has been said about the energy of the river systems in the West and the drainage basins in the East, it becomes clear that the problem areas are the small seas such as the Mediterranean, the Black Sea, the Baltic, the Caspian and the North Sea, because they are not linked or are only weakly linked to the world oceans.

The danger posed for the Black Sea is apparent in view of the huge extension of this drainage basin, and the immense load of polluting substances which is carried by the Danube, by the Don from the highly polluted area of the Donbas as well as by the Dnepr and the Dnestr from the vast areas of industrial agriculture. But the threat for the Caspian Sea and the Lake Aral, which are both located in Asia but share a similar risk with the Black Sea, is even bigger because of the surrounding political geography.

With respect to the geographical situation, the Baltic is only in a slightly more advantageous situation for coping with the accumulation of pollution from the drainage systems. But now, after the opening of the East, their neighbours – the Scandinavian countries and Germany – who share the coastline will be interested in investing in the improvement of the situation. The Scandinavians have already expressed, during the Cold War period, their interest in a co-operative cleaning up of the Baltic Sea. Poland, the Baltic countries and the USSR will certainly profit from this shared interest. Financial obligations will have to be carefully negotiated because of the weak economic conditions of the reform countries. The wealthier neighbours will have to reinforce their vivid interest in the project by substantial investments. Technically, the lesser developed countries will profit in a type of mutual help by technology transfer and better organizational and institutional understanding.

The Black Sea, contrary to the situation of the Baltic, does not benefit from the participation of poor and wealthy countries which could make technology transfer and the necessary investments easier. German and Austrian cleaning of their parts of the Danube will not save the Black Sea. Since money has become scarce, the political idea of Europe is taking a shape that includes Poland, Hungary and the CSFR, but leaves surrounding Bulgaria and Romania at the very edge. Thus, the political conditions together with geography are making the Black Sea one of the environmentally most threatened places in Europe.

Watersheds in Europe/Drainage Basins

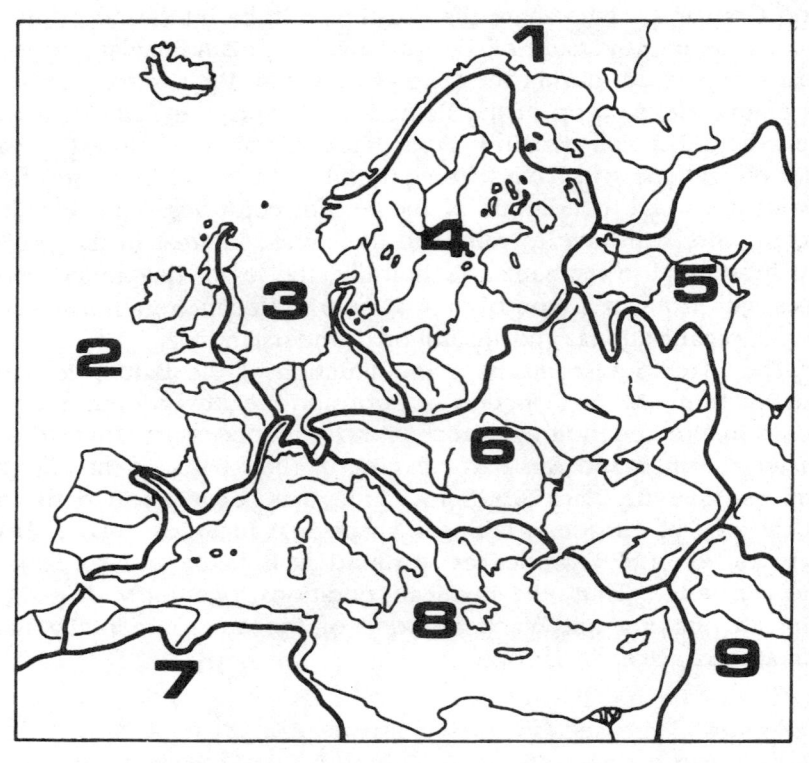

Legend: 1 = Arctic Sea, 2 = Atlantic Ocean, 3 = North Sea, 4 = Baltic Sea, 5 = Caspian Sea, 6 = Black Sea, 7 = Sahara Desert, 8 = Mediterranean, 9 = Persian Bay

5. Generations of Technology

Looking again at Europe as one ecosystem, it has now become clear that different systems are operating on the European surface which have different functional patterns: The political system with the borders of the national territories, reinforced by the past system of two different more or less integrated political blocks, caused different types of pollution. The drainage basins systems with their watersheds and the highly volatile wind system operate in general in a north-easterly direction.

Coming back to a historical perception another type of approach can be distinguished. Industrial society has developed, improved and substituted different generations of technology. Very roughly we can distinguish a first generation of mechanical, heavy industries, a second generation of petrochemical industries, a third generation of information-related, computer-assisted industries, which most probably will be followed by a next generation of biotechnology-based forms of production.

This very rough generation pattern, of course, occurs in a parallel mode and overlaps. There are no clearcut borders and they all exist side by side. Each type of industry in itself is improved, refined and often only partly substituted. Each type of industrial production also follows a certain pollution and resource consumption pattern which affects the environment in a very specific way.

For example, the economic recession at the end of the 70s strongly affected the heavy industries. The SO_2 values in Western countries decreased not only because of abatement strategies but also because these industries came under pressure and were not as competitive as other sectors of the economy.

The old industrial areas in Western Europe experienced a deep decline from which they never recovered, but were instead more or less substituted with other types of industries, with different pollution patterns.

The same development will occur now in Eastern European countries. But other types of pollution are to follow. More advanced types of industries produce pollution which cannot easily be monitored, and which is more complicated to discover. The major difference in kinds of pollution in the East and West is therefore bound to generations of technology.

6. Differences between Eastern and Western Europe in Pollution and Resource Consumption and Expected Developments

Having given an overview of the different factors which operated and are still operating on the European surface over time, the following sections will look more closely at the inherited differences and will dare some predictions on how certain changes will occur unless policies intervene by either hindering or supporting the coming developments.

6.1. Air Pollution

The typical difference between the type of air pollution in the East and the West has already been mentioned: the eastern air was and still is visibly polluted with sulphur and dust, whereas pollution in western air has become less visible and smelly over the last decade. Air pollution by SO_2 and dust is still the typical feature of former socialist countries with their old-fashioned type of heavy industries. Depending on the changes which will be achieved, the decrease of SO_2 pollution and dust is the most obvious goal and most countries started their new economic programmes by investing in new types of technologies. If these policies are successful, SO_2 emissions and dust will rapidly diminish.

In the emerging private sector many of the old factories will be closed or completely changed because their products cannot be sold on the world market. Long-term contracts of delivery still exist, for example, with the Soviet Union, which may prolong the production of some goods, but the majority will have to be redesigned.

The public sector as well will hopefully limit the energy production from lignite coal and coal with a high sulphur content and will equip the old power plants with filters and scrubbers to improve their environmental quality by reducing dust and SO_2 emissions.

The Northern European countries are especially affected by emissions coming from the so-called magic triangle: the south of the former GDR, Northern Bohemia and Silesia. The import and export rates give a clear picture that investment by the Northern European countries is now best placed in this triangle, thus improving the air and fighting against acidification, much more so than through investment in their own systems.

But closing down coal combusting power plants could lead some of the Eastern European countries into further investment into nuclear power. It seems that here history is literally repeating mistakes which have been made in the West. Nuclear power was one of the most costly failures of investment policies. In the long run the difficulties surmounted the solutions that nuclear energy was expected to deliver.

SO_2 Emission in Kg by Head of Population and Tonnes per Km^2 of Land Surface

Country	Year	SO_2	Emissions per head	Emissions per km^2
Austria	1980	354	46.89	4.22
	1985	138	18.25	1.65
CSSR	1980	3100	202.48	24.71
	1985	3150	203.23	25.11
France	1980	3558	64.75	6.52
	1985	1716	31.10	3.14
FRG	1980	3200	51.98	13.10
	1984	2600	42.50	10.64
Hungary	1980	1633	152.47	17.68
	1985	1400	131.58	15.16
Netherlands	1978	389	27.91	11.46
	1982	362	25.30	10.67
Poland	1980	4100	115.23	13.46
	1985	4300	115.59	14.12
Spain	1979	3250	87.41	6.51
	1985	2877	74.53	5.76
Sweden	1978	530	64.01	1.29
	1985	272	32.57	0.66
UK	1980	4670	85.28	19.33
	1985	3580	65.02	14.82

NO_x Emission in Kg by Head of Population and Tonnes per Km^2 of Land Surface

Country	Year	NO_x	Emissions per head	Emissions per km²
Austria	1980	216	28.61	2.58
	1985	208	27.51	2.48
CSSR	1980	1200	78.38	9.57
	1985	1120	72.26	8.93
France	1980	1867	33.98	3.42
	1985	1600	29.00	2.93
FRG	1978	3000	48.93	12.28
	1984	3000	49.04	12.28
Hungary	1980	370	34.55	4.01
	1985	400	37.59	4.33
Netherlands	1978	487	34.94	14.35
	1982	481	33.61	14.17
Poland	1980	187	5.26	0.61
	1985	670	18.01	2.20
Spain	1980	792	21.10	1.59
	1985	942	24.40	1.89
Sweden	1978	317	38.29	0.77
	1985	305	36.53	0.74
UK	1980	1916	34.99	7.93
	1985	1837	33.36	7.60

NO_x production rather than SO_2 and dust may become more relevant. Until now the air in Western countries, despite the fact that they export more to the East than the other way round, contains a higher content of NO_x than Eastern countries. But public investment into waste incineration of toxic materials will emerge in the East and the individual traffic will increase rapidly.

To be mobile is the new freedom of citizens of the Eastern European countries, and the dream of a car belongs to the highest ranking consumer wishes after the introduction of the market economy. Therefore, the hope of avoiding a situation in which the car becomes a mass consumer product in Central and Eastern Europe seems to be unrealistic. However, the infrastructure is by no means prepared, and the question is whether the public investments will strive for an extensive completion of the rail system or whether the network of roads will be quickly extended and improved. The immediate increase of the transport of goods of any kind from the West to the East started very early. Regrettably, the carriers were able to react much more quickly than the worn-out rail system, which transported approximately 75 per cent of all goods until the opening.

The heavy type of pollution will quickly diminish, SO_2 and dust will quickly show decreasing values. But a new type of pollution will follow, a type of air pollution for which the West, until now, has not been able to suggest a viable solution. No nation or supranational organisation has yet found a regulation which could show significant effects. The discussion about climatic change and the depletion of the ozone layer shows the difficulties, both technically and with regard to regulations.

6.2 Water Pollution

Water pollution must be stopped through legal norms and by inspectorates controlling the industries which until now have discharged directly into rivers, lakes and onto the coastline. Concerning the future public sector, huge investments for many years will be needed to restructure the sewage systems because most public systems are in a disastrous situation. Just to give some figures, once more from the former GDR: A quarter of the population is without any canalization and there is a mechanical and biological cleaning system of the sewage water for only one third of the population, phosphates can only be treated by two sewage plants, nitrates by none.

The drainage basins approach clearly shows which countries need to cooperate on the cleaning up of which rivers. The mentioned different energy budget of the water cycles in Eastern and Western Europe shows different patterns of danger: the East is able to accumulate many more pollutants, because the soil is thicker and sedimentation occurs more widely. Thus, the concentration capacity is less than in the more energetic cycles of the West where substances flow together on the same point. In the East this concentration process does not happen so quickly. As an effect, the Eastern system can digest pollution for a longer time and can better purify, but once the system is overloaded it is more difficult to get rid of the accumulations.

Thus, agriculture is becoming a very dangerous enterprise for soils and groundwaters. Fertilizer, herbicide and pesticide utilization has been overstressed. Agriculture which operates on huge field units, and the widespread use of monoculture have added to the accumulation of toxic substances in the soil. Irrigation systems have exploited the groundwater and have led to severe damage of the focal points of drainage basins. The worst example known has become Lake Aral, one third of which has already turned into a poisonous desert. In addition, the basin of the Black Sea is endangered because its oxygen level has diminished and the risk of dying is encroaching.

Industrialized Agriculture on Banknotes 1000 Yugoslavian Dinar and 5 Mark GDR

6.3 Soil and Land Use

This leads us to the next problem: the soil. The centralized agriculture, as already mentioned, has led to huge agricultural units. We all know the typical money bill with strong farmers and huge land machines of the socialist countries. The steady use of heavy machinery has pressured the soil, the capacity of water drainage is decreasing, and the use of fertilizers is high. The wind blows over the huge fields and takes the soil away because there is not enough protection from rows of bushes or trees.

The concentration of huge pig farms and the unsolved problems of manure lead to groundwater contaminations. As well, the storage of fertilizers in the open normally leads to more nitrate loads than necessary.

But there is one positive argument: the proportion of houses, streets and infrastructure compared to open land is still rather low. The state ownership of land has prevented the total destruction of nature by building houses. Visiting, for instance, the surroundings of Berlin, you may not believe that you are only a few kilometres from the city. Unfortunately, the developers have already started with construction work in the countryside. All cities and villages in the East still have a very clear-cut fringe; the areas of semi-rural, semi-urban, undefined developing do not exist so extensively as in the West. The lack of cars and transportation systems had led to a greater concentration of habitats. The problem of the so-called "Datschas" is still manageable.

In addition, the streets and infrastructure are still in the same state as in the early fifties, beautiful country roads, with trees on both sides and cobblestone paving: a beautiful landscape, but a poor infrastructure. Along the 3000 km long former border, the old strip of death has become during the past 20 years an untouched area where animals remained indisturbed. Next to the strip of death was a rather loosely populated area. A suggestion has already been made to guard this untouched strip, dedicating it in parts to a park.

On the other hand, large areas of nature and villages were destroyed each year because of the opencast mining of lignite coal in the GDR and in Czechoslovakia.

In general, privatization of the land will certainly lead to more extensive land use. Infrastructure policies will increase the public demand for land. It seems to be unavoidable that the rail system will take quite a long time before it becomes competitive with the individual system in terms of comfort, density and speed. Supporting policies in this respect are urgent, but interest from the West in supporting this development is rather low, except from those countries like Austria which fear being utilized as transit countries.

6.4 Waste Management

Waste Management like land use has had both a positive and a very negative side.

A very positive aspect of the Eastern European waste processing systems was that because of the general scarcity of primary raw materials, recycling systems were developed early and rather intensively. This means that the recycling rate was quite high. Figures show that in 1988 91.3 million tonnes of industrial waste were collected in the GDR. Approximately 40 per cent of this industrial waste could be recycled. This is a very high quota of recycling, and the substances for which a reutilization procedure exists seem to be much more numerous than in Western countries. There needs to be a more thorough analysis of whether really valuable substances could be recovered and used as secondary materials. It would be good if these attitudes of collecting old materials and gaining from them secondary raw materials could be retained. The media will have to work on trying to combat a consumer mentality which does not respect the scarcity of resources. In general, the idea of recollecting old substances and regaining secondary material as a very important aim was widespread and the behaviour of people shows an education of scarcity and careful use of goods.

The packaging industries were not yet developed and normally more paper packaging was used and very little plastic packaging. Thus, the overall amount of waste is still at a rather low level. Waste in general will increase in the former socialist countries, especially household waste, and plastic materials will be introduced into packaging to a greater degree. Until now packaging has mainly been based on paper or cardboard. In general, mixes of different substances and the proportion of the plastic materials will increase.

The other side of waste management looks once again disastrous. The management of household waste collection and careful handling and processing or dumping were not at all guaranteed. The services of the public sector were barely developed. In the countryside collections were not organized, but people brought their wastes to small local deposition sites where no controls were maintained and no specific sealing against leakages to the groundwater was used. No high temperature incinerations existed. Thus many new substances could not be appropriately handled.

In addition – and this was considered to be a big business, for example, for the GDR – West Germany and other Western countries dumped their hazardous wastes on special deposition sites in the GDR, in Yugoslavia and in other socialist countries. It has become clear that the waste management in most Eastern countries was not well organized and many poisonous secret dump sites are expected to be found. Many large industrial complexes buried their wastes in the backyard of their factories. Today the buyers of these enterprises will meet the burdens of the past on their locations: toxic substances in the backyard. In many cases, the clean-up costs for these sites will have to be paid for by the state.

It is very urgent that this type of waste tourism is stopped. The Western countries produce by far the biggest share of chemical and toxic wastes. As long as they could use the possibility to export their hazardous wastes they were not forced to think about more preventive methods of production. Closing the borders for this type of waste management by banning it in Eastern or other countries will put much more pressure on the internal policies of the Western countries to feel more responsible for their types of production.

Greenpeace has taken the initiative to interfere in the EC discussion on a directive on waste management. A regulation to open up waste export for recycling reasons should not be allowed because this will be, and is now, heavily used by exporters of hazardous wastes. Countries must be forced to treat their own waste in order to develop a rational long-term waste management policy.

But toxic waste in Eastern and Central Europe will increase as well because filters and scrubbers will stop a larger part of polluting substances from being discharged directly into the air and water systems. These rather toxic substances will be collected and will have to be processed.

6.5. *Energy*

As already mentioned above, the energy question may be considered as one of the most irrational decisions. On the one hand, energy was highly subsidized. Therefore it was cheap, by no means covering the production costs, and was thus wasted. The energy input into production, because of the out-dated technology, was very high compared to the output. The machinery no longer worked efficiently. As a comparison, the energy consumption per inhabitant in the GDR was 25 per cent higher than in the Federal Republic, which had a much higher standard of living. The GDR held, after the United States and Canada, the third rank in energy consumption per inhabitant. The price of energy in the GDR was 30 per cent below the West German level. In the so-called magic triangle the type of electricity production from lignite coal is the most polluting and landscape-destroying. The high sulphur emissions for the main part stem from the production of electricity where no exhaust gas filters were used.

The centralized system worked inefficiently and lost a lot of energy in the form of uncontrolled escaping warmth. The energy system, beside the old industries, will be one of the first systems to be reconstructed and made more efficient. It has to be completely renewed. Hopefully this will be done in a decentralized form, and the average production cost in most branches of industry will have to decrease the input of energy per unit. The energy price system has already changed significantly. Energy prices were highly subsidized and thus not much attention was given to saving energy. But the problem will be that under the given economic conditions many former socialist countries will invest in nuclear power, as Czechoslovakia has already decided. Safety conditions will have to be better adjusted, but it is not clear whether Eastern countries will be able to leave aside nuclear power as an option. The future is not yet decided on this subject and cooperative energy policies are needed. A European energy network is in discussion but it will take years – if not forever – for it to happen.

7. Policy Instruments

The environmental situation is characterized today by many uncertainties. To describe the situation we can identify three major factors influencing the decision-making process: science/technology, public control and politics.

Science until now has not been able to give precise advice on what is right or wrong. It would seem necessary for politicians to follow a precautionary principle, but instead politicians follow the cycles of elections and not necessarily scientific views unless they are not strongly supported by public control.

This gives the most efficient power to the media. The most effective relation in the past was the interrelation between science and the mass media. Grassroots movements very often played an important avant-garde role in cases where the public was not yet able to understand certain issues and the media therefore had not picked them up. In most cases they were not yet mature for public acceptance, because the economic fear of recession and unemployment was more powerful and convincing than the environmental threats. These were the plots when grassroots movements and non-governmental organization called upon the state to fulfil its duties and to protect its citizens and nature despite the negative economic issues.

Monitoring systems must be extended to the Eastern countries, and as far as they exist they must be improved and refined. Many studies and investigations have to be carried out. A free press will follow these investigations and will sensitize the public.

Consumer interests and fears about economic survival may for a certain period overshadow the necessities of following environmentally safer political decisions, as the energy strategies may already indicate. But the press in conjunction with a responsible science will hopefully work in the direction of not excluding environmental aspects when developing economic strategies. An independent information system and a quick feedback of the consequences of political decisions turned out to be most successful strategy in the long run in the West and is likely to be the most effective means of securing an environmentally more attentive pathway in the East.

Regulations and institutions on the national and international level must follow the outlined systems of interaction. This essay aims to communicate the necessity of a shared geographical responsibility. But this is not enough nor is it just for all countries to behave according to standardized principles. Geography distributed the climate, the watersheds and the prevailing winds into a certain pattern which cannot be neglected. International cooperative policy patterns must recognize these patterns if European policies are to refer to the principle of solidarity. It must be stressed that Great Britain and France have a higher responsibility for the air content for the whole of Europe. Their local emission influences the air quality of Europe in a much deeper sense than a local view would consider. England especially, which in some ways has a rather privileged situation as an island in the far west of Europe, has a greater responsibility than the local data would suggest.

Fair systems of cooperation have to be formed according to the ecological interactions described above.

Concerning European institutions, much attention should be paid towards the policies of the EBRD, the European Bank for Reconstruction and Development. The mistakes of the World Bank which until the late eighties very often supported projects with counter-productive environmental effects, must be avoided. In the EBRD a department of environmental impact assessment must be involved in the decision to give loans to development projects.

The importance of the policies of the EBRD might become crucial to the environmental policies of the Central European countries. The money of private investors is only coming very slowly because most enterprises have profited from the extension of their markets without feeling the necessity to invest in the countries themselves. The attraction of Eastern European countries for investors will be determined to a great extent by the conditions set by the EBRD.

The purpose and function of the bank is laid down in Articles 1 and 2 of the "Agreement establishing the European Bank for Reconstruction and Development", made in Paris on 29 May 1990. Article 2 of this agreement mentions under 1. (vii) as the last but one function: "to promote in the full range of its activities environmentally sound and sustainable development". This operational duty is controlled by a report which must be published annually (Article 35: Publication of Reports and Provision of Information, para. 2): "The bank shall report annually on the environmental impact of its activities and may publish such other reports as its deems desirable to advance its purpose."

Discussion about a new Marshall Plan from the part of the EC must follow the same obligations. The World Bank and IMF have made such horrible mistakes concerning the environment that new economic approaches must be applied. Future energy systems, in particular, must be carefully investigated.

One possibility for the former socialist countries would be to apply green taxes now instead of a purely income-related tax system. As well, the privatization strategies will play an important role. The same applies to investment strategies into infrastructure: How to slow down the investments into mobility by individual traffic, and better support public traffic? How to improve the agricultural system? How to avoid the Eastern part of Europe becoming an area of older polluting technologies?

The illusions of the first year after the opening up of Eastern Europe have disappeared. On the contrary, the perspectives for the future have unfortunately not improved. With nationalistic feelings and the struggles of neighbours against each other common European policies on the environment will not receive first priority. It seems that this was only the first reaction after the opening, when the West for the first time could take an honest view of the difficulties. A heavy burden for grassroots movements is gaining shape now, because for several more years it will be their task once again to make sure the media and people do not forget the necessities of serious environmental policies. This could easily happen now, as it did in the seventies in the West, when the recession made the politicians forget about the commitments they had given to the environment in 1972 in Stockholm.

Regulation Problems of a General European Environmental Policy

Kurt TUDYKA

This paper does not pretend to give even a few of the urgent answers to the breathtaking problems which are commonly associated with environmental issues in the new Europe. The following considerations will evaluate the chances for a transnational environmental policy, and thus it even enlarges the number of question-marks by asking for the factors which hamper the conduct of an effective – international – environmental policy in Europe.

This may lead to some uncomfortable conclusions with regard to the pre-requisites for a pan-European environmental union, which is apparently the most promising perspective for the European continent. Finally an attempt will be made to elaborate a perspective for a cooperative and common environmental policy in Europe.

1. Obstacles

1.1. The National Actors

The end of the division of Europe along the lines of the East-West antagonism might also have raised expectations for a more effective pan-European environmental policy than during the period of the East-West conflict. However, a powerful international environmental policy is permanently confronted with a number of principal problems independent of political systems and it will face henceforth obstacles up to now quite unknown under the political regimes in Eastern Europe. After all, the theoretical question remains whether the primacy of politics did not offer conditions principally more favourable for an effective environmental policy than the forces of the market place. Or conversely, is such a primacy of politics within highly industrialized countries counter-productive, or in other words, do environmental politics matter at all?

In general terms it might be inadequate to deal with European cooperation and then mainly focus on the European Community because Europe includes more than the EC. But in specific cases this statement can be reversed if Europe is to be regarded as more than the sum of its individual countries. The EC is seen as a model for the rest of Europe. But what has the European Community to offer? The answer depends on the standpoint on the continent. For the area of non-member countries, it has to offer an immense amount, but not so much from a position within the EC, measured on the relationship between policies and the number of real problems. The EC symbolizes the as yet highest stadium of European cooperation, but the real achievements are regrettably meagre. If this statement is valid and it can be supported by many facts especially in the field of environmental protection, what are the reasons?

The European Community's first environmental action programme mainly proposing anti-pollution measures was installed in 1973; the second one – somewhat broadening and adjusting the first one – in 1977. The third one in 1983 introduced the idea of preventive measures and the fourth one of 1987 emphasized the suggestion of a self interest of industry to produce goods which fulfil environmental standards. This appeal must fascinate political scientists because it includes evidently the notion and concession that politics dealing with environmental issues has reached certain limitations while the environmental problems are still growing.

The European Community proclaimed the year 1987 the year of the environment. Since then the messages about environmental damage have evidently multiplied and so has the number of fora, symposia and conferences. They communicate one message with two observations, an increase firstly in the degree of concern and secondly in the character and the complexity of the underlying problems. This agitation obviously reflects not only the endangered life on the continent but is also aimed at the growing gap between the worsening of living conditions and a political practice to cope with it. Despite the impressive number of international and European agreements on norms, laws, institutions and even monitoring, the most complete and scrupulous account of the accomplished results cannot shut its eyes to the meagre effects of environmental policy making[1]. If the conclusion is correct, which is supported by overwhelming evidence, the question must be raised: what are the reasons for the lack of an adequate environmental policy? The hypothesis that there is no effective international environmental policy in Europe – and elsewhere – because there is no national one is attractive. But is it not also reasonable to argue with the opposite formulation, namely that there is no adequate national environmental policy because there is no international one? Both statements are certainly correct depending on the circumstances. But do they not suggest that there is no adequate environmental policy at all or at least that a cooperative environmental policy does not go without saying? In other words: do environmental problems rather foster or hamper international cooperation in Europe – or elsewhere? This is the question which has to be dealt with seriously instead of purely maintaining the cliché that environmental policy must be international because the problems are international.

A fragile relationship exists between the state of the environment, economic processes, public opinion and the regulation by political actors. This quadrangle is even more delicate if it is placed into international dimensions. A commonsense argument says environmental pollution does not come to a halt at national boundaries, therefore environmental policy must be conducted internationally. Although this proposition is valid for many media its generalization is doubtful. A differentiation is necessary.

There is furthermore a fundamental contradiction between the international character of polluting processes and the necessary national character of their regulation. On the one hand, pollution caused under national circumstances diffuses into other nations; on the other, the more international a regulation has to be formulated and implemented the less it will contain substance and rigidity.

---

[1] H. Hohmann, p. 44.

The three following examples illustrate the main constraints for an international environmental policy.

In the first situation, the environment of one country or more countries independently from each other is polluted by sources originating in the same country. In this case, international action can normally not be expected. Environmental policy measures will be restricted to the national political systems of the countries concerned. A coordination or concertation of the policies is feasible by interference of an external factor, e.g. competitive strategies with regard to foreign tourism, the exchange of commodities or transit.

In the second situation, the polluted media cross national boundaries. A common international approach is determined by the net balance of pollution from each country. The extreme cases are when only one or a group of countries belongs to the exporters and the other belong to the importers; the other extreme is an equal balance of all countries concerned. The formulation of a common environmental policy will be very laborious in each case; the probable outcome will be much less than optimal with respect to environmental protection. Economic considerations will determine the attitude of the policy makers.

In the third situation, certain economic activities show damaging effects for the environment on a continental level. All countries regardless of their share are victims of the pollution and they are hit to the same degree. The need for international action is evident in order to improve the situation. A common policy could be based on generally accepted parameters, e.g. 30% less sulphur dioxide for each country. However, the implementation and control of such a programme will be very difficult.

The cooperation problem can also be approached by a collective goods analysis. Depending on the character of the pollution problem and on the excludability of others the various national actors might more or less strongly cooperate.

If the public damage is divisible, e.g. in the case of noise or the destruction of natural beauty, and others can exclude themselves from a respective policy, the perspectives for cooperation are minimal; a kind of coordination of national policies is only feasible on the grounds of other common interests.

If the public damage is indivisible, like in the case of the Chernobyl accident, and actors can exclude themselves from direct measures, some actors will try to internationalize their policies.

If the public damage is divisible but no actor can exclude itself from action, like in the case of the pollution of the Rhine river, cooperation is feasible in on the basis of compensation.

And finally, if the public damage is indivisible and no exclusion of actors is possible, like the unlimited whale fishery, strong international cooperation even with some kind of supranational authority is likely.

There are some essential distinctions between traditional border crossing transactions like the exchange of commodities, migration of people, even warfare and the international proliferation of polluted media.

If international processes are to be kept under control the attention is directed towards their destination. Usually the need for control arises in the receiving country. It can restrict the transactions partially or totally by imposing levies, duties, etc. Thus, by regulating the output a negative feedback is sent back to the input of the undesired process. This kind of procedure does not function with the proliferation of polluted media.

The classical border-crossing transactions, war and trade, had generally a clear, identifiable national origin and a clear, defined national destination. The border-passing emissions are usually an accidental by-product of some other activity which is certainly not related to the direction of the environment polluted by those emissions.

International trade and international wars – again the classical transnational processes within the international system – are based on conscious intentions and corresponding efforts. The environmental damage in one country caused by activities in another country is a side-effect and certainly not the result of a direct purpose. In contrast to the general and his army, the truck-driver dumping polluted waste in a neighbouring country does not intend to spoil the environment.

Those characteristics of trade and war give the opportunity for their national and international regulations. Environmental pollution passing borders and lacking those clear characteristics is therefore comparatively more difficult – if possible at all – to regulate.

1.2. The Lack of a European Public Opinion

Nature has no interest group and therefore no lobby and advocates. This statement often made by environmentalists, friends of animals and protectionists of trees and plants should justify their spectacular actions. Public attention helps to develop a general consciousness for the endangered environment and strengthens the issue on the priority list of politicians. The young history of the green movement confirms this kind of shaping of the agenda in favour of an environmental policy. The final measures and their implementation are of course subject still to other influences, mainly various economic considerations.

In comparison with other policies, environmental policy has thus another frame of reference. If no specific group of the electorate but only the general public can be mobilized for the sake of ecological issues, a politician can hardly become a permanent and absolutely exclusive representative of this concern because he cannot gain additional voters. Only in a period of emotional interest in the general public opinion can politicians be mobilized in favour of a powerful environmental policy. This necessary emotional sphere as a prerequisite for successful policy making has a strong populistic flavour.

But the working of this political process is bound up with the national society and the respective country. And the environmental issues at stake and the way they are perceived and evaluated by the people remain distinctive from country to country. The polluted coasts, rivers and lakes get more or less attention. Even an identical item of concern can stimulate different public reactions in different countries, as the Chernobyl accident and its perception demonstrated.

Therefore, the spectacular happenings of Greecepeace, Robin Wood or other activities always have a distinct national effect even if they take place at sites with high international esteem. Under these circumstances international environmental policy making cannot be stimulated, supported or legitimated by an adequate public opinion. Such a public opinion does not exist globally or even in a European framework because of the absence of a "world society" respectively a European society. And since the political process is lacking, as is the pressure by engaged interest groups such as business representatives or peasants, it is reduced to a marginal diplomatic bargaining standing aloof from the real problems. This situation is not changed by the exotic picture of demonstrating environmentalists outside international conference buildings.

1.3. The Competition of Economies

The economic competitiveness of exporting countries by applying stronger and thus more expensive environmental standards will not be weakened because of the increasing demand by consumers for quality products. This argument may be valid for the product but it does not include the production. The introduction of a clean production process is much more complicated, with respect to the competition among various national economies. The mixture of industries, their share of the national product and their productivity is different among the various competing economies and thus so too is their share to the national pollution. Environmental measures in favour of a cleaner production in one European industry may thus have very different effects for different countries. Finally, the environment of some countries is more endangered than that of others – the latter therefore feel that they have to bear a material burden for the sole advantage of the first group of countries if the same measures are applied to all countries.

1.4. The Erosion of Politics

The principal problem is the erosion of politics. The political classes in Europe are manoeuvring in order to keep their status with its privileges; the political fabric is insufficient and not functional. The need for another policy will be satisfied in the long run only by another political system.

The EC and other institutions are on the way to an enlightened administration. In our days it is not bureaucracy which can be regarded as clumsy, but the political process. Certainly the latter, i.e.

the disoriented troubled politicians, are responsible for late and wrong decisions.

2. Openings

In spite of all the afore-mentioned reservations under the present circumstances, three potential developments include the opportunity for promising perspectives for a European international environmental policy in the near future by contrast with a universal international environmental policy.

The development towards a common European economic area will produce a net of private and public transactions and the need for an adaptation and innovation of norms and standards. Different national environmental standards can function as barriers to the free flow of these transactions. This new flow of capital, goods and services could be linked with European conditions for their production and circulation, and this would be bound to protect the environment. The question is whether the standards are harmonized by lowering or by strengthening the pre-existing standards. The decision will be influenced by economic considerations. For purely competitive reasons countries possessing high standards and an adequately developed industry will prefer higher international standards while countries with lower standards will oppose such a policy.

Nevertheless, the promotion programmes of the EC for the Eastern and Central European countries and the operations of the Bank for European Reconstruction and Development could be principally based on such kinds of environmental prerequisites. Initiatives, concessions, aid and other positive responses of the EC to non-EC countries with regard to certain sectors like agriculture, the oil industry, energy, transport, tourism and regional development could be made dependent on the introduction of the EC's environmental impact assessment directive and its results.

Furthermore, one can regard the relation between economic development and the ecological equilibrium as a spiral interdependence: economic growth interferes with the natural environment, the altered environment conditions further economic activities. Is this relation between economic and ecological effects reversed, as has been recently maintained[2]? During the first period of the global environmental debate all attention was on the ecological effects of the economy, while now the economic effects of the damaged ecology would come into the foreground. In economic terms: the external costs of one economic activity have a negative feedback for the calculation of other economic activities. If this proposition is more than a theoretical construction and it now becomes relevant in reality, the consequence of such a shift of dependencies could be a positive stimulus for the motivation, formulation and the implementation of an effective environmental policy.

Secondly, the re-integration of Europe and the formation of a European confederation – following the proposal of the French President F. Mitterrand – can result in the constitution of a political and administrative fabric which could include the necessary institutional framework for the assessment, formulation and implementation of a pan-European environmental policy. The decision of the EC to set up a European Environment Agency, which is to provide objective and comparable data on the state of the environment, is only a first step. Its task should be enriched in order to take over the responsibility for running the "green" label scheme designed to alert consumers to environmentally-friendly products. But the strengthening of the authority of this agency could be only one important but limited act. (The delay in its establishment shows a symptomatic lack of concern among Europe's national politicians for the urgency of a European approach towards environmental problems. They estimate the national economic effects of its location higher than the European environmental effects of its function). Equally important is the enlarging of its membership to countries which do not as yet belong to the EC. This could perhaps be achieved by cooperation with the respective ECE department and finally by transformation of both activities into one common institution.

The historical experience with the political systems in Europe and the integrative factors of the various modern communication systems deliver a fundament for the incitation to a European consciousness in favour of a continental togetherness and identity

---

[2] Simonis/von Weizsäcker, p. 1

which could facilitate the realization of a comprehensive environmental programme in Europe beyond the purely economic rationale.

Bibliography

BUITENEN, A. V., 1991: Versterking van het milieubeleid van internationale organisaties: institutionelle voorstellen, in *Internationale Spectator*, pp. 93-100.

HOHMANN, H., 1989: Die Entwicklung der internationalen Umweltpolitik und des Umweltrechts durch internationale und europäische Organisationen, in *Aus Politik und Zeitgeschichte*, B 47-48.

PIETRAS, Z. J., PIETRAS, M. (eds.), 1991: International Ecological Security, Lublin.

SIMONIS, U. E., E. U. VON WEIZSÄCKER, 1990: Globale Umweltprobleme. Neun Thesen, in *Europa-Archiv*, pp. 1-12.

The End of the East-West Conflict and the Ecological Challenge for Europe

Michael STRÜBEL

An attempt to combine a concept of peace research with concrete problems of environmental cooperation in Europe involves three key questions. The first is a summary of the political arena of the decade in which current and future environmental policy will take place. To understand this arena it seems indispensable to present the most important differences in the field of environmental policy-making in capitalist and socialist countries. The second point is a stocktaking of concrete actions. Three short case studies will be presented: the West German-East German environmental policy, the work of the Helsinki Commission concerning the Baltic Sea and the policy of the United Nations Economic Commission for Europe (ECE) in dealing with air pollution in Europe. The three cases will be discussed using a comparative approach focusing in particular on efficiency and effectiveness. The third part will bring together considerations about arms control policy and management problems of a European environmental policy. The questions to be asked are: how should or could given structures be used for further operational activities, and what kinds of environmental conflicts might occur? Even more important: is the given structure of functional differentiation sufficient for environmental management in Europe or are there concepts for reforms that should be kept in mind? Whether the concept of common security should be applied to environmental policy – or what other norms or principles of international relations could be used – must also be considered.

1. The End of the East-West Conflict and the Multiple Ecological Interdependence

One assumption underlying this paper is the substantial decline of East-West conflictuality. Whether the reason lies in the decline of communism as an ideology, or in the policies of communist parties within their political systems, or in a given anachronistic structure of international relations is irrelevant in the long run. The democratic revolutions of the years 1989/90 in Central and Eastern European countries have not only changed the countries themselves. They have changed the architecture of international relations and brought to an end the historical period of cold war which characterized the situation in Europe after 1945. This does not signify the "end of history" but it does substantially diminish several dimensions of the East-West conflict: as a power-conflict of two superpowers – the USA and the USSR – and as a conflict over their interest spheres in terms of the Jalta-Agreement, as a structural antagonism between capitalist and socialist models of economic order, as a conflict over different internal societal organization and democratic representation and – last but not least – as a security conflict of hostile military alliances.

It has become obsolete to use war as an option for resolving political contradictions between two major powers and their allies, though this was true to a lesser extent under the sign of "peaceful coexistence" or the policy of arms control and crisis management. The fact remains that war, conventional or nuclear, as a political option can theoretically still be explained as a result of the security dilemma. But can it be politically legitimated in a historical moment in which given conflicts no longer seem to exist and in which the strategic and ideological background of traditional enemy images has been broken down by the democratic revolution in former socialist states? The results of given and traditional war scenarios for citizens as well as for the environment are in both cases a disaster. In the nuclear age there has always been a structural inconsistency between strategic targets on the one hand and military ways and means on the other. The study of the consequences and prevention of war (Weizsäcker 1969), the more fundamental critique of war-fighting concepts (especially on the strategy of "flexible response"), the considerations on an "atomic winter", and the discussion of the negative consequences of military activities for civil societies (Krusewitz 1985) have all led to the same result.

There is no plausible reason for a war scenario in Europe, at least not in the sense of a rational choice contrasting targets and strategies and potential military actions. Secondly: with the system changes in former Central or Eastern European countries like Hungary, Poland, the former GDR, Czechoslovakia, Bulgaria, Romania and the Baltic States, not to mention the transformation in the Soviet Union itself, there can be no doubt about a fundamental change in East-West relations. This change involves not only national political systems but the whole European policy arena. The end of the cold war era probably corresponds to the beginning of a postcommunist age. Some, most likely exaggerating, call these periods the breakthrough to and the coming-out of the "postmodern age" (Maull/Heynitz 1990). It indicates also a new way of thinking in looking at and analyzing international politics and policy. Especially in the European case cooperative structures, like those discussed at the CSCE-Conference in 1975, have to be developed as fast and as constructively as possible in order to maintain the revolutionary drive and impact that came from Central and Eastern Europe after the events of 1989 and the beginning of the nineties.

A new epoch of détente policy is marked, in the original sense of the German word *"Entspannung"* (which means "to relax the tension"). Although the situation in Yugoslavia, Romania and several republics of the Soviet Union is still incalculable and the status quo of the nation-states in Europe has begun to falter, the political instrument of threats of violence ranging up to the use of atomic missiles has become an anachronism. Europe is becoming "normal", i.e. relations exist on bi- and multilateral levels between states and transnational actors and not between two different ideological and military blocks with their own internal mechanisms of rules and sanctions. But the situation in Europe is not a state-oriented renaissance of changing alliance policies like that which took place in the 19th and the beginning of the 20th century. It is an asymmetrical peaceful confrontation of a highly integrated political space, covering the member states of the European Community and the EFTA countries on one side, and the newly democratized states in Eastern

Europe on the other side. The latter are involved in a number of nationality conflicts with each other as well as within their own countries, with the possible exception of Poland. Whereas the Western and Southern European states have been successful over decades in establishing a high level of economic integration, of democratic ripening in terms of irreversibility during the process of democratization, the situation in the East is quite different. Lacking a coherent theory of transition – be it Marxist or not – from a socialist to a capitalist economy, from a socialist state and society under the "dictatorship of the proletariat" to democratic rules and organizations, from a highly centralized and inefficient state bureaucracy to a more efficient, decentralized and democratically controlled executive system, these countries are facing considerable difficulties all at once.

It is the "magic triangle": economic growth – social security – ecological modernization, which brings new conflicts and leads to unknown dilemmas. Most important is the tension which results from the fact that ecological modernization has to be realised at a time when the quick and efficient functioning of a liberal market economy is supposed to be the foundation of political stability. It is nearly impossible to eliminate – on a short- or middle-term basis – the destructive and dangerous environmental damages caused during more than 40 years of socialist politics and policy and to eliminate the existing and constantly rising costs and charges resulting from this destruction (Förster 1991: 14).

On the other hand, European integration, especially the integration process in the European Community itself, continues to advance. Integration takes on special importance in the field of the environment, because of current ecological conditions. The pollution of rivers and seas, of the air and the biosphere does not stop at national borders, state frontiers or ideological boundaries. The sources of pollution can be easily located, but the consequences are transboundary and even global. These facts lead to general interdependence. It is not only the combination of complexity and vulnerability that is becoming important. The multiple interdependence involves new forms of transnational cooperation beyond the governmental level. Hierarchy among issues must be overcome and the irrelevancy of the use of military force shown (Keohane/Nye 1977: 22 seq.).

The Chernobyl accident, on April 26, 1986, taught us that reactor safety is not only a national problem. Over distances of thousands of kilometres, across national frontiers and military alliances a general threat suddenly existed. Neither the most sophisticated weapons and arms technologies, nor the best organized agencies at the national as well at the international level appeared to be able to deal with the problem promptly and efficiently. In other fields, which seemed less intractable, for example, the transport of hazardous waste, air and water pollution, the same tendency towards inaction could be seen. National governments, supranational organizations like the European Community or international organizations such as the OECD, IAEA, ECE, UNEP or WMO appeared to be unable to help. Even membership of security systems and alliances like NATO or the Warsaw Treaty Organization (WTO) did not play an important role.

The artificial separation of internal and foreign policy becomes obsolete in the environment field. Uncontrolled technological development, based primarily on political decisions on regulation, brings in the policy arena risks and dangers, and also possible chances, both for man and nature. Very few of them are scientifically analyzed in such a way as to ensure that a consensus exists in the scientific community. Even democratic systems have to concede that to a large extent on this topic a non-decision – and non-regulatory-policy exists. The reasons are the difficulties of communication on ecological subjects, internal problems of the "risk-society" and the utopia of a zero-option in a highly industrialized society (Luhmann 1986; Offe 1986; Beck 1986, 1988). At the national level, attempts have only rarely been made to control and regulate risks of technological innovation. Problems are becoming more complicated and difficult at the supra- and international level. But the multiple interdependence in the inner-European context as well as in the international one involves several dimensions.

This approach is reasonable for Europe for three reasons. Firstly, CO_2 is responsible for half of the destructive capacity of greenhouse gases. In Western European countries this is about 15 per cent, in Eastern European countries 21 per cent, mainly due to the burning of fossil energy. The figures are higher concerning the contribution of European countries with CFCs and NO_x (Enquête-Kommission 1988: 460). The use of energy per capita in European countries and in North America is extremely high, entailing very heavy negative consequences for the global protection of the earth's atmosphere and the protection and consumption of natural resources.

Secondly, new data, for example, on forest damage in European countries (ECE 1989), still indicate great ecological vulnerability. There are some peripheral European countries that are less involved than those at the centre, thanks to geographical advantages, such as the UK, an island with west winds, or that have experienced less industrialization and forest damages earlier, like the Mediterranean regions. But apart from the qualitative aspects the amount of quantitative destruction and damage is still enormous. "Le Waldsterben", an ironical invention of French journalists, has nothing to do with a special German romanticism or irrational love of woods and forests. The consequences of forest damage, primarily caused by SO_2 and NO_x emissions from industry and cars, are obvious for the water reservoir capacity and air quality in inhabited zones. The emissions also have a negative impact on the storage of CO_2 in biomass.

Thirdly, it has to be mentioned that European countries are involved in different forms of regional and global transport and use of chemicals, for example, in agriculture, and the export of hazardous waste. The Basel Convention, guidelines and recommendations of OECD, UNEP or EC, have not as yet had a considerable impact on the management of chemicals or hazardous waste. It is possible that things will change in the near future, especially if we bear in mind the increase of environmental consciousness as expressed in the latest opinion polls of the EC Commission concerning the preference decision between economy and ecology (European Omnibus Survey 1988). To date, on the East-West as well as on the North-South level, transboundary movement of dangerous waste, chemicals and toxic substances can be seen as an important field of regulation and control. But before presenting the existing forms of cooperation and the need for improvement the systemic differences between socialist and liberal economies, between Western and Eastern European systems have to be analyzed, especially in order to understand the restrictions and difficulties in environmental policy cooperation and to understand the challenges that face us, the heritage of more than 40 years of real existing socialism.

2. Environmental Policy in Socialist Countries

The diversity of the system changes in Poland, Hungary, Czechoslovakia, the former GDR and – partly – the Soviet Union makes it difficult to generalize. Nevertheless, the dominance of financial interest in the secondary sector and the preference for military expenditures over the field of research and development put ecological issues in a position where they were considered of peripheral importance. The situation in capitalist countries had been quite similar for a long time. Economic growth seemed to be the *ultima ratio* of the whole system and, to some extent, this attitude continues to prevail.

But under the conditions of party competition and electoral campaigns environmental policy became more and more important. Meanwhile in the EC countries it is seen as one of the most important issues. Three out of four European citizens share the opinion that it is an urgent issue. In the polls economic growth and the protection of nature and the environment are estimated to be of equal value and a majority regard the protection of natural resources as the condition for economic development. Most of those interviewed want decisions taken on problems of environmental quality not only by their national governments but by supranational committees of the European Community (European Omnibus Survey; Süddeutsche Zeitung 18.11.1989).

In socialist countries such results would hardly have been possible. Environmental policy did not take place in the state-market-democracy triangle, but was principally determined by other premises. The financial priority with centralized planning did not allow for a flexible intervention for the protection of the environment. No incentives came from the field of production, nor from the policy of the state, nor by demands coming from a free market for an ecological modernization of the product, the production process or the economic system itself (Strübel 1989a). The monopoly of the Communist Party, the non-existence of occasions for the election and representation of opposition groups excluded any form of democratic participation. Only during and after the process of democratization did civil movements and "Green" Parties begin to organize themselves in the public space and obviously became a multi-coloured rainbow coalition of quite heterogeneous political forces (Economist 4.11.1989).

Up to the end of the eighties there was nearly no transparency about environmental damages and the diseases caused by pollution. The results of environmental monitoring were labeled as "top secret", no open discussion was allowed about the extent and the effects of pollution. Public information by journalists or scientists was excluded, official briefing was not possible. Technical intelligence was not obliged to develop any end-of-the-pipe technologies nor was any technology transfer organized that could improve the quality of the environment.

On the international level the socialist countries participated in the EEC, the Baltic Sea regime of the Helsinki Commission and in international organizations like WMO, UNEP and others. On a regional level inside COMECON since 1971 a number of working groups and commissions on environmental problems were established. They had, if any, only marginal influence in the work of this organization. The environment was, much more so than in the West, considered as a common good, open for the exploitation for all and seen as an infinite resource.

The results of this policy that later became evident show how necessary an ecological orientation is and how far the degradation of the natural resources has already gone. Let us take the Soviet Union as an example. The USSR is probably the most ecologically destroyed industrialized country in the world. In some regions of the USSR the destruction of the environment is not controllable and millions of environmental refugees are about to emigrate. Half of the immense land area is becoming useless for agricultural production because of the excessive use of pesticides and of industrial emissions. An area which is larger than the area of the EC countries must be declared more or less an emergency area.

Every fifth citizen of the Soviet Union and one third of the urban population live under pathogenic conditions (Altshuler/Mnatsakanyan 1990, Spiegel 48/1990). In Moscow one fifth of all diseases are a result of air pollution. No large Soviet city is below the limits of pathological air pollution defined by the WHO. 70 million people live in areas where the maximum of emission concentration is five times higher, or even more, than the WHO limit (Förster 1991: 17). The pollution of the groundwater in urban regions is a permanent threat to the use of the drinking water. To overcome the ecological disaster investments of 400 billion Rubel are necessary in the coming 15 years, as requested by the State Committee on Environmental Protection. Nobody knows where this total sum of money could come from, except from a massive reduction of the military budget. In the Soviet Union environmental damages are estimated at 10 per cent of the GNP, in Poland even 20 per cent. Investments in both countries are less than 1 per cent of the GNP. These dramatic data show that it is time to act and not only in the sense of compassion with those who are negatively involved in this disaster. The situation can be said to represent a unique historical chance to combine the modernization of production with ecological needs and extensive redevelopment measures. But the crucial points are in the concrete policies that are developed. Let us take as an example of provisional regulation problems, the difficulties and conflicts in the environmental policy of the two former German states.

3. The Environmental Cooperation between West and East Germany

The German-German environmental cooperation before the unification process is an interesting example of the problems that have been brought up by decades of different economic and ideological orientation. The problems of the German Democratic Republic (GDR) were similar to those of all highly industrialized countries: air pollution, pollution of ground, inland and coastal waters, high energy consumption, changes in land use and waste management. Without going too much into details which only came to the public attention at the end of 1989, the situation is characterized by a high interdependence among neighbour states on all sides. In the field of air pollution the GDR was a major producer of sulphor dioxide (per capita) in Europe and among all industrialized countries. One of the reasons is the great amount of brown coal burnt in power plants. Another reason goes back to the absence of end-of-the-pipe technologies, and the almost total absence of any up-to-date effective cleaning technology. Concerning the pollution of water and rivers, the load of harmful substances was not controlled nor was the polluter charged for any emissions. As a consequence, the water and rivers that finally enter the Baltic Sea and the North Sea via the Elbe are badly poisoned. Lastly, the GDR was considered a convenient place to export and to store waste coming from West Germany and West Berlin. Public protests were not allowed and the government needed the foreign exchange.

Concrete cooperation between the two states in the field of environmental policy was disrupted by diplomatic difficulties and conflicts for a long time. The foundation of the Umweltbundesamt in Berlin (West) in 1974 as a federal authority and the non-transparency of data concerning the quality of the environment in the GDR have been an obstacle to cooperation for many years. In the eighties there were improvements, especially with the agreements of 1986/1987 concerning science and technology, reactor safety and environmental policy. The more or less exclusive attention at the government level offered only few possibilities for the exchange of views either privately or by political actors in different fields (Bergedorfer Gesprächskreis 1989). This led to only a few pilot projects and restricted scientific communication. But the environmental problems that were increasingly regulated in West Germany, though in most cases not solved, became more serious in the GDR. This was the most important point in the activities of environmental movements before and in 1989.

After the opening of the Berlin Wall in November 1989, the situation changed insofar as the transparency of public politics became a central issue. The evidence confirmed worst-case scenarios. Emission standards implemented at the European Community level were surpassed, and nuclear reactor safety was poor. Public protests arose, especially against West German exports of waste, and against the painful consequences of an irresponsible policy that had lasted for decades. The former bilateral foreign environmental policy became, of course, more and more a part of domestic policy, ending up in the unification process on October 3rd 1990. But the problems remain as to defining the area of policy. The GDR example is interesting from two different angles: the smaller investments are in clean air or water technologies over a long period, the higher ones are the costs of a damage limiting policy afterwards. The more restrictive participation in decision-making is suppressed, the more radical and chaotic the situation seems to be after a system change. Unfortunately, this situation is characteristic of other countries as well, whether they are socialist, post-socialist or neo-capitalist systems.

As far as environmental cooperation is concerned, the cooperation between the two German states was quite weak. In the budget of the Federal Republic for 1990 the budget for environmental expenses as a whole was about 1 billion DM, the budget line for defence was about 54 billion DM. Only a small part of the environmental budget was intended to go into FRG-GDR projects. Concrete projects like the installation of purification plants or filters for air pollution control suffer from the fact that the unstable political and social situation in the former GDR makes it difficult to define concrete responsibilities for the correct use of investments. In addition, the uncertainties in the social field, the threat of unemployment for millions of people, complicate the introduction of a homogeneous environmental policy, especially if the effect is the closing of major polluting factories, plants or nuclear power stations.

But internal reasons in the former GDR are not alone in preventing a radical change in environmental policy-making or a more ecological orientation. The rapid "Westernization" of the new "Bundesländer" has had quite a negative impact on the different fields of environmental policy. The strict free market economy has destroyed a well-accepted system of recycling of bottles and other domestic waste. Without any financial support by the state the decentralized collecting points were no longer able to exist. After 1990 the lack of resources or of foreign currency was no longer a dominant motive for maintaining a recycling system. As a consequence, the whole system broke down without any substitute. The amount of waste increased enormously.

The second point refers to the energy policy. The three big West German electric power companies controlled the electricity supply leaving aside the competence of towns and cities. These companies are now highly dependent on Western monopolies and have lost an important source of income. The ecological and social costs, the risks and charges of waste management are taken by the state, whereas profits are made exclusively by the more or less private companies. Democratic control, which exists partially in municipal companies, is not possible.

The last issue covers traffic problems, both private or public. In the private field, the massive rush to buy Western cars and the high mobility increased the volume of traffic, especially on roads and highways to and from Berlin. In the public field, the partly decayed railway system of the "Reichsbahn", the lack of money for the modernization of equipment and a dumping-price policy by West German carriers led to an increase of lorry traffic as compared to the transport of goods by rail, which does not have such negative effects for the environment and the use of energy. All three tendencies show in a dramatic way that in the process of building an "Environment Union" (*Umweltunion*) the transformation of the Socialist economy did not follow ecological priorities.

4. Environmental Regime of the Baltic Sea

Since the beginning of the seventies alarming reports about the environmental quality of the Baltic Sea have been published. 10 per cent of the seabed has been considered dead and a high percentage of DDT and other harmful substances has been found in fishes. In some areas fishing as well as swimming has had to be officially prohibited (ECE 1987). The reasons for this policy are easy to reconstruct. Over 70 million people live near the coast of the Baltic Sea, some of them in highly industrialized countries with big agglomerations and harbours. The hydrography of the Baltic Sea is extremely environmentally dangerous compared with the North Sea or the Mediterranean. As the average depth of the sea is 55 metres the exchange of water is very limited. A total change of water requires between 20 and 40 years. 80 per cent of the emissions of harmful substances come from rivers.

The states in the area belong to different alliances: Denmark and the FRG are members of NATO and the EC, Sweden and Finland are neutral, the GDR, Poland and the Baltic states of the Soviet Union belonged in the past to the WTO and were considered socialist countries. In 1973 the Gdansk Convention, which dealt with fishing and conservation of the living resources in the Baltic Sea, was signed. In 1974 the Helsinki Convention expressed a "more general concern" about the protection of the marine environment of the Baltic Sea area. As a result, the Helsinki Commission (HELCOM) was built up with a permanent office in Helsinki, different working groups, regular publications and meetings of ministers and secretaries of state. HELCOM tries to control the decisions and guidelines, especially emission standards, concerning harmful substances. The possibilities of control of the Commission are only relevant outside the coastal zone, which remains under the sovereignty of the national states. This is one of the major problems of implementation. The MARPOL Treaty is also relevant for the Baltic Sea, particularly the prohibition of the dumping of oil and harmful substances from ships. This has not been achieved in the case of the North Sea where the MARPOL Convention was not ratified by all members.

In trying to evaluate the work of HELCOM, three important points should be considered. Firstly, in spite of fundamental differences in political systems and the crisis of détente policy, a continuing and functional cooperation structure which is an important peacekeeping factor has been developed. Secondly, there have been some successful results, such as the reduction of DDT and PCB concentration (ECE 1987). But at the same time new dangers, such as the eutrophication due to agricultural production and the ongoing intensive pollution from land-based sources, have appeared. This has partly to do with insufficient environmental protection measures in socialist and post-socialist countries and with the enormous use of phospates and nitrates in Western and Northern European regions. Finally, there is still a significant quantity of emissions that are transported through the air and come from mobile sources. It must be mentioned that on the whole no real technology transfer, for example, of purification plants, has taken place between West and East.

The late ratification of the Convention in 1980 and the geographical restriction of control actions for the territory outside the coastal states are better than nothing, and even more efficient than the North Sea regime (Strübel 1989b: 261). But this is not sufficient. The Baltic Sea is still polluted to a large extent, with all the negative consequences for fishing, tourism, the living conditions of millions of people and the ecological balance of the ecosystem itself.

There are a number of reasons for this unsatisfying situation that come from the very workings of the Baltic Sea regime. One refers to the procedure of control and verification. Common monitoring systems only exist outside the coastal area. The data published concerning land-based emissions of the single states are as varied as emission standards and as the state of technical environment protection. Equally divergent are monitoring methods. On the other hand, one means of pressure and innovation remains the cooperative style of the work of HELCOM. Supposing that all members in spite of their financial and social difficulties are interested in succeeding, being more or less continuously in a free-rider position or even sabotaging the common approach becomes a question of political prestige.

It remains to be seen whether the change of political systems in the former GDR, Poland and the Baltic states will improve the situation. At least the political liberalization of the systems can allow for more space for the action and working of NGOs like Global Challenges Network, the Coalition Clean Baltic or Greenpeace. Concrete working areas of the new social movements are the redevelopment of the Vistula in Poland or actions against extensive fertilizing with nutrients in agriculture. Apart from political repression, which is continuously diminishing, there are financial difficulties and technical transaction problems because of the different infrastructure and the level of public awareness concerning environmental pollution. Public actions pointing to unbearable conditions or scandalous pollution are necessary for transparency and the development of an environmental conciousness. Concrete policy regulation by governmental or international authorities is another field. This judgement also refers to the third case study: air pollution control policy in Europe.

5. The Control and Reduction of Transnational Air Pollution in Europe

Apart from national and bilateral strategies or regional regimes, co-operation can also be achieved by classical international organizations. The issue of air pollution control is to a large extent one of the main fields of the United Nations Economic Commission for Europe (ECE) together with organizations like the OECD or the Council of Europe. One advantage of the ECE is the membership of different countries. With 34 member states the ECE is the only organization in Europe that has brought together Western and Eastern European countries since 1946/1947, as well as neutral and nonaligned and the North American states. The orientation of the ECE is strictly governmental, and policy-making in the different committees depends exclusively on the mandate given by national governments. The ECE is thus a classical field for environmental diplomacy (Carrol 1983), significant because of its structural deficit of democracy compared with the European Community.

It is not necessary to repeat the details of national characteristics of air pollution control (Enyedi/Gijswijt/Rhode 1987; Rhode 1988) or the long and complicated history of preparing treaties and common declarations (Prittwitz 1984; Chossudovsky 1988), but it has to be emphazised that the ECE introduced important regulation strategies. The "Convention on Long-Range Transboundary Air Pollution" (LRTAP) was signed in 1979 and came into force in 1983. This was completed by the "30 Per Cent Club" after the conferences in Stockholm (1982) and Munich (1984) concerning SO_2. Secondly, the build-up of the "Cooperative Programme for Monitoring and Evaluation of the Long-Range Transport of Air Pollutants in Europe" (EMEP) has attempted since 1977 to set up permanent monitoring stations with a reliable data base. In 1988 the ECE had about 95 monitoring stations in 32 countries. The Federal Republic had 15, the USSR in its European area 11, Norway 8 and the UK 5. This shows – leaving out the methodological problems of different investigation methods – that the control system is developed with asymetrical points of reference. But the important fact is that with these publications of emission data an approximate location of sources becomes possible, import-export relations of deposits can be proven

(Weidner 1986: 16) and movements of harmful substances through the air can be followed even over a long time period. Apart from the Sulphur Protocol, some states inside the ECE have tried to implement concrete reductions of other substances, especially those coming from traffic emissions, and have begun to realize the standards of the NO_x Protocol of Sofia (1988).

Concerning the political efficiency of the conventions on transboundary air pollution in Europe, the ECE itself makes two major points (Sand 1987, 1990). Firstly, the quantitative reduction of sulphur dioxide emissions from 80 million tons in 1980 to 63 tons in 1986 is considered a success of the "30 Per Cent Club" with its given targets. By 1988 twelve states had already reached the 30 per cent target and 10 countries were willing to reduce their sulphur emissions from 1980 to 1995 to 50 per cent or even more. Secondly, the consolidation and strengthening of the EMEP system can be seen to be relatively successful. One methodological objection has already been mentioned: the monitoring systems are asymetrically located and at least partly of problematic comparative validity. Another critical point concerning the reduction of sulphur emissions refers to the given economic trend in highly industrialized countries. The permanent development and restructuring process includes a decline of heavy industries and at the same time a continuing growth of the tertiary sector.

Another critique of the air pollution policy of the ECE could point to the long ratification procedure of the treaties, the lack of political innovations concerning moratoriums and immediate applicable strategies, the complicated ways of integrating those states which have a "free-rider" position, the absence of a more global approach regarding the greenhouse effect, and the exclusion of NGOs and public participation in the decision-making process.

It seems as if there is a highly significant discrepancy between regime formation and regime innovation on the one hand and regime effectiveness on the other hand. One can take the view that "the process is the policy" (M. Strong, in Choussudovsky 1989: 208) and interpret the work of the ECE as a successful example of environmental diplomacy. But at the same time one can argue that the acid rain regime is quite weak in regrading the ecological impact (Schwarzer 1990: 35). Apart from the reduction margins of 30 per cent – which are political figures – the critical load which is assessed by experts is much higher, namely about 70 to 80 per cent. The end result is that 10 to 13 mostly Western and Northern European countries, members of the EC or EFTA, have promised high emission reductions, whereas non-cooperative countries like the United Kingdom, Poland or Italy prefer a position of staying outside the club without having the intention of leaving it, and at the same time not realizing the standards. The integration of those who are unable or not willing to reduce emissions significantly has become a difficult and sometimes frustrating effort in the work of the ECE.

6. Environmental Cooperation: A Comparison

In a systematic sense three stages of cooperation can be recognized. The first is problem identification, a stage which clearly exists in all three cases. The second deals with common monitoring and evaluation, data gathering and information collection, risk estimation and impact assessment (Kay/Jacobsen 1983: 15). All states more or less attempted to accomplish this for themselves as far as possible and then to discuss their experiences with others either at an informal diplomatic level or within international organizations, like the OECD, the Council of Europe, the EC or the ECE. The third and most interesting stage of environmental cooperation is the facilitation and coordination of national and international programmes, normative pronouncements, standard setting and rule-making, the supervision of norms and rules and direct operational activities.

In the case of the Baltic Sea regime this stage was realized after the ratification of the Helsinki Convention, and was combined with the concrete activities of HELCOM, at least outside the coastal waters of the territorial states involved. Concerning the two German states, cooperation was on a very low level for many years and a long road of common standard setting and implementation control lies ahead. The financial aspect seems not to be as important as it was in the past because of political or ideological differences. The concrete enforcement of projects in an accurate administrative way is much more complicated in the former GDR. The lack of effective administration structures, of well-established management and of qualified employees makes ecological modernization very difficult. In the years of the system change an optimistic supposition expected more progressive reforms in the former GDR (Petschow et al. 1989).

With the EMEP programme the ECE tried to fulfil minimum standards for monitoring and attempted to obtain concrete reductions of SO_2 and later of NO_x. One way to achieve this in the work of the ECE is the setting-up of permanent working groups. The second way is to develop a regulation by obliging the member states to report on the quality of their environment by presenting their data and policy outcome, and to publish the data. At the same time common control mechanisms remain very weak and the organization as such has almost no concrete implementation capacity. This remains the domain of the member states, which have very different approaches, political instruments and technical capabilities.

In terms of a preliminary assessment of ecological effectiveness, we can see, in the case of the Baltic Sea, some reductions of DDT and PCB, and in the case of the ECE Convention, a lower level of SO_2 emissions. But in both examples new dangers have arisen, such as pollution from mobile and diffuse sources or emissions of harmful substances that accumulate in biosystems over a long time. Bioaccumulation and synergetic effects make things more complicated and even unable to be accounted for. One can come to the conclusion that the given transnational organizational cooperation structures, in spite of their partial successes, are not nearly sufficient to regulate the environmental problems in Europe as a whole. And even efforts to achieve a certain homogeneity of standards on a national level show, as in the case of Germany, that a number of serious political and social difficulties and conflicts cannot be excluded. These considerations bring us to a discussion of problems and perspectives, including organizational reforms and institutional innovations.

Conclusion

This paper does not deal with ecological threats to the environment caused by armed forces or by weapons, but rather with civilian ecological problems in Europe that require a new concept of security. Ordinary security can no longer be reduced to arms control policy. It should include issues that are fundamental for all sides, East and West, North and South, or any combination of these. Not only the global warming and the destruction of the ozone layer are involved, but also issues such as the pollution of air, water, seas, the transport of dangerous waste and the safety of nuclear power plants or the big chemical and agricultural industries.

Such an understanding of international politics and policy leads one to ask whether the concept of Common Security should be modified by integrating the aspect of ecological security (Pietras 1990; Theisen 1990). The concept as a whole was formulated at the beginning of the eighties by the Palme Commission. The main point of Common Security was the assumption that security in the nuclear age can no longer be defined in terms of national or regional security, of alliances of friends on the one side, enemies on the other, of "winners" and "losers" in a potential war. The Eurocentric and military-oriented approach of the Palme Commission was later corrected by the second Brandt Report and especially by the Brundtland Report. "Our Common Future" was linked up with the conflicts between development and environment, on the global as well as on regional levels.

Authors who are in favour of a concept of ecological security mention three main aspects: firstly, security can be interpreted as a state-centred phenomenon, insofar as "ecological aggression" by other states becomes an issue in interstate relations. Secondly, ecological threats – for example, the greenhouse effect – are a challenge for international cooperation. National interests are involved and introduce strategic advantages or disadvantages in the arena of international politics (Brown 1989; Myers 1989). Thirdly, growing ecological problems cause international conflicts and tensions on a bilateral as well as on a multilateral level.

Contrary to these ideas there are more sceptical positions concerning "ecological security". One argument is that "ecological thinking is dynamic and global, whereas security thinking is static and particularistic" (Brock 1990: 25). This contradiction could be overcome by a wider definition of security (Ullmann 1983). But even then the question arises as to whether such a definition is tactically useful and substantially coherent. It can be criticized that this is a dubious application of old military thinking to new ecological problems without result. Furthermore, an integral definition of security and global change could hinder the analysis of causes that lie behind ecological damages and the responsibility of individual actors (Daase 1990). In discussing these essential differences of definitions and views, a convenient solution would be to use the concept of "sustainable development". This term has been introduced in international relations by the Brundtland Commission and seriously discussed by the scientific community within the framework of the problematic aspects of a financial and political operationalization of sustainability (Pearce et al. 1989; Simonis 1990) as well.

A comparison of domestic aspects of environmental policy in Eastern and Western countries, if these expressions can still be used (Tudyka 1988: 16) shows that, apart from the current fundamental changes, there are still significant structural differences between the political programmes of socialist, post-socialist and capitalist countries as well as in their practical implementation. A great advantage for Western European countries is the openness of the political system, the possibility of including ecological issues on the agenda, of integrating green groups into the party system and of making room for the activities of new social movements. There is also a greater degree of "Glasnost", which means transparency, in general politics because Western journalists are able to investigate delicate issues. One difficulty in organizing environmental interests in socialist countries is that concrete problems are sometimes mixed up with other conflicts such as national topics or general system opposition.

We have to add that in post-socialist countries problems do not disappear automatically just because parliamentary democracy is set up or a market economy is reconstructed. Furthermore, the private profit-oriented use of technologies as a reaction to four decades of underdevelopment and planned economy creates new problems: "In our countries, the underdeveloped state of civil society, and an inadequate ecological consciousness, will make it difficult to limit effectively the use of aggressive technologies" (Vargha 1990: 7). In addition, it is not always clear that the strong bonds between civilian environmentalists and democratic political movements will manage to survive the breakdown of socialism. GDR environmentalists, for example, presently play the role of an outsider even more than during the previous period. Since officials used to regard them as a strong and dangerous opposition group, they provoked, through very repressive punishment, a certain level of solidarity with these groups within the civil society.

As far as the administrative system is concerned, socialist countries had a structural advantage of long-term plans with concrete restrictions and step-by-step programmes. They did not have to take into account every interest group that came along and they could, if they wanted to, launch strict programmes for energy saving or the ecological modernization of production. But in the latter case the centralization of the state had negative effects on environmental policy. The official ideology that gave priority to financial rather than to ecological policy reduced the scope for action that in Western Europe is vested in local authorities or town administrations.

Three case studies are presented here, including forms of environmental cooperation between East and West that have already been implemented. The first, dealing with the environmental problems of the former two Germanies, shows that the transfer of experts and know-how has begun but is still quite insufficient. As long as – until 1989 – exchange between non-governmental organizations was more or less forbidden and the free flow of information or the publication of environmental data was prevented, efficiency was reduced to a minimum, causing frustration. New efforts for ecological modernization have since been made. But this policy is characterized by setbacks. In some cases mistakes in energy policy that were already made in the past are simply repeated.

In the second case study, concerning the Helsinki Commission, it becomes obvious that significant cooperation structures have existed for more than a decade and that monitoring and control programmes function. However, the jealous safeguarding of national sovereignty, especially involving land-based sources that cause about 80 per cent of the Baltic Sea pollution, is still the most important obstacle in solving these problems. The third overview concerning air pollution policy in Europe came to an ambivalent result for the eighties. A slight reduction of SO_2 is better than nothing but is not enough to achieve a real and constant improvement of air quality in general.

To sum up we can say that policy style in East and West has shared three characteristics: "too little, too late, too slow!" (Christie 1988: 22) The result is the progressive worsening of environmental conditions on a global as well as on a European scale. Data that analyze forest damage in European countries are important evidence. At the same time, environmental awareness, for instance in the European Community member states, is growing and becoming an important political factor, even in elections.

Two important factors of environmental policy must be discussed. These are the problems of "time" and "money". The "time" factor is significant because a discrepancy exists between two different dimensions: our "real time" in the sense of counting minutes, hours, days, months and years is quite different from the "natural time" that nature needs, for example, for the beginning or regeneration of ecosystems, of forest complexes, water systems and agricultural areas. Even a successful commitment that gets all the way to the causes of pollution requires a long time to achieve positive results. Such a comprehension of time allows no consideration for election periods, parliamentary sessions, dates of international meetings or deadlines for conference declarations. When a long period of "muddling through" and of a no-decision policy concerning the environment has already elapsed it seems nearly impossible to achieve certain standards within a given time or to reduce emissions within a few years. In some cases damage is irreversible and a policy concept of damage-limiting seems impossible to implement.

The second issue is linked to financial investments. The dilemma of all environmental policy lies in the common-goods problem: the use of nature and the environment is possible as long as the externalization of costs is not hindered by any market mechanism or by directives and laws given or prepared by the state. Capitalist as well as socialist economies profited from this structure. Private and non-private enterprises try to make the best out of the situation, which means externalizing costs as much as possible by polluting the environment up to the maximum of legal or illegal informally accepted limits. International competition intensifies this tendency.

But at the same time, this mechanism produces costs and charges that sooner or later have to be paid by the state, that is, the tax-payers. And the higher the costs are the lower is the probability that they are paid. For the Federal Republic losses due to environmental damages are estimated at a minimum of 100 billion DM annually (Wicke 1986: 123; Leipert 1989: 275). The EC Commission estimates Community damages caused by acid rain to buildings, forests and agricultural production at 10 billion ECU per annum. OECD experts estimate that environmental damages cost up to 6 per cent of the GNP of their member states. This figure continuously increases to the extent to which public and private expenditures for environment protection drop and to which preventive policy instruments are either not implemented or fail. These and other authors see the necessity for new policy options in a modified definition of property rights, a calculation of the GNP that includes environmental costs, the introduction of eco-taxes in all EC or OECD countries to avoid competition disadvantages, and the standardization of control technologies on a high level (Weizsäcker 1989).

In this context the proposal to design an ecological Marshall Plan that, apart from the North-South dimension, particularly the saving of tropical forests, should have an East-West aspect, has been made. In a 20-year period the OECD countries should invest 200 billion US dollars. According to different problems, different measures have to be taken: reduction of air pollution coming from stationary sources by setting up new end-of-the-pipe technologies in power plants and industrial production, building-up of purification plants, if possible with all three purification levels, development of efficient recycling systems and modernization of installations with intensive emissions (Wicke/Hucke 1989: 270). Apart from the fact that these measures are still necessary for some EC member states, the main obstacles for this unique West-East transfer are obvious: the conditions for financing the plan, the sacrifices that have to be made by the population all over Europe, the implementation problems, for instance, the administrative completion on a decentralized level, and the participation of the persons affected.

The unideological character of environmental policy, compared with security policy or even with welfare policy, is a good starting point and a basis for cross-national cooperation. New models are being discussed in this context, such as an "Eco-Fund" for the transfer of technology, the establishment of a European Environmental Protection Agency or common working groups on special issues with members of the EC, the EFTA and COMECON countries. Together with closer-knit NGO networks of NGOs and scientists, the introduction of more sophisticated environmental training programmes, with financial support from the European Investment Bank or the World Bank, is planned. But reforms of organizations or the establishment of new agencies, such as the European Environmental Agency for members from in and outside the Common Market, are destined to remain inadequate as long as the political will for profound environmental changes does not exist or is not organized in such a way as to have an impact on regulatory policy on a transnational level.

Bibliography

ALTSHULER, IGOR/MNATASKANYAN, RUBEN, 1990: Environmentalism in the Soviet Union, in *Ambio* 2.

BECK, ULRICH, 1986: Risikogesellschaft, Frankfurt.

BECK, ULRICH, 1988: Gegengifte, Frankfurt.

BERGEDORFER GESPRÄCHSKREIS, 1989: Globale Umweltproblematik als gemeinsame Überlebensfrage – Neue Kooperationsformen zwischen Ost und West, Hamburg.

BROCK, LOTHAR, 1991: Peace Through Parks – The Environment on the Peace Research Agenda, (Unpublished) Frankfurt.

BROWN, NEVILLE, 1989: Climate, Ecology and International Security, in *Survival* 12.

CARROLL, JOHN E. (ED.) 1983: Environmental Diplomacy, Ann Arbor.

CHRISTIE, IAN, 1988: Cleaning up a Continent: Environmental Policy in Eastern and Western Europe, in *Policy Studies*, August.

CHOUSSUDOVSKY, EVGENY, 1989: "East-West" Diplomacy for the Environment in the United Nations, Geneve, New York.

DAASE, CHRISTOPHER, 1991: Ökologische Sicherheit – Zur friedenspolitischen Konzeptionalisierung eines Begriffs, in *Wasmuht, U. C. (ed.)*: Ist Wissen Macht? Baden-Baden (in print).

ECONOMIC COMMISSION FOR EUROPE (ECE), 1987: Environment Statistics in Europe and North America, New York.

ECE, 1989: The State of Transboundary Air Pollution: Effects and Control, New York.

ENQUÊTE-KOMMISSION, 1988: Schutz der Erdatmosphäre, Zwischenbericht, in *Zur Sache 5*, Bonn.

ENQUÊTE-KOMMISSION, 1990: 3. Bericht zum Thema Schutz der Erde, Deutscher Bundestag, Drucksache 11/8030, 24.5.1990, Bonn.

ENYEDI, GYORGY/GIJSWIJT, AUGUST J./RHODE, BARBARA (EDS.), 1987: Environmental Policies in East and West, London.

EUROPEAN OMNIBUS SURVEY, 1988: Les Européens et l'Environnement, Bruxelles.

FÖRSTER, HORST, 1991: Umweltprobleme und Umweltpolitik in Osteuropa, in *Aus Politik und Zeitgeschichte* B10.

JÄNICKE, MARTIN/MÖNCH, HARALD, 1988: Ökologischer und wirtschaftlicher Wandel im Industrieländervergleich, in *Manfred G. Schmidt (ed.)*: Staatstätigkeit, Opladen.

KAY, DAVID/JACOBSON, HAROLD (EDS.), 1983: Environmental Protection – The International Dimension, New Jersey.

KEOHANE, ROBERT O./NYE, JOSEPH S., Power and Interdependence, Boston, Toronto 1977.

KRUSEWITZ, KNUT, 1985: Umweltkrieg, Frankfurt.

LEIPERT, CHRISTIAN, 1989: Die heimlichen Kosten des Fortschritts, Frankfurt.

LUHMANN, NIKLAS, 1986: Ökologische Kommunikation, Opladen.

LUTZ, DIETER S. (ED.), 1991: Gemeinsame Sicherheit – Kollektive Sicherheit – Gemeinsamer Frieden, Baden-Baden.

MAULL, HANNS W./HEYNITZ, ACHIM VON, 1990: Osteuropa: Durchbuch in die Postmoderne, in *Europa-Archiv* 15.

MEYERS, NORMAN, 1989: Environment and Security, in *Foreign Policy* 74.

PEARCE, DAVID/MARKANDYA, ANIL/BARBIER, EDWARD B., 1989: Blueprint for a Green Economy, London.

PETSCHOW, ULRICH/MEYERHOFF, JÜRGEN/THOMASBERGER, CLAUS (EDS.), 1990: Umweltreport DDR, Frankfurt.

PIETRAS, MAREK, 1990: Notion of Ecological Security, Lublin.

RHODE, BARBARA, 1988: Air Pollution in Europe, Vienna Centre Occasional Paper No. 4, Wien.

SAND, PETER, 1987: Air Pollution in Europe: International Policy Responses, in *Environment* 10.

SAND, PETER, 1990: Regional Approaches to Transboundary Air Pollution, in *Helm, J.L. (ed.)*, Energy Production, Consumption and Consequences, Washington D. C.

SCHREIBER, HELMUT (ED.), 1989: Umweltprobleme in Mittel- und Osteuropa, Frankfurt, New York.

SCHWARZER, GUDRUN, 1990: Weiträumige grenzüberschreitende Luftverschmutzung, in *Tübinger Arbeitspapiere zur Internationalen Politik und Friedensforschung* (Nr. 15), Tübingen.

SENGHAAS, DIETER, 1990: Europa 2000 – Ein Friedensplan, Frankfurt.

SIMONIS, UDO ERNST, 1990: Beyond Growth – Elements of Sustainable Development, Berlin.

STRÜBEL, MICHAEL, 1989a: Technologietransfer und grenzüberschreitende Umweltpolitik in Europa, in *U. Albrecht (ed.)*, Technologietransfer und Internationale Politik, Opladen.

STRÜBEL, MICHAEL, 1989b: Umweltregime in Europa, in *B. Kohler-Koch (ed.)*, Regime in den internationalen Beziehungen, Baden-Baden.

STRÜBEL, MICHAEL, 1990: Grenzüberschreitende Umweltpolitik in Europa, in *M. Strübel (ed.)*, Wohin treibt Europa? Marburg.

STRÜBEL, MICHAEL, 1991: Auf dem Weg zur "Umweltunion": Bisherige Umweltkooperation und Handlungserfordernisse im vereinten Deutschland, in *Liebert, U./Merkel, W. (eds.)*, Die Politik der deutschen Einheit, Opladen 1991.

THEISEN, HEINZ, 1990: Gemeinsame ökologische Sicherheit und demokratischer Konsens, in *Beiträge zur Konfliktforschung* 2.

TUDYKA, KURT P. (ED.), 1988: Umweltpolitik in Ost- und Westeuropa, Opladen.

ULLMAN, RICHARD H., 1983: Redefining Security, in *International Security* 1.

VARGHA, JANOS, 1990: Green Revolutions in East Europe, in *Panoscope* 18.

WESTING, ARTHUR H. (ED.), 1986: Global Resources and International Conflict, Oxford.

WEIDNER, HELMUT, 1986: Air Pollution Control Strategies and Policies in the Federal Republic of Germany, Berlin.

VON WEIZSÄCKER, E. U., 1989: Erdpolitik. Darmstadt.

WICKE, LUTZ, 1986: Die ökologischen Milliarden, München.

WICKE, LUTZ/HUCKE, JOCHEN, 1989: Die ökologischen Milliarden, Berlin.

WORLD COMMISSION ON ENVIRONMENT AND DEVELOPMENT, 1987: Our Common Future, Oxford.